Other books by the author:

Hiking In the Great Smokies

Wonderment of Mountains

Valley So Wild
(with Alberta Brewer)

Just over the next ridge

A traveler's guide
to little-known and
out-of-the-way places
in Southern Appalachia

By Carson Brewer

 **The Knoxville News-Sentinel**
A SCRIPPS HOWARD NEWSPAPER

Cover photograph: The Beauty Spot, Erwin, Tenn.

Contents

Introduction   v.

Author's preface   vii.

I. Tennessee   1

II. Kentucky   63

III. Virginia   85

IV. North Carolina   97

V. Georgia   131

Index of Places   143

Photo Acknowledgments   149

Introduction

My wife and I were driving through the extreme northwestern part of North Carolina, in that region where the mountains rise sharply and majestically, but where the creek meadows are level and peaceful. And in that beautiful setting we encountered a quaint and picturesque old homestead that appeared to be straight from the last century.

There was the large gabled house with an inviting porch on three sides. A smokehouse, blacksmith shop, wash house, spring house and other auxiliary buildings surrounded it; and there was a pioneer log house nearby. That was where the pioneer family had lived, I thought to myself, before they built the big two-story Victorian-style home.

There was nothing to distinguish this inviting domicile from a few other old family homesteads in that area — except a small and hand-lettered sign. It read simply, "Restaurant and Lodging." We soon learned all about the warm and cozy rooms, furnished with period furniture, tastefully decorated with mountain crafts and fragranted with fresh flowers. We learned, too, of the sumptuous family-style meals, served as part of the modest room rental fee.

My thoughts immediately turned to the many requests I receive from throughout the country, inquiring about just such places. These travelers stay in plush hotels or at convenient motels and they have meals in the franchised restaurants. But when they come to the fabled Southern Appalachian mountains they want something different — something which reflects the flavor, the atmosphere and the culture of the region. How very good it would be, I thought, if someone thoroughly familiar with our Southern Appalachian region ferreted out and described such out-of-the-way places and made this information available for all.

The day after we returned home from this weekend trip I received a phone call from Susan Alexander of The Knoxville News-Sentinel. She asked if I would write an introduction for a travel guide that would encompass East Tennessee, southeastern Kentucky, southwestern Virginia, western North Carolina and north Georgia, which her newspaper was publishing. The first question I asked was whether or not the tiny North Carolina inn was included. She assured me that it was. Then she informed me that the noted columnist, Carson Brewer, was the author. I readily and enthusiastically agreed to lend whatever assistance I could to this much-needed publication.

I know of no one better qualified to write such a book than Carson Brewer. A native of one of the region's most remote and historically rich sections (Hancock County, Tennessee), Carson early learned about the physical beauty, the cultural richness, the historic importance and the sheer romance of the region. For 40 years he wrote about these mountains, the interesting folk who inhabited them, and his hiking forages through the most remote traces. During these years with The Knoxville News-Sentinel he won numerous prestigious awards and he became one of the south's most respected journalists.

Although he is a colorful and often subtly humorous writer, he never allows his inclination for interesting lines to challenge his steadfastness for accuracy. I've read Carson's column for a quarter century and he literally tells it like it is. So "Just Over the Next Ridge," it seems to me, provides the kind of information so often sought by the increasing numbers of visitors who come here from throughout the country and who wish to explore our lovely hinterland. And it will be equally beneficial, maybe more so, to those of us who are natives to the region. After all, Carson has likely already been wherever we might choose to go, and he's been to many intriguing little places of which we have never heard. Not only does he provide general descriptive comments, he also provides the technical type information that a potential visitor needs to know.

The Knoxville News-Sentinel and its editor Harry Moskos should be commended for conceptualizing and implementing this project. With "Just Over the Next Ridge" in hand, we can all better enjoy the beauty, heritage and mystique of this section of Southern Appalachia.

—*John Rice Irwin*
Museum of Appalachia, Norris, Tenn.
March, 1987

Author's preface

What I hope you'll do with this book is have some fun and partake generously of the treasures and pleasures of Southern Appalachia.

These include trout sizzling in a skillet, muscadines ripening in warm September sun, walking the rim of a river gorge in the Cumberlands, feasting on the loveliness of wild azaleas on Gregory Bald and rhododendrons on Roan Mountain. They also include visiting with the Cherokees of western North Carolina and visiting Rocky Mount and the Museum of Appalachia to see how our forebears lived in considerable joy in the days before movies, television, automobiles and surrogate motherhood.

I hope you'll get maps before you drive or walk or float into unfamiliar territory. You usually can find trail maps at headquarters or visitor centers for the Great Smokies, Big South Fork National River and Recreation Area, Cumberland Gap National Historic Park, the Obed Wild and Scenic River, Joyce Kilmer-Slickrock Wilderness Area, the six national forests in our area, as well as state parks. Sometimes they're free; sometimes they cost a small sum. If you want every switchback on the trail and every bend in the river, you should buy quadrangle maps. You can get them at the TVA Map Office on the first floor of West Tower, located on Summit Hill Drive in downtown Knoxville. You also can buy quad maps of the Great Smokies at park visitor centers. And, of course, you need highway maps.

I wrote the book generally from the point of view of a person in the Knoxville Metropolitan Area wanting to relax for a few days in nearby territory. Our nearby territory is among the finest in the country. We've got mountain trails for hikers, river gorges for rock-climbers, fast rivers for canoeists and both rivers and lakes for fishermen. In the Great Smokies, we have what probably is the world's greatest remaining remnant of pristine deciduous forest.

The book is aimed more at where to go to find interesting things to see and do and experience than at finding the best places to eat and sleep. But I haven't neglected good places to eat and sleep when they happen to be on our routes. In fact, there are some excellent ones.

I've tried, with nearly 100 percent success, to keep you out of large cities. This is a book for people who like places wild to rural to small town. I assume that people here already know about Blount Mansion and its kindred historic homes in Knoxville, about the Dogwood Arts Festival, about the good restaurants here.

My thanks to:

My bosses, the News-Sentinel committee charged with seeing that this book gets written and published, for not bossing too much. Members are Susan Alexander, public service director; Berl Schwartz, managing editor; Ed Pieratt, assistant managing editor/graphics, and Sam Venable, philosopher, turkey hunter, columnist.

John Rice Irwin, for writing the introduction.

Susan again, for putting together all the lists of places and institutions, with addresses and phone numbers, at the end of each chapter.

Martin Gehring, News-Sentinel artist, for his maps.

Susan, one more time, and my wife, Alberta, for catching all (I hope) my misspellings, typos and sins against good taste. Also, to Sam, Doug Mason, Bill Dockery, Idonna Tillery and Susan Dawson, all of The News-Sentinel staff, for helping with the same task. And Alberta, again, for reading the map while I drove and driving while I read.

— *Carson Brewer*

Tennessee

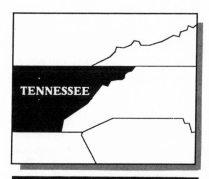

TENNESSEE

Chapter One

L et's get rolling into the
Cumberlands, to Scott, Morgan
and Fentress counties, place of heroes,
history, wine, wildlife, wildflowers, wild
waters and the Yellow Door where Alvin
C. York went to pray.

First stop, Frozen Head State Park.
No, on second thought, since we're
traveling up State Highway 62, we may
as well take the opportunity for a right
turn and a drive of two or three miles to
Petros and Brushy Mountain State
Prison. If anything can deter you from a
life of crime, it's a look at Brushy.

When you come to a fork in the road,
take the left fork. The other one goes to
Petros community. Almost immediately,
you'll see the prison. Sitting there
crossways of a narrow mountain valley,
it looks like a dam somebody forgot to
finish at both ends. It also looks
foreboding, like some place where I
would not like to spend the rest of my
life or even the rest of the day.

The trillium and violets and hepaticas
in Frozen Head look better. Frozen Head

1

State Park consists of 11,862 acres of mountain land, and about 8000 acres of it is the Frozen Head State Natural Area, where the deer and wildcats roam and the wildflowers bloom gloriously.

April is the best time for wildflowers. Frozen Head has a wildflower pilgrimage the second, third and fourth weekends of every April.

The Panther Branch Trail is the best one for wildflowers. It's about two miles long. Pick up a trails map at park headquarters and go up the North Prong of Flat Fork Creek to the trailhead. You'll walk less than a mile up an old Jeep road. Don't forget to stop for a look at DeBord Falls. Then go on to where the Panther Branch Trail branches to the right off the Jeep road. Immediately, the hepaticas start, and they go on and on. Both red and white trillium also are on this trail, plus foam flower, and a scattering of other nice things to see.

One of these is Panther Branch. You stay close to it for a long time. Finally, you come to a place where the trail steepens and the little stream stairsteps up the mountain in a series of small falls. Then the trail turns sharply right. You can go to where it intersects the North Old Mac Mountain Trail and turn back. Or you can continue on the Old Mac Trail down to a point near park headquarters. From there, you'll have to walk back up the road to your car. Your round trip will be about five miles.

Soon after you leave the Panther Branch Trail for the Old Mac Trail, you'll see a marker pointing to a rock overlook. It's worth the short walk, and it's a good place to sit down and eat lunch. Lots of laurel on and near the overlook. Saw a deer nearby, the fourth for the day, for I had seen three others at the start of the hike. Park Manager Duane Wyrick said there was a reliable panther sighting in the park in the summer of 1985.

Panther Branch and Old Mac are two of a dozen trails in the park. Alberta and I did the Chimney Top Trail several years ago. I will not soon forget it. As we were about to start walking, someone said to me, "You're not going to take that woman up that trail, are you?"

His concern was rattlesnakes. Alberta is afraid of all snakes. Intellectually, she knows there is reason for fear in East Tennessee only for rattlers and copperheads. But her reaction to snakes is not born of the intellect; she fears blacksnakes, king snakes, garter snakes only slightly less than the poisonous ones.

Chimney Rock is a very big boulder. Unless you're a good rock climber, there is only one route up the rock to the top. On the back side of the trails map, there is a warning about climbing the rock: "Be cautious when climbing, as rattlesnakes have been seen around the rocks during summer months."

I'm one of those who saw them. Alberta wouldn't climb the rock. She stopped several yards short of it. I climbed it and was looking around at all the pretty scenery when I heard an odd whispery sound. I looked around and saw two black rattlers. They lay within a yard of each other. One was trying to rattle. (That was the noise.) But he couldn't rattle really because his rattles were gone, perhaps lost in some accident.

On to Wartburg, founded in 1844 by German native George Frederick Gerding. He came to this country and made a bundle before he bought 300,000 acres of East Tennessee land and turned it into the East Tennessee Land Colonization Co. for Swiss, German and French immigrants.

Somewhere in Wartburg is the headquarters for the Obed Wild and Scenic River. It was in the Federal Building the last time I was there, but there was talk then of moving into another building. If you're interested in putting a canoe into the Obed or two of its tributaries, Clear Creek and Daddys Creek, you can pick up a map and other information at this headquarters.

At last count, in early 1987, the government had bought nearly 2000 acres of an authorized 5000 acres along the Obed and the two major tributaries. It's slowly buying more land. Eventually, I suppose, it will have all 5000 acres. Only a narrow band of land along the streams can be bought — the river gorge and a maximum of 200 yards back from the top of the gorge on either side. In some instances, not all the 200 yards will be bought.

These are remote waters. Roads cross them at only a few places. They are mostly for canoeists and fishermen. Among the fish to catch and keep are redeyes and smallmouth bass. You might catch an Ohio River muskellunge, but you can't keep it. The Obed and its tributaries are among the few Tennessee streams where that strain of musky still lives. So they're on the state's endangered list. (Muskies that have been stocked in some of the TVA lakes are of a different strain.)

There's only one short hiking trail in the Obed land. It runs about 2.5 miles, from Nemo Bridge to Alley Ford. But Walter Mayer, Obed manager, says it will be extended all the way to the Devils Breakfast Table, on Daddys Creek, a distance of about 12 miles. The Devils Breakfast Table is a big boulder, flat on top, sitting atop a sort of pedestal rock. In autumn, when the streams run low, you don't need a trail. You can walk for miles on dry streambed. You may want to bring your fishing rod, for there's enough water left for the fish.

One good thing about the Obed land is that it's adjacent to the state's much larger Catoosa Wildlife Management Area, about 80,000 acres. The area is operated primarily for hunters. But anybody can drive through it, picnic in it and observe wildlife when no hunt is in progress.

Only a few miles from the Obed is Fairfield Glade, 12,341 acres of premier resort. Three 18-hole golf courses and a fourth under construction. One of the three, Stonehedge, in 1985 was selected by Golf Digest as the best resort course in the nation. Indoor and outdoor tennis courts, ditto for swimming pools. There's a full-size gym. You can rent horses and ride them on Fairfield trails. Rates generally are high. Various rate packages are available for those who play golf or tennis. If you're rich, you might want to make Fairfield Glade headquarters for a week's exploration of the Cumberlands.

I stopped in Sunbright, several miles up US Highway 27, north of Wartburg. For it's at Sunbright that Bob Lantz manufactures canoes at the Blue Hole Canoe Co. He knows more about whitewater canoeing in this region than anyone else I know. I know very little, only what you learn in a few floats down the Clinch, the Little Tennessee, the Hiwassee and the Nantahala. Of that group, only the Nantahala is wild and woolly.

Because I know little and Bob knows so much, I asked whether it'd be all right to give you his phone number, in case you have any questions about a prospective river float. He said OK. So his phone number at the Blue Hole is 615-628-2116. I don't guarantee you'll always find him there. He spends a lot of time on rivers. Don't visit him, not unless you have at least half a mind to buy a canoe. Just phone.

I knew that Bob was familiar with the Obed, Daddys Creek and Clear Creek, plus Big South Fork and Clear Fork. What I wasn't sure was whether he also was familiar with all those whitewater rivers in North Carolina, Virginia and upper east Tennessee.

"Have you been on the Doe?" I asked.

He pointed to a wall of his cluttered office and, hanging there, a picture of a fellow taking a canoe over a waterfall. "That's me on the Doe," he said.

To further establish his credentials, he handed me a copy of "Appalachian Whitewater," a 159-page book about canoeing fast rivers in Tennessee, Kentucky, Virginia, North Carolina, South Carolina and Alabama. Bob is one of the co-authors. I met another co-author, Don Otey, in Bob's office. The other co-authors are Bob Sehlinger, Bob Benner and William Nealy.

Bob said Knoxville is closer to more exciting rivers than just about any other place he knows. Besides those already mentioned, there are the Tellico, in Cherokee National Forest; Little River and the Oconaluftee, in the Great Smoky Mountains National Park; the Watauga and the French Broad, in upper east Tennessee and western North Carolina; the Ocoee and the Sequatchie, in southeast Tennessee; the Nolichucky, in upper east Tennessee; Russell Fork of the Levisa Fork of Big Sandy River, in Virginia and Kentucky; the Chattooga and the Chattahoochee, plus Amicalola Creek, in north Georgia; New River and its North and South Forks, North Fork

Kingstone Lisle Home, Rugby

of the Catawba and the Green River, in western North Carolina.

Let's move on up US 27 to State 52 and Rugby, the town that failed as a colony for younger sons of English gentry but is doing well in its reincarnation as an interesting place to visit.

English author Thomas Hughes established Rugby in the wilds of the Cumberland Plateau in 1880 and called it a "lovely corner of God's earth." Sons of well-to-do English families had a problem then: Only the eldest son of an English family could inherit. This left younger sons without inheritances. These same young men in class-conscious England could enter only the few professions socially acceptable to their class. Hughes established Rugby for them. With Rugby so far from England, he thought the young men might be able to get into agriculture and manual work without causing anyone to faint.

The young Englishmen came. Some of them canned tomatoes in a factory established for that purpose. Some worked in a pottery. They tried growing grain, fruit,

raising cattle. But nothing much seemed to turn out well. Perhaps it was because the young men stopped for tea at 4 each afternoon. They spent lots of time on plays, musicals, football, tennis and swimming in nearby Clear Fork River.

By 1884, the community had its peak population of about 450 persons who lived and worked and played in some 70 buildings. By 1900, the population was down to approximately 125, and Rugby generally was regarded as a failure. Its buildings began to decay.

But Rugby is rising again. Interested persons in 1966 established Historic Rugby Inc. Its main purpose is to preserve and restore some of the best parts of Rugby. About 20 of the original buildings still stand. Of the 20, more than a dozen have been restored. Historic Rugby did seven of them. Private owners restored the others. Christ Church, Episcopal, is a tiny jewel of a church. The Thomas Hughes Library is filled with Victorian literature and Rugby history. Hughes' home, Kingstone Lisle, is restored. So are the Rugby Printing Works,

Pioneer Cottage and Newberry House Inn.

You can spend a night in Newberry House or Pioneer Cottage, and you might want to make this headquarters for a few days in the area. You can eat at the Harrow Road Cafe.

Pioneer Cottage, originally called Asylum House, really was a place of asylum for some of the first young men to arrive. They had no place else to stay. Thomas Hughes stayed there for the same reason. It now rents as a unit to one family or one group. It can accommodate about 10 persons in one downstairs room and two rooms upstairs. Newbury House has five guest rooms. Three of them have private baths. Occupants of the two other rooms share a bath. Rates are moderate. You can have complimentary morning and evening coffee or tea in the parlor.

You can drive through Rugby and eat at Harrow Road Cafe just about any time. You can stay any time of the year at Pioneer Cottage and from Feb. 16 to Dec. 15 at Newberry House. But Rugby is considered "open" only from March 1 to Dec. 15. That's when you can take tours and get more of the flavor of the place. There are some good annual events: Christmas at Rugby, the first Friday and Saturday of December; the Spring Music and Craft Festival, the first weekend after Mother's Day; and the Pilgrimage of Homes, the first full weekend of August.

We follow State 52 on to Fentress County. We come to Allardt, a Germany community established the same year the English established Rugby. One Fentress Countian told me, "Rugby failed and Allardt succeeded because the people of Rugby planted flowers while the people of Allardt planted potatoes."

In the vicinity of Allardt, on a road just off 52, look for markers that will lead you to Colditz Cove. This is a 75-acre State Natural Area on land contributed by the brothers Arnold and Rudolph Colditz of Oneida. It's a gorge, a waterfall and a long rock house. And it's some lovely hemlocks and other trees. A 1.5-mile trail takes you on a tour of the area. About half the trail is on top of the bluff, offering views of the gorge and Northrup Falls. Then the trail takes you down into the gorge and under its overhang, which is the rock house. Woodland Indians used it as shelter. The last time I was there, I was careful to stay well back under the overhang or well away from the front of it. For the sun was just warm enough to loosen heavy sections of ice from the gorge walls above, and these ice chunks were piled up along the trail. When I was there on an earlier visit, only a trickle of water was coming down Big Branch over Northrup Falls, and the leaves of the maples and oaks wore autumn colors.

If you're interested in food and drink, as you go west from Allardt, turn left off 52 onto State 296, which will take you to US 127. A left turn onto 127 will take you immediately to Tennessee's first commercial winery in modern times.

It's Highland Manor Winery, operated by Fay and Kathy Wheeler. If you have as many as a half-dozen in your group, Fay will take you on a tour of his winery and tell you how he makes his product. His big seller is muscadine wine. He also makes muscadine champagne, but there's not much chance you'll be able to buy either muscadine wine or champagne unless you've reserved some as much as six months earlier. That reserve list usually contains names of about 1000 customers. That's how great the demand for muscadine wine is. If you're new around here, you may not know that the muscadine is a big grape that grows wild in the woods. This is approximately the northern limit of its natural area. It's been domesticated and is grown in commercial vineyards in Tennessee and states to the south. The 24-below cold in January 1985 killed back Fay's own muscadine vines above ground and they have not yet recovered. He has been buying muscadines from vineyards farther south.

Muscadine wine is on the sweet side, a disadvantage in the view of most connoisseurs. But don't turn it down until you've tried it. The unusual flavor of muscadines overcomes the disadvantage for many. I like muscadine wine. I like muscadine marmalade and I like to eat muscadines right off the vine. I like to smell them. There's nothing much better in the world of aromas

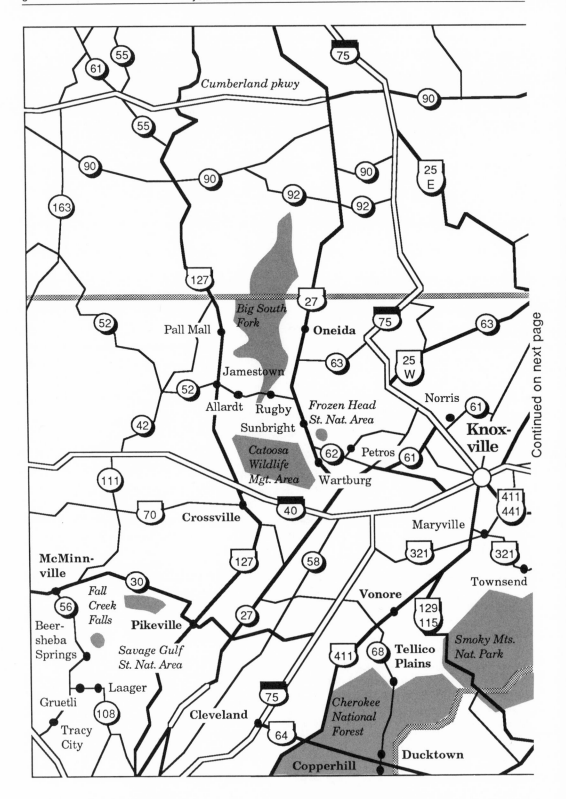

Continued on next page

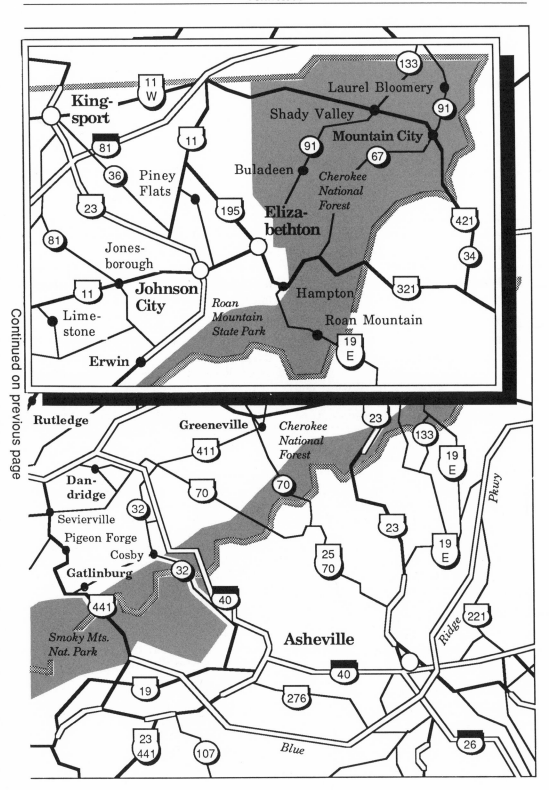

Continued on previous page

than walking into a closed room where a bucket of muscadines has rested overnight.

Fay, of course, makes several other varieties of wine. His best last year, I thought, was the Chardonnay, dry as an October day in the Cumberlands. If Fay knows you well enough, he might show you a copy of the wine list of San Francisco's Mark Hopkins Hotel. One of the Chardonnays is from Highland Manor, priced at $30 a bottle. It costs lots less at the winery.

The winery has a wall covered with blue ribbons. Fay sometimes jokes that he bought them at a flea market. He didn't. He also has gold medals for beating the French, the Californians, the Italians, the Germans and all the others in international competition.

Fay is a Fentress County product. He found Kathy in Scotland, one of his stopping places in a 20-year Air Force career. They got Tennessee's first license to make wine Jan. 24, 1980. (Nine other Tennessee wineries now are licensed.)

Taste a few of the Wheelers' wines and select some to take home and a bottle or two to take to dinner — or lunch — at the Beggar's Castle.

The Beggar's Castle is a German restaurant west of Jamestown. You go north from the winery on 127 and look for Glen Oby Road, to your left. Follow Glen Oby a couple of miles and look for a Beggar's Castle marker beckoning you to a gravel road to the left. Follow that one down, down into Buffalo Cove. And there, backed up against a cliff, is the Beggar's Castle.

Roger and Sylvia Salomon run it. If they'd hired marketing specialists to select the worst place to put a restaurant, they might have landed in the same place. It's close to no big population center. It's about equally too far from Knoxville, Nashville, Lexington and Chattanooga.

But they didn't select the site for a restaurant. Roger is from Germany. After coming to this country, marrying Sylvia and teaching for a time, he decided to retire. They looked over much of the country and found this place in the woods of Fentress County. They bought more than 450 acres.

Roger got restless. He also got tired of eating food he thought was not prepared just right. He was thinking particularly of ham. He comes from a long line of curers of meat in Germany. So he started buying hams from Lay Packing Co. of Knoxville and curing them himself. Gradually, he started selling them at what he came to call Salomon Farm. From there, he went into the restaurant business in 1984.

In spite of the location, Roger is still in business. In fact, he's in business 12 months of the year now. Until 1987, he had closed in January and February. He is closed Mondays. (One thing to remember: You cannot buy wine at Highland Manor on Sunday or food at the restaurant on Monday. But if you can't have wine with your meal on Sunday, you can drink some of the fine German beer Roger serves.)

His menu includes such items as wiener schnitzel, sauerbraten, bratwurst and rindsrouladen. If you don't like that sort of thing, Roger usually has ribeye steak, trout or chicken. He always serves his special ham as part of an appetizer. For dessert, I like the brandied apricots. Incidentally, one thing Roger does with some of his hams is remove the bones and stuff the cavities with Turkish apricots. Then he soaks the hams in cognac for three months.

Last time I talked with him, he said he was dredging up food memories from his German childhood. He didn't know what route his mother traveled to arrive at some of her food destinations, but he's going his own route and trying to arrive at the same destinations. One of these memories involves a pizza-like German dish made with Black Forest ham.

Back to 127. Turn left and go to Pall Mall, on Wolf River. Stand on the bridge over the Wolf and look back generally in the direction you've come. You may be able to see a bare cliff wall. That's the Yellow Door.

The Yellow Door is where Alvin C. York went to meditate and pray when he was trying to reconcile his religious convictions with his duty to country in deciding whether to fight in World War I or stay out as a conscientious objector.

Three days and nights he stayed up

there, says his son Andy (Andrew Jackson) York. And when he came down, he went to war.

In France's Argonne Forest, on Oct. 8, 1918, the Tennessee squirrel hunter put out of commission an entire German machine-gun battalion. With his rifle and pistol, he killed 25 and took 132 prisoners. For this, he became the most decorated soldier of World War I and probably America's greatest war hero of all time. All told, he received more than 40 Allied decorations. His own country gave him the Medal of Honor. France gave him the Croix de Guerre.

A few yards downstream from the bridge is the grist mill York operated on the Wolf. It now is part of Alvin York Memorial Park, established by the state in 1968. There in the shade of trees, people of the Cumberlands can picnic, and youngsters and their fathers can catch smallmouth and redeyes from the Wolf.

Andy York is the park ranger. When he has to be away, cousin Cletus York takes over. The old York home stands near the river. Andy says it soon will become part of the park.

Back down in Jamestown is the Alvin C. York Agricultural Institute. York established it in the 1920s to help young people of his area get an education that would help them make a living. From about 1926 to 1937, York operated it as a private school. Then a temporary illness forced him to end his connection with it. The state took it over. Two unusual circumstances are connected with the school: On 400 acres of pine forest and grassland, it is said to have the largest campus of any high school in the world, and it is the only Tennessee high school operated directly by the state. Fentress County's only connection is to provide bus transportation for some of the students.

Also in Jamestown is a block-sized park containing the Mark Twain Spring. The spring was the source of water for early Jamestown settlers, including the parents of Samuel L. Clemens (Mark Twain), who lived just north of it from 1827 to 1832. They also lived somewhere in the vicinity three years longer. Mark Twain never

lived there. But he probably was conceived there. According to the marker, his parents left for Missouri "in the spring of 1835" and he was born the following November.

On the road again. A short distance north of Jamestown, turn east off 127 onto State 154. Follow that road to its intersection with State 297 and then follow 297 into and through Big South Fork National River and Recreation Area.

You can hunt in BSFNRRA. In fact that's one of the few things you can do in it that you cannot do in a national park. The usual East Tennessee game animals are there. But be certain you know the seasons and the rules before you start. You can hike on about 150 miles of trails and ride on about 125 miles of separate horse trails. Horse trails are marked by a white blaze and a yellow horse head. Hiking trails are marked by a white blaze and either a red arrowhead or a blue silhouette of John Muir. The latter are only for the John Muir Trail, named for that fine Scottish gentleman who in the late 19th and early 20th centuries walked over great swaths of the United States before he finally stopped in California.

You can fish but be sure you have the right license — a Tennessee one for streams in Tennessee and a Kentucky license for streams in the Kentucky part of Big South Fork. The main river is a good walleye stream. It also has smallmouth bass, redeyes, bluegills and catfish. Same story for one of Big South Fork's two major tributaries, Clear Fork. (The other major tributary is New River which carries gunk from a coal-mining region.) Trout are stocked in some of the smaller streams and they're reproducing in some streams. North White Oak Creek and Laurel Fork are good trout streams.

And, of course, you can float the river in canoes, kayaks and rafts. But get all the information you need from people at park headquarters, or from somebody like Bob Lantz, before you make your first trip. Take a map and compass. If you crack up, you may have to walk out.

Big South Fork now contains about 105,000 acres. Land buying is continuing

Big South Fork National River and Recreation Area

and the area is planned to grow to about 125,000 acres.

My favorite trails in BSFNRRA are the two from Leatherwood Ford to Angel Falls. One's on one side of the river and the other's on the other side. The high bridge you cross on 297 is at Leatherwood Ford. What you need to do is get down to the low bridge, just downstream from the high one. You do that from the east side (the Oneida side) of the river. One trail goes down the east side of the river two miles to Angel Falls. To go down the other side, you walk across the river on the low bridge and turn right on the John Muir Trail.

Howard Duncan, who has lived in the area all his life and is a member of the Big South Fork staff, went with me on both of these not long ago.

First, the trail along the east side. It stays close to the river all the way to the falls. Howard pointed out the old Anderson Branch Coal Mine, up the hillside to our right. You can see evidence of recent reclamation work. Lots of wildflowers bloom along this trail in spring and summer.

Angel Falls used to be just "the Falls," Howard said. But canoeists added "Angel" to it in the 1960s. This was to offset that evil waterfall, Devil's Jump, downstream in Kentucky. As waterfalls go, Angel Falls isn't a big one, not as far as the drop is concerned. It's of more concern to canoeists because the river there is full of huge boulders. Picking safe passage through them is the major problem. Big South Fork people tell you to portage around it. Most people do, but a few daredevils run it. Many canoes have cracked up there, Howard said. When the river is in flood — as it had been a few days before Howard and I were there — most of those great boulders are covered with water. One of the things to look at from this side of the river is the high gorge wall on the other side. It towers 450 to 500 feet above the river.

Back at Leatherwood Ford, Howard explained how it got that name. He stripped bark from a shrub and then separated the inner and outer bark. The inner bark is as strong and pliable as leather. Indians used it for string and to make nets.

Another little goodie Howard told me is about the coal particles that are mixed naturally with sand along the river. When you build a fire on the sand to cook a fish or a hotdog, there sometimes is such a rich coal mixture that the sand catches fire.

From the east side of the bridge, the hike to Angel Falls Overlook, on the west side of the river, is about three miles. On your left, as you go down the river, stands an old chimney above a fireplace whose stones have long been cold. Howard said he's never found anyone who knew the family who lived in the house that went with the chimney.

Somewhere along this trail, I saw what I'm pretty sure is pachysandra. Low-growing plant with splotchy leaves that stay green through the winter, then drop off when new leaves come out in spring. Has an odd-looking bloom. I've never seen that plant in the Great Smokies, though the Great Smokies has what's probably the greatest plant variety in the country.

The Great Smokies does have gaywings (Polygala paucifolia). But on a trail near Rugby, I've seen more gaywings on a 100-yard stretch than I've seen on all the trails I ever walked in the Smokies.

Nor does the Great Smokies have anything comparable to the gorge of Big South Fork.

No, I'm not knocking the Great Smokies. It's one of my favorite places on earth. What I'm saying is that people who always head for the Smokies and never go to the Cumberlands surely are missing much.

After maybe a mile, we left the river and turned left up Fall Branch, where part of the trail is on a long wooden bridge. As we ascended the bluff from its back side, we climbed stone steps, and once or twice, wooden steps. Finally, we came out on top and looked far down at the river. The first overlook you reach offers a fine view, but you don't see Angel Falls from there. Go just a few yards to the next natural overlook and you can see the falls. Either overlook is a good place to look far up and down the river, to spot an occasional hawk, to eat lunch, and to feel pretty good about the universe.

You're in Scott County here. It's an unusual county. It produces some coal but no big amount according to standards set in Kentucky and Virginia. It produces quite a bit of lumber. And it produces successful Republican politicians. It produced Howard H. Baker, Second District congressman for many years; the Baker son, Howard Jr., White House chief of staff and former Senate majority leader, and John Duncan, long-time Second District congressman.

Democrats don't do well in Scott County. A story is told about a Democratic candidate long ago coming to the county to speak. The natives thought this was pretty funny. They thought they ought to provide a proper platform for the visitor. So they piled up a mound of manure.

The Democrat climbed to the top of the manure pile, sniffed a time or two, smiled a bit uncomfortably but in good humor, and said:

"This is the first time I've ever spoken from a Republican platform."

Pick a fair three-day weekend and point the car toward the history treasures of Upper East Tennessee.

Don't misunderstand; Upper ET has more to offer than history. It has rhododendrons in numbers you will not see elsewere. It has off-the-beaten-path beauty spots. It's a place to go for fine dinnerware. It has fast rivers and deep lakes. But the major thing it has is a forest of historic markers concerning great Tennesseans and events before the Revolution and not so long after it.

I'm not sure where Upper East Tennessee begins. But for us, for this weekend, it begins in Rutledge, on US 11W.

I particularly like Rutledge in October, when the Rutledge maples wear autumn colors. Rutledge used to have lots more maples. A road widening took many of them 15 or more years ago. But it still has enough for an autumn show.

It also has the site of the very first business venture of this country's 17th president and one of Tennessee's more forthright governors. I mean Andrew Johnson's tailor shop.

Most historians ignore Johnson's stay in

Rutledge because it was brief. But the Rutledge Lions Club didn't ignore it. Club members laid brick, drove nails and skinned knuckles in 1976 when they built a tiny tailor shop as much like the one Johnson used as they could make it. They found old pictures of the shop, counted the numbers of bricks in the sides and used exactly the same number in the one that stands today on the southeast lawn of the Courthouse.

Johnson must have been 17 or 18 years old. He had been apprenticed to a tailor in Greeneville. He wanted a business of his own. So he came to Rutledge. He got to talking with Grainger County Sheriff Sam Bunch. He told Bunch he wanted to go into the tailoring business. So the sheriff offered him the use of his office.

They must have been crowded. For the sheriff needed at least enough space for a desk and probably a spitoon. And Johnson needed space for a sewing machine and probably a cutting table.

You can understand why Johnson moved at the first opportunity. That came in about six months, with the death of the Greeneville tailor to whom he had been apprenticed. Johnson moved right back to Greeneville and took over the dead man's business.

Going on northeast on 11W, you can slow down, or even stop, at the site of the old Tate Spring Hotel, a premier resort hotel in its time. Its time was from its construction shortly after the Civil War until TVA built Cherokee Dam in the early 1940s. Cherokee Lake took all but four holes of the 18-hole golf course and that killed the old resort which the Great Depression had already crippled.

At the peak of its popularity, Tate Spring Hotel was the vacation place for the car-making Studebaker family from Indiana and wealthy bankers and planters from the Deep South. They hunted, played cards, played golf, drank whiskey and sometimes played fly poker.

Fly poker?

Yes, when they were too tired from playing golf and had drunk too much booze to be very alert, they played a simple card game. Each player put one card and an agreed-upon amount of money on the table. The winner was the person on whose card a fly first lit.

Not every hotel guest drank liquor, but nearly every one drank Tate water. It contained certain minerals and it tasted bad, so it was supposed to be good for you. An early-morning ritual was a knock on the door of each guestroom by a servant bearing a healthful pot of heated water from the little spring. At the mid-morning "watering hour" everyone went to the spring to drink more water. There was another water-drinking time in the afternoon.

Except for the Studebakers who used their own product for transportation, most of the very rich hotel guests came in their private railroad cars. They came to Morristown on the Southern Railway, then on to Tate Spring on the little Peavine Railroad.

The same railroads hauled out Tate water to thirsty customers across the country. It was the Perrier of its day. You could buy a 33-gallon barrel for $5, a half-barrel for $3.50 and a 5-gallon demijohn for $2.25.

Just a few miles on up the highway was a much earlier place of lodging, Bean Station Inn, built in 1814. It was said to be the largest tavern between Washington and New Orleans. Among those who sampled its hospitality were John Sevier, Andrew Jackson, James K. Polk, Henry Clay and Andrew Johnson. Long before the inn was built, Daniel Boone and William Bean camped there in about 1775. Members of the Bean family moved to this spot and built a fort in 1787. The Bean home, part of the fort, was built over a spring, about 70 yards south of a marker in a grove of trees beside Cherokee Lake.

This place where the Beans settled and left their name also was a key spot on an alternate route to the Wilderness Road, blazed in 1775 by Daniel Boone and 30 helpers. The regular route was northward from the present Kingsport into Virginia and then westward down Powell Valley, then north through Cumberland Gap. The alternate route was from Long Island of the Holston (Kingsport) down Holston Valley to Bean Station, then north across Clinch Mountain and on to Cumberland Gap.

Our next stop is Rogersville, county seat of Hawkins County and the site of another early inn. John McKinney built McKinney Tavern House in 1824-25. The first guests stayed in 1824, before the building was finished. Presidents Jackson, Polk and Johnson also slept and ate there.

But this inn differs in one important respect from Bean Station Inn and Tate Spring Hotel. This inn in Rogersville still stands, still takes guests. It's had other names over the years; it's now called Hale Springs Inn. Though it's 163 years old, it is elegant. The pegged-down heart-of-pine floors glow. The antique furniture in every room is clean, comfortable, useable. Two of the mantels, in the Andrew Johnson suite and the Mollie Gray apartment, are especially lovely. They were brought from Philadelphia when the inn was built. Ready-to-burn wood rests beside the fireplaces. (But the building now has central heat and air conditioning.) The rooms have no phones or TV sets to destroy the illusion that the inn is about the same as when Andrew Jackson last stopped, en route the last time from the White House to the Hermitage.

Rates for the inn's eight rooms are moderate. For instance, a couple can sleep under the high canopy of the bed in the Andrew Jackson Suite for $55. If an additional one or two persons sleep in the other bedroom of the suite, the cost goes up $10.

During the Civil War, when Federal troops held the town, the Union used the inn (then McKinney Tavern House) as a hospital. When the Confederates held the town, they used the Kyle House, just across the street, as their headquarters. For years thereafter, some Rogersvillians crossed the street to walk on the side they favored. The Kyle House, built in 1830, also still stands.

I cannot tell you who were the first persons to live where Rogersville now stands. But David Crockett and his wife must have been among the first. For Indians massacred them there in 1777. They were Davy's grandparents. Somebody can direct you to Rogers Cemetery, where the Crockett remains rest. The little cemetery is enclosed by an attractive low stone wall.

The oldest courthouse in Tennessee?

The one in Hawkins County, of course.

It stands near Hale Springs Inn. Hawkins Countians have been going to court, paying their taxes and getting their marriage licenses there since 1836. And that fine old brick structure looks sturdy enough to continue serving the same purposes for another 150 years.

Rogersville is named for Joseph Rogers, who came from Ireland in 1780 to operate a cluster of stores for Thomas Amis (pronounced Amee). Amis lived in a house of stone (which still stands but is partly covered with wood) 1.5 miles east of Rogersville. Amis went away temporarily to represent the district in the North Carolina Legislature. (This area then was still part of North Carolina.) While he was gone, Rogers courted an Amis daughter, Mary. Joseph and Mary eloped. Amis was unhappy when he came home and learned he had a son-in-law. But his anger soon cooled and he gave them his blessing and lots of acres in what's now Rogersville. Rogers later gave a little of the land for a courthouse and a village square for the new county of Hawkins which was established in 1787. North Carolina granted a charter for the county seat and named it Rogersville in 1889. (Some authorities say Rogersville actually was established in 1786 when the region was part of the State of Franklin. More later about Franklin.) It's one of Tennessee's oldest towns.

Going eastward out of Rogersville (on old Highway 11-W, not the bypass), we come to Burem Road, veering to the right. Veer with it. It's on this road that the old Amis house stands, many yards left of the road. We soon come to a road that turns left along a large creek. This is Big Creek. Follow this road to the home of sisters Mary and Matilda Beal and the Ebbing and Flowing Spring.

They are great-great-great-great granddaughters of Thomas Amis and their 250 acres and the unusual spring are part of the 3000-plus acres Amis owned. The spring is one of the rare ones of the earth whose flow starts and stops on a regular clock-like schedule. The cycle from maximum flow back to max is about two hours and 40 minutes. When I visited once, Mary said the spring was ebbing and that it would be more than an hour before it reached its low point and started to rise again.

So I did an errand in Rogersville and came back an hour later. By then, the flow was nearly stopped. We looked at the spring openings — at least seven, all fairly close together at the base of a rock ledge. No water came from them. Only minutes later, we saw water flowing from two openings, then from all openings. Within no more than 10 minutes, the current was strong. Water in the shallow streambed deepened and widened about 20 inches on both sides. Mary says the maximum flow has been measured at about 500 gallons per minute.

There are few such springs. The only other one I've seen is the Fittified Spring in the Greenbrier section of the Great Smokies. But the Fittified Spring differs considerably from the one on the Beal farm. The maximum flow of the Fittified Spring was only about 10 gallons per minute and its complete cycle was about 18 minutes. And their histories differ. It was a 1916 earthquake that gave the Fittified Spring the starts and stops, and something, possibly nearby dynamiting, has caused it to start acting almost like a normal spring again. Not so the Ebbing and Flowing Spring. It has done what it's doing for all the 200-plus years since its discovery and it shows no sign of stopping.

There are two or three theories on why such springs do as they do. The one I like is that there is a natural siphon somewhere in the underground stream course. A natural basin fills and flows out at a top opening. Because of the siphon, it continues to flow until empty. Once it is empty, the siphon is broken and the flow stops until the basin fills again.

If you should go to Ebbing and Flowing Spring, be on your good behavior. The Beals charge no admission, nor do they in any other way commercialize their rare spring. Don't litter or throw rocks at the dogs and chickens. And don't cause a traffic jam on the narrow road.

Back on Burem Road, we soon cross the Holston River. Immediately on the left after we cross the bridge is Webster Angus

Farm, 900 acres, on both sides of the river, owned by George D. Webster, a Washington lawyer with long roots back into Hawkins County history. He's a great-great grandson of Joseph and Mary Rogers and a great-grandson of Drury Alsbrook Spears. Spears in 1858 built the large brick home that stands well off the road to the left. Webster restored the old house in 1968-72 and added a wing in 1977. He also added many acres to the farm. Bricks for the original house were made on the site. In the restoration, Webster had the outer layer of bricks taken down and then turned around when they were put back up, so that they show the original color. During the Civil War, Lazarus Spears, a Confederate officer, was home on leave. Bushwackers ambushed him and hanged him from a persimmon tree near the house. The hat he wore that day is preserved in the house.

The house, a second home for the Websters, is not open to the public, but you can get a pretty good look at it from the road.

Let's leave Hawkins County. Back to 11W. On to Kingsport and lunch at the Chicago Dough Company, on Stone Drive (11W). Good pizza. The restaurant serves beer and mixed drinks.

Then I hunted up Long Island of the Holston. It is truly a *long* island. Tennessee Eastman now owns and uses a great deal of it. The Mead Corp. owns some of it. The Cherokees once owned all of it and they loved it. They were partial to islands. I don't think they ever had a town on the island, but it was one of the places where they camped and where their leaders sometimes met with leaders of other tribes and with white leaders. It was sacred ground to them. But they had to relinquish it to the white folks under terms of a treaty of 1806.

One hundred seventy years later, something occurred which, as far as I know, was without precedent: The white folks gave some land back to the Indians. It happened in this way, according to Norman Spencer, who then was manager of the Mead plant in Kingsport: Mead wanted to give some Long Island land both to the city and to the Cherokees. So it gave it all to the city — some 10 or 15 acres — with the under-

standing that the city would pass on to the Cherokees 3.6 acres of it. This was done on July 16, 1976. It now is the property of the Eastern Band of the Cherokees.

The Cherokees built a monument on it, and on panels of the monument are the names of the seven Cherokee clans: Wolf, Blue, Deer, Bird, Paint, Wild Potato and Long Hair.

When I was there not so long ago, mallards were swimming and flying up and down the river much as they might have when the Cherokees owned the whole island. You reach the island by way of Netherland Inn Road, which leads you to Kingsport's Boatyard Riverfront Park. And from there you walk a swinging bridge across the river to the island.

As a practical matter, there's not much the Cherokees can do with the little plot of land. It's too far from where most Cherokees live for them to grow corn and squash on it. But then that's not what the Cherokees did with the land when they owned all of the island. They had meetings on it then, and they've had a few meetings on it in the past 10 years.

Mostly, the gift back to the Cherokees was a symbol, an indication that more friendship and understanding exist now than did 200 years ago.

Next time the Cherokees visit, maybe they should go to Kingsport's Bays Mountain Park. The Cherokees lived close to nature, and nature is what Bays Mountain Park is, all 3000 acres of it. It's more than a park; it also is a school, a place where young and not-so-young learn about the natural environment. Classes at the park are part of the curriculum of Sullivan County and Kingsport students. Students from 19 surrounding counties use the park to lesser extent. About 25,000 students per year study there. Total park visits average 120,000 to 130,000 per year.

The park has an annual budget of about $500,000. It has a staff of 19, including four naturalists. It has a planetarium. It has a 700-gallon salt-water "touch tank" some of whose fish and other salt-water critters will stay still for the touch of youngsters.

It has many aquatic wall tank exhibits made possible by membership dues of the

Bays Mountain Park Association. It has a freeze chamber in which dead animals are freeze-dried (instead of stuffed) for exhibits. This is the newest technique for animal exhibits, and the Bays Mountain freeze-dryers went to the Smithsonian to learn how to do it.

Teacher-naturalist David Taylor says the park is in the first stage of establishing a native animal habitat. Otters will be first to inhabit it. Wolves, mountain lions and bobcats may come later.

A small zoo at the park is populated mostly with animals for which the Tennessee Wildlife Resources Agency had to find a home. These include an injured red-tailed hawk no longer able to make it in the wild, a few deer, a raccoon confiscated from someone who was keeping it as an illegal pet, and a few coyotes.

Visitors can walk about 25 miles of hiking trails, one of which meanders along the shore of a 44-acre lake. In 1914, the Kingsport Waterworks Corp. bought a 1300-acre watershed and impounded the lake as the source of Kingsport's water supply. The city of Kingsport bought the complete water system in 1926. In 1944, the city stopped using water from the lake. In the 1960s, it turned the area into a park and bought about 2000 more acres to add to it. Tennessee Eastman gave $225,000 for construction of the Nature Center Building.

It's most unusual for a city — especially a city of only about 35,000 population — to support such an outstanding park/nature center/school.

The park is more than six miles west of the city. Take State Highway 93 and then follow the markers. There is a $1 parking fee. Admission to the planetarium is $2 for adults and $1 for children.

Motorists going south from Kingsport toward Johnson City can choose between four-lane, limited-access US 23/I-181 and two-lane, older State Highway 36. I used 36, bordered by homes, communities, historic markers. One of the markers, in the Boones Creek area, took me to a small waterfall. Daniel Boone once hid under that waterfall to escape Indians. Also, it was not so far from here that once stood a beech tree on which Boone carved, "D Boon cilled

a bar in year 1760."

I went on south on 36 to 11E, north of Johnson City, turned northeast on 11E and went to Rocky Mount.

Besides mothballs, what do moths not want to smell? Well, for one thing, the stem of an old clay pipe, the kind people smoked 200 and more years ago.

That's one of the things one learns at Rocky Mount. You also learn about baking bread in a beehive oven. The beehive oven at Rocky Mount is chest high in the wall just left of the huge fireplace where most of the cooking was done. Julia Farrell, my tour guide, said the bread bakers of long ago built a fire in the beehive oven. After it had burned a while and nothing much was left but embers, the baker stuck her arm inside the oven. If it was hot enough to singe hairs on the arm, it was hot enough to bake bread. So the baker raked out the fire and ashes and put in bread dough.

Such things interest me more than the fact that William Blount governed the Territory South of the River Ohio from this big log home from 1790 to '92. This was while that Knoxville building called Blount Mansion was being built for him.

This was no humble log cabin of pioneer lore. It was — and remains — a two-story house. Two big rooms upstairs and two down. A dogtrot away was a big dining room with its own fireplace. The kitchen was in a separate building a few yards from the dining room. The path between dining room and kitchen was the "whistle walk." Slaves carrying food between the two places were supposed to whistle to let the mistress and master know they weren't chomping on the vittles.

The master and mistress were William and Barsheba Cobb. Cobb built the house in 1770-72. And he picked a lovely site for it. It sits atop a hill and the view extends for miles in all directions. Blount apparently was a non-paying guest of the Cobbs while he governed from the hilltop. Rocky Mount is the oldest original territorial capitol in the United States and one of the oldest buildings in Tennessee.

It was a social center of the region. One frequent guest was young Andrew Jack-

Doe River covered bridge, Elizabethton

son, a Jonesborough lawyer. Barsheba Cobb thought Jackson drank too much, and she told him so. This didn't make Jackson stop drinking, but it prompted him to hide his bottle from Barsheba. His hiding place was the rear section of a two-section small middle drawer of the hunt board.

The hunt board is a handsome piece of furniture in the dining room. Julia Farrell said the prevailing theory is that William Cobb stood at the hunt board and ate a quick breakfast before going hunting. But she said a visitor once advanced a reasonable theory that venison, quail and other game foods were served from the hunt board. Maybe both are correct.

On the dining table sits a solid cone of white sugar, with the metal sugar snip one used to snip off a piece of sugar for tea or coffee.

Then there's the hot-toddy poker beside the dining room fireplace. Heat the end of it until it glows and then poke it into a crock of toddy, usually a mixture of rum, apple juice and sugar.

People who smoked tobacco back then used clay pipes with very long stems. When the end of the stem became bitter with tobacco taste, the smoker simply broke off an inch or two of the stem and went on smoking a fresher pipe with a shorter stem. A few days or weeks later, he broke off the end again. Barsheba saved these smelly broken ends and put them in closets and drawers to make moths turn up their noses and leave.

The smelliest thing at Rocky Mount now is the slave cabin. Julia Farrell said the odor is from rotted flax. For in the slave cabin are all the tools for turning flax fibers into cloth. The slaves did it. Non-slaves still do it in educational demonstrations.

Descendants of the Cobbs owned Rocky Mount until 1959, when they sold it to the state for preservation as an historic site. Since then, a modern building has been added to house the Massengill Museum of Overmountain History. A tour of Rocky Mount lasts about an hour and a half. Tour guides wear clothes like the Cobbs wore. Admission is $4 for adults, $3.50 for adults in a group of 10 or more, and $2.50 for students. It's worth it. Bring a picnic lunch. There's a place outside to eat it.

Back in the car and headed northeast on 11E, you can go on to Bristol for the auto races, or you can go only as far as the 11W-US 19E intersection, turn south on 19E and go to Elizabethton.

I went to Elizabethton, site of one of the biggest deals in history, place where you can drive, or walk, across a covered bridge more than 100 years old, starting place of a march that some say turned the tide of the Revolution.

Before Elizabethton was Elizabethton it was Sycamore Shoals of the Watauga River. It was at Sycamore Shoals that hundreds of Cherokees and quite a few white people met in March 1775 to negotiate the biggest real estate deal in history. If it happened today, newspaper and television reporters by the hundreds would cover it. It had great political, social and economic significance. It lasted for days.

Land speculator Richard Henderson was trying to persuade the Indians to sell him more than 20 million acres of land — all the land in the Cumberland River watershed, plus land extending northward to the Kentucky River. That's a lot of Kentucky and a big chunk of Tennessee. The Indians were divided. Most of the old chiefs favored the sale. Young Chief Dragging Canoe bitterly opposed it. The old chiefs prevailed. Henderson bought the land for 2000 pounds sterling and 8000 pounds in goods. Then he sent Daniel Boone and 30 axmen to blaze a route into it.

Two days after that deal was struck, leaders of the settlers living in questionable legality on Cherokee land along the Holston, Watauga and New Rivers bought this land from the Indians for 2000 pounds sterling.

Representing the settlers in the second deal was the Watauga Association, a simple, infant government, the first independent democratic government in America, except of course those of the Indians. It was the means established by the settlers on the Watauga and the Holston to protect themselves. They formed it without permission of the King of England, the colonial governor of North Carolina or anybody

else. That sort of thing wasn't much done back then. The people called their little government a court. It had five elected members, who were supposed to "govern and direct for the common good of all the people."

It was at this same Sycamore Shoals, five years after the big real estate transaction, that the Overmountain men gathered to water their horses and hear a prayer before riding across the mountains to whip the British at Kings Mountain and, as folks in this region are fond of saying, "turn the tide of the Revolution."

You can learn more about all these events at the Sycamore Shoals State Historic Area, which also is a National Historic Landmark. At the same place, you can see a replica of old Fort Watauga, which actually stood some distance from this spot.

I left the historic area, headed back uptown and walked across Doe River on the old covered bridge. It has a protected lane for walkers and a wider one for vehicles. But a high-bed truck couldn't squeeze under the cover. Covered bridges sometimes were called "kissing bridges" or "courting bridges." But of course the bridge builders didn't build them for courting couples.

Well, why did they cover bridges?

One theory is they did it to protect the bridge, to keep the weather off the important timbers that carried the weight of loaded wagons and galloping horses. Another theory is that bridges were covered (sides as well as top) to keep horses from looking far down at the river and becoming frightened. Bridges were built many feet above water so they wouldn't wash away in floods. Horses were not accustomed to being so high above water. Of course, a good enough reason for covering them was to shelter travelers from storms.

The Doe River Bridge is one of a very few covered bridges left in Tennessee and probably is the one most used and kept in the best condition. Until Halloween vandals burned it 15 or 20 years ago, there was a covered bridge across Flat Creek on Old Rutledge Pike in east Knox County.

At Elizabethton, you decide where to go next. If it's late June, it's no problem. You head south to the Highlands of Roan and a

Cross-country skiing in Roan Mountain State Resort Park

rhododendron show the likes of which you are not likely to see elsewhere. Take 19E south to the little town of Roan Mountain, then State 143 to the top. You'll follow Doe River much of the way.

En route to the top of the mountain, you will pass Roan Mountain State Resort Park, one of Tennessee's best. It has about 2200 acres scattered on the northern slopes of the Roan and in the valley of the Doe. The Doe runs within a few feet of the visitor center and once powered an old iron mining operation there. The Doe has good trout water, and the state stocks it generously.

The park has about 15 miles of hiking trails. One of them is called the Fred H. Behrand Trail. Fred was an Elizabethton newspaperman. I used to call him when the weather was very cold and the snow very deep to ask whether any snow buntings had come to Roan Mountain. These little northern birds sometimes came that far south during extremely cold weather. Fred then was about the only person to brave the elements and go to the mountaintop.

But I suspect more people go there now.

The Roan has become a popular spot for cross-country skiing. A group called High South Nordic Guides operates a cross-country ski center based in the state park.

You can rent one of the 20 park cabins by the day or by the week. Rates are moderate. Rates Sunday through Thursday are considerably lower than Friday and Saturday. Cabins have linens and cooking utensils, but if cooking is one of the things you are trying to escape, you can eat at the park restaurant. However, the restaurant is closed Monday and Tuesday from December to April and is closed on Monday throughout the year.

The park has 50 campsites with water, electric hookups and bathhouses. Daily fee for these is $8. A tent area has 20 sites with tent pads, water and two bathhouses. These cost $5.50 per day.

To see the rhododendron show during the second half of June, go on to the top of the mountain at Carvers Gap. Then turn right on a road that leads you more than a mile to parking areas. Up there, Tennessee and North Carolina share more than 600 acres of natural rhododendron gardens. Some claim this is the biggest rhododendron garden on earth. Others limit the area to the United States. After all, China has lots of rhododendrons; they might be hiding a 700-acre garden. These are Catawba rhododendrons, the kind with the rose-purple blooms. There is an annual rhododendron festival the third weekend of June in the state park.

But on this most recent trip into Upper East Tennessee, I didn't go south to Roan Mountain. Instead, I turned northeast on State 91. The road parallels Stony Creek, a big, fast stream that crosses lots of rocks. This rural area is surprisingly heavily populated. You pass house after house as you drive through the communities of Carter, Sadie and Buladeen. (If one Buladeen per day isn't enough for you, turn back to Elizabethton, go up over the Roan into North Carolina and down to another one. Only this other one is spelled differently — B-u-l-a-d-e-a-n. A straight-flying crow could go from Buladean to Buladeen in 20 minutes.

The populated area ends abruptly when you enter Cherokee National Forest and the road starts switchbacking up a mountain. Then you reach the top of Cross Mountain and cross the Appalachian Trail and the Carter-Johnson county line. Down there below you is what you came to see: Shady Valley.

Shady Valley is wide and gently sloped. Pastoral. Nearly unblemished. Most of the land is grazed or cultivated.

Go to the first crossroads and turn right on 91 and US 421 and go over another Iron Mountain ridge to Mountain City. Then go north on 91 to Laurel Bloomery, the easternmost community in Tennessee. You may not know when you've reached Laurel Bloomery. But that's all right. You'll know when you reach a building on the left that houses Iron Mountain Stoneware.

Alberta and I spent a weekend in Mountain City 20 or more years ago and took time to drive up to Laurel Bloomery. We bought a load of Iron Mountain Stoneware — cups, saucers, plates, bowls. In all the years since, not one has broken. A few have tiny nicks. I suppose you could break

the stuff if you took an axe to it. But it survives the normal run of accidents. Take it out of the freezer and put it into the hottest oven without worry.

On a Scandinavian trip several years later, we were browsing on the second floor of a store of that holy of holies of dinnerware, Royal Copenhagen of Denmark. And there we found Iron Mountain Stoneware in our pattern, called Roan Mountain.

This wouldn't have surprised me so much had I known then that Nancy Patterson Lamb, the head lady of Iron Mountain Stoneware, had spent 30 months working and studying with master craftsmen and artists of Royal Copenhagen. After that stay in Denmark, she went on to Finland for a year with Arabia Potteries. She later went to Taiwan and helped the Peitou Ceramic Plant develop a line of stoneware dinnerware. She came back to this country in 1961 and, instead of going back home to California, came to Johnson County and established Iron Mountain Stoneware.

Why there?

One reason is that it's a "pretty place," she said. The land was available at a reasonable price. Johnson County had people needing jobs. Raw materials were reasonably close. And her first partner, a businessman, lived just up the road in Damascus, Va.

She says she no longer sells stoneware in Denmark, nor in Belgium and France, where she also used to sell. The same blow that hit lots of other U.S. manufacturers hit her: The currency exchange rate became too unfavorable. However, Iron Mountain Stoneware *is* sold in all 50 states.

Why is it so hard to chip or break?

Because it's fired so high — up to a peak of 2550 degrees. It's "all melted together." It has no porosity.

Doesn't anybody else fire dinnerware so high?

Yes, the makers of fine porcelain dinnerware do. But they paint it *after* the high firing. It's the paint that doesn't stand up. She paints her products *before* she gives them the high firing. And the paint lasts through all sorts of adversity.

Iron Mountain sells seconds at its own retail shop at the factory. And twice a year

— Mother's Day and Thanksgiving weekends —big four-day sales are held. Things get pretty informal. They fry hamburgers on the scrubbed silicon carbide kiln shelves. Anybody is welcome, but invitations go out to all those who have signed the guest register.

Back to Mountain City and Elizabethton. But we don't have to go back the same route from Mountain City. We'll get some different scenery and mountains not so steep on State 67 and then US 321. A good look at Watauga Lake, one of TVA's lovelier lakes, is one reason for taking 67. On through Elizabethton on 321 and then on through Johnson City on it. Our next stop is Jonesborough, oldest town in the state, Mother Town of Tennessee, the first entire town to be placed on the National Register of Historic Places.

In 1770, somebody whose name is lost to history built a cabin where Jonesborough now sits. By 1779, there was a cluster of buildings and the State of North Carolina issued it a charter as a city and named it in honor of Willie Jones of Halifax, N. C. Jones was a bit different. For instance, he left orders that when he died, he was to be buried standing up, so he could be standing when he met his Maker. His orders were obeyed.

It was to Jonesborough in 1784 that delegates came to form the State of Franklin. (It was first called Frankland but leaders changed it to Franklin in hopes of persuading Benjamin Franklin to use his influence to make Franklin the 14th state. It didn't work.)

Franklin background: After the Revolution, North Carolina had a vast territory west of the mountains it didn't want. One member of the North Carolina legislature said people across the mountains were the "offscourings of the earth, fugitives from justice, and we will be rid of them at any rate."

So North Carolina gave the unwanted area to the federal government. The feds didn't accept it. That left all those people west of the mountains without a government. They formed Franklin and elected John Sevier governor. Later, Carolinians changed their minds and said they wanted back the land and people across the mountains.

Denied statehood and reclaimed against their wishes by Carolina, the Franklinites were unhappy. In 1888, Sevier was elected to a second term as governor. He declined to serve. Franklin fell apart and the area again became part of North Carolina. Two years later, the region became part of the Territory South of the Ohio River, presided over by William Blount at Rocky Mount.

Jonesborough, after it became a city, was more of a planned community than most that sprang up on the frontier. All land owners were required to build, within three years, a brick, stone or frame house 20 by 16 feet, with brick or stone chimney. Most were built of stone or brick, and that's one reason they still stand.

Let's get a copy of "A Strolling Tour of Historic Jonesborough" and take a walk.

The first building on our walking tour isn't of wood or stone. Nor is it a frame house. It's a two-story log house. It probably escaped the planning regulations because it was built outside Jonesborough and probably before Jonesborough became a city. Anyway, it's the house where Andrew Jackson boarded while he briefly practiced law in Jonesborough. So it's been moved into town, restored and stands proudly by the pre-Civil War Jonesborough Presbyterian Church.

In the church, you will find the original pews, pulpit and slave gallery. But slavery was not 100 percent accepted in Jonesborough. At the other end of the same block is the spot where once stood the print shop that printed Elihu Embree's "Manumission Intelligencer" and "Emancipator." These were the first periodicals devoted exclusively to abolition of slavery in America.

Here's the Mansion House, once an inn and stopping place on the Great Stage Road. And Sisters' Row, Jonesborough's only row houses, one building housing three separate residences.

Knoxvillians may want to look at the Old Jacobs House, for it once was the home of Thomas Emmerson, Knoxville's first mayor. For a similar reason, they might take a look at the Gresham-Keys House. W. G. "Parson" Brownlow lived in it while he published the Whig newspaper there before the Civil War. He later moved the Whig to Knoxville. He was an angry foe of the Confederacy.

We mustn't miss the old Chester Inn. Andrew Jackson, Andrew Johnson and John Sevier all slept there, but not at the same time. Jackson and Sevier were contemporaries but they hated each other.

According to one story handed down, Jackson came to town to serve as judge in the quarterly superior court. (This was after he lived there as a lawyer.) He was sick. Friends took him to the Chester Inn and put him to bed. That night, Jackson's enemies gathered outside the inn. They talked of coming in to get him and tarring and feathering him. Jackson's friends suggested he slip out the back door. He would have none of it. He told them to hand him his pistols. He sent word to the mob leader to come in first, instead of following. Nothing happened.

I don't know about you, but I'm getting hungry. So let's walk to the old First Christian Church, which now is the Parson's Table, one of East Tennessee's better restaurants.

Dinner starts at 5:30 Tuesday through Saturday. The Sunday meal is a buffet from 11:30 to 2. Lunch is 11:30 to 2 Tuesday through Saturday. The restaurant is closed Monday.

Jeff and Debra Myron own and operate the Parson's Table. The food, the service, the decor — the whole atmosphere of the place — are immensely pleasing. First Christian members first worshiped here in 1874. It ceased being a church in 1953 and then served time as a woodworking shop. It became the Parson's Table in the 1970s. The restaurant was closed in the fall of 1985. The Myrons bought it and reopened it about a year later.

If you need a highball or a glass of wine, bring it with you to the Parson's Table. You can drink liquor in Washington County but you can't buy it legally in public.

I ordered a blackened chicken breast, Cajun style. It arrived, black, peppery and delicious. For dessert, Alberta and I shared something called Kentucky Derby Pie — syrup, pecans, coconut and bits of chocolate. Very satisfying. Entree prices range from nearly $10 to nearly $15. If you start with snails or smoked salmon and end with the Derby pie, the check will be for considerably more.

Besides being a handsome restored old city, Jonesborough is the place where, on the first full weekend of October, yarn spinners from all over the nation, and sometimes from foreign lands, attend the National Storytellers Festival.

While you're in this section, you may as well drive south to Erwin. If you're a trout fisherman, you can make a pilgrimage to one of the oldest rainbow trout hatcheries in the nation. It was established there in 1897, and if you've done much trouting, chances are you've caught a fish that had its beginning at this hatchery.

Between about 15 million and 18 million fertilized fish eggs are shipped from this hatchery to various parts of the nation every year. Female brood fish are reared there and kept until they're two years old. Then their eggs are stripped from them and fertilized with sperm taken from males. By the time the fish are two years old, they are about 18 inches long and weigh about 2½ pounds. After this one production of eggs, the fish are sent out to be stocked in some stream. A fisherman who catches one of these big brood trout can feel good for a week. Nearly 109,000 of these big trout were stocked in streams in fiscal year 1986.

You can gape at approximately 40,000 trout in 24 concrete raceways. Some of them are in the 18-inch range. It's a pleasant place to walk around. If you happen to have a picnic lunch with you, there's a place to eat it. The hatchery is on State Road 107.

While you're near Erwin, you should drive up Rock Creek Road (State 395) to the top of the Unakas. Then, right on the mountain top at Indian Grave Gap, take a left on a narrow, rough gravel road. Go about two miles to where the road forks. Take the right fork and go to the top of the hill.

You've arrived at Beauty Spot, where the picture was made for the cover of this book. It's a big grassy bald, partly in Cherokee National Forest and partly in Pisgah

Davy Crockett Birthplace State Historical Area, Limestone

National Forest. The Appalachian Trail crosses the bald. In fact, if you don't want to drive that rough two miles, you can hike the AT from Indian Grave Gap to Beauty Spot. Some wild azaleas grow there, along with blackberries and blueberries.

The grassy bald now consists of about 35 acres. It was larger before the U. S. Forest Service stopped livestock grazing there years ago. Top of the bald is 4437 feet above sea level. OK. Back down the mountain.

Next stop: Davy Crockett Birthplace State Historical Area near Limestone. Look for markers as you drive southwestward on US 11E and 321, between Jonesborough and Greeneville.

Davy Crockett was the first native-born Tennessee hero. John Sevier, Andrew Jackson, William Blount and some of the other early big-name people in this state were born elsewhere and moved here.

Davy was born in a log cabin beside the Nolichucky River in 1786, in what then was the State of Franklin and now is Greene County. He probably is best known for dy-

ing 50 years later in the siege of the Alamo. In the years between, he was a hunter, storyteller, pioneer and Tennessee congressman. Just as Sevier and the younger Jackson didn't get along, Jackson and the younger Crockett didn't see eye to eye. While in Congress, Crockett fought Jackson's efforts to move the Indians to the West. He lost.

The state has preserved the Crockett birthplace. The old Crockett cabin is gone, but state log cabin builders have erected another in the same place, and they hope it looks like the first one. Davy didn't stay long in that pleasant spot. His family moved when he was six. But maybe he caught a fish from the Nolichucky before he left. It's a good fishing stream. Lots of people fish at the 63-acre park. The Nolichucky also provides a fast ride for rafters and canoeists.

Next stop, Greeneville, and a look at Andrew Johnson's other tailor shop. It was bigger than the one in Rutledge, but it was of wood. If it were not enclosed in a larger brick building, it might have fallen to pieces. It's part of the Andrew Johnson National Historic Site, operated by the National Park Service.

There, you'll see some of Johnson's tailoring tools and a wedding coat he made. Also there is the field desk he used during his travels as military governor of Tennessee during the Civil War. You'll learn that Johnson had no formal education. He learned to read and write between intervals of work, in time snatched here and there during the day. His wife, Eliza, read to him. He sometimes paid others to read to him.

He held many elective offices — Greeneville alderman, mayor, U. S. representative, governor, senator, vice president, president. But he never was *elected* president. He ascended from the vice presidency to the presidency after Lincoln was assassinated. During his presidency the House of Representatives voted articles of impeachment against him. The Senate voted 35 to 19 to convict him, one vote short of the two-thirds majority necessary for conviction. The charge against him was that he fired Secretary of War Edwin M. Stanton in what some in Congress said was a violation of the Tenure of Office Act. That act forbade presidential firing of certain officials without concurrence of the Senate. After his term as president ended, Johnson became the only man ever elected to the Senate after serving as president. But he died of a stroke shortly after he started serving that Senate term.

If you want to follow Davy Crockett another step or two, stop at Crockett Tavern on 11E, on the eastern edge of Morristown. Davy's parents, John and Rebecca, operated a tavern there for several years after they left Limestone. That was Davy's growing-up place.

As far as I know, there's only one other Crockett stop in East Tennessee. That's at Dandridge. There, at the Jefferson County Courthouse, you'll find an interesting historical collection. One item in it is the marriage bond Davy made when he pledged to marry Polly Findley in 1806, five days before his 20th birthday. By this time, the Crockett family was living on Spring Creek, east of Dandridge, where John and Rebecca were again operating a tavern.

Dandridge is another old East Tennessee city, with lots of fine old buidings. But something there that interests me is not so old. It's a huge dike TVA built to keep the waters of Douglas Lake from covering much of the town. Dandridge had been scheduled for drowning when TVA planned the dam. But Mrs. Alf Swann wrote a letter to Mrs. Franklin D. Roosevelt. Mrs. FDR mentioned it to FDR, FDR said something to TVA, and TVA built the dike. So the old part of Dandridge lives on at the foot of the dike, a pretty sloping grassy wall.

For a few days or a week, let's go south along the disputed lands of the Little Tennessee Valley, to Tellico Plains and Tellico River, then down across the Hiwassee River to the red earth of the Copper Basin.

First, a brief history session:

No land this side of Palestine has been more fought over than the fertile acres along the lower Little Tennessee River. When the first white traders and explorers crossed the mountains from Virginia and the Carolinas, they found the Overhill Cherokees in nearly a dozen towns from approximately the present Calderwood downriver to a little below the Highway 411 Bridge.

One of the towns was Chota, secular and religious capital of the entire Cherokee tribe. In these towns along the lower river lived the Cherokees' greatest men. And women:

Attakullakulla, the Little Carpenter, who in 1730 went to London and dined with the king, before reaching a trade agreement with England's Board of Trade and Plantations in America. He was the Cherokees' great diplomat and nearly always favored the English when other Cherokee chiefs sometimes were less than friendly toward them.

Oconostota, the great war chief. He may have been the only Indian chief ever to lead his men to victory over an army of British regulars.

Sequoyah, who devised the Cherokee

syllabary by which nearly the entire tribe learned to read and write in their own language in a matter of months.

Nancy Ward, the tribe's Beloved Woman, whose powers included pardoning prisoners. It was she who saved the life of Mrs. William Bean, wife of the man usually called Tennessee's first permanent white settler. Indians had captured her. She was tied to a stake atop Toqua Mound and dry cane and wood had been lighted at her feet when Nancy Ward raced to the top of the mound, scattered the fire and released the prisoner. About 130 years before white women in American could vote, Nancy Ward represented the Cherokees at a conference with the new United States government in 1785.

The Cherokees defended their towns along the Little Tennessee against their sometime enemies, the Creeks, the Shawnees and perhaps the Chickasaws.

They persuaded the English to build Fort Loudoun on the Little T in the middle 1750s. It was to be an English-Cherokee defense against French-Creek attackers. No such attack ever came. But in their on-again-off-again relationship with the English, the Cherokees finally laid siege to the fort. The English surrendered it on Aug. 9, 1760. Breaking the terms of the surrender agreement, the Indians the next day massacred many of the soldiers who had started back to Charleston, S. C.

Though Cherokee-English relations soon improved, the English never again manned the fort. But by then the English and their Indian allies had gained the upper hand against the French and their Indian friends in the battle for dominance in North America. Perhaps Fort Loudoun had played a part by discouraging French-Creek attack in this region. Maybe it was a small part of the reason we speak English around here, instead of French, like those people in Quebec.

In a peaceful period that followed, English Lieutenant Henry Timberlake floated in a dugout canoe from Long Island of the Holston (Kingsport) down the Holston and the Tennessee to the mouth of the Little T and then paddled and poled up the Little T to the Indian towns. He stayed long enough to gather material for a book, "Memoirs of Lieutenant Henry Timberlake," that gives an excellent picture of life in the towns along the river. He also drew a remarkably accurate map of the area. The TVA Map Office still sells prints of it. On his map, Timberlake listed the number of "fighting men" in each Cherokee town. The total was 809. So the total Cherokee population in that 25-mile stretch of the river must have been at least three times as many.

The peaceful period did not last long. The relentless surge of white settlement sparked repeated clashes with the Indians. The Indians usually lost. They were no match for the mounted fighters led by John Sevier, frontier leader who later became Tennessee's first governor. And the great Indian leaders were growing too old to lead.

Old and ill, Oconostota spent the winter of 1782-83 on Long Island of the Holston at the home of Joseph Martin, Virginia's Indian agent. Martin was married to a daughter of Nancy Ward, who also spent that winter at the Martin home.

When spring came, Oconostota asked to go back to Chota to die. So they put him in a canoe and floated him down the river, the Timberlake route. He did die. And they used a portion of the canoe in which he had floated as the bottom part of his coffin. (He had asked to be buried "like the white people are buried.")

In 1794, the U. S. Government built Tellico Blockhouse diagonally across the river from old Fort Loudoun. Besides being a garrisoned military post, it was a center for regulating trade with the Indians. At the blockhouse, the Indians also were taught "arts which furnished comforts and conveniences to the white race." Among the many visitors to the blockhouse was the Duke of Orleans, later King Louis Philippe of France. By 1805, so many Indians were moving south, out of the way of the white settlers, that the blockhouse was abandoned and its operations transferred to near the mouth of the Hiwassee River.

By 1819, white farmers were prospering on the Little Tennessee bottoms that had served the Indians so well. Except for a remarkable feud, (the McGhee-Howard feud, between two white families on the river), the people who tilled this land were peaceful for nearly 150 years.

Then, in 1965, TVA asked Congress for money to build Tellico Dam. The dam would flood nearly all the rich Little Tennessee bottomland, as well as the nearly-forgotten sites of the Cherokee towns.

Opposition grew quickly. The battle between TVA and its supporters, on one side, and trout fishermen, landowners, Indians, history buffs and environmentalists, on the other side, lasted more than a dozen years. TVA finally finished the dam and closed the gates in 1979. The battle raged in the halls of Congress, in the U. S. Supreme Court and in thousands of private and public arguments in this region. Involved in it was a small endangered fish called the snail darter. Snail darter became household words in East Tennessee and familiar to people over the nation.

One result of all this has been a growing nest of history down beside the lake.

A re-created Fort Loudoun, as much like the elaborate old fort as circumstances permit, stands on a hill above Tellico Lake. Some of it is on the site of the old fort. But the lake waters cover part of the original fort area. It's called the Fort Loudoun State Historic Area, and it's a great place to sit under big trees and think back to the time English soldiers lived there, some of them with their wives, comprising the first white families in what's now Tennessee. The first christening of a child in Tennessee was there.

Reflect for a second or two. This quiet valley, now partly covered with still water, is where nearly all the human action was in East Tennessee only 250 years ago. The birds and bears still reigned in the woods where Knoxville, Maryville, Johnson City would rise.

Sequoyah is remembered. Near the fort is the new Sequoyah Birthplace Museum, owned and operated by the Eastern Band of the Cherokee. It's on land TVA turned over to the Cherokees on a permanent-easement basis. The museum is near the flooded site of Tuskegee, where Sequoyah was born.

Several yards behind the museum is the burial site of the remains of 191 Indians archaeologists dug up along the river before the land was flooded. The Cherokees have built a lovely memorial there.

But not all the remains are in that mound. When archaeologists dug into the site of the Chota council house, they unearthed the remains of Oconostota. They knew it was he because his eyeglasses were with him (a rarity among Indians, he wore glasses in his later years), and he still lay in the canoe in which he was known to have been buried. The level of Tellico Lake is higher than the original Chota council house. But TVA built up the site above the lake level and also built a causeway to it. This area also has been turned over to the Eastern Band. It expects to rebury Oconostota there and erect an appropriate memorial.

(Remember, the Mead Corp. gave back to the Indians a piece of Long Island of the Holston. So the Cherokees are regaining land both at the beginning and end of Oconostota's last journey.)

TVA also has turned over to the state a piece of land at Tennessee, which was kind of a suburb of Chota. Lt. Timberlake spelled it that way. Others spell it T-a-n-a-s-i. However you spell it, it's the word that became the name of the state just south of Kentucky. The state is expected to erect a proper marker there.

Back across the lake, Tellico Blockhouse has not been rebuilt. But 180 years of accumulated dirt has been scraped away, exposing the blockhouse foundation and floor plan. There are explanatory markers. One of the markers gives an interesting bit of Tennessee and national history.

William Blount established the blockhouse when he was governor of the Southwest Territory. After Tennessee became a state, Blount was elected as its first senator. But before he took his Senate seat, he became involved in dealings between influential frontier whites and the British. The settlers wanted the British to join them in driving out the Indians to open more land for settlement. In a letter, Blount described the plan to James Carey, an interpreter at the blockhouse. The letter fell into the hands of Col. David Henley, agent of the

War Department in the territory. Supervision of the troops at the blockhouse was part of his duties. Another part of his job was to see that U.S. treaties with the Indians were enforced. So he turned the Blount letter over to the War Department. Blount was accused of conspiring against the government, and he became the first member ever expelled from the Senate.

Because he protected the Indians against land-hungry settlers, Henley then wasn't overly popular in Knoxville. Somebody once burned his barn, apparently a revenge action. In spite of his being expelled from the Senate, Blount remained popular in East Tennessee. Blount Mansion, which was his home and also the seat of territorial government, still stands in Knoxville, but so does Henley Bridge, which, along with the street, was named for the colonel.

So let's visit a direct descendant of Col. Henley. He is Luther G. "Luke" Henley, owner of a Knoxville roofing company and self-proclaimed "Head Turkey" of Turkey Pen Resort. The resort is in the hills south of Chilhowee Lake. Take Citico Road from Vonore (same road you take to reach Old Fort Loudoun) and follow it for miles up the valley. Cross Citico Creek and keep going, following the turkey tracks Luke has painted along the way.

Luke is a great-great-great grandson of David and a great-great grandson of Arthur Henley, who once owned the Chota land. He will tell you there is more than one Henley Bridge. The other is across the Thames, at the town of Henley, 35 miles northeast of London. That was the nest of the ancestoral Henleys.

He also will tell you he owns 4000 acres of mountain land on which rests his Turkey Pen Resort. He named it that because there are in the vicinity a Turkey Pen Hollow, Turkey Pen Bluff and Turkey Pen Gap. He thought one more was needed. He says he owns all the land in that section that's not owned by the U. S. Forest Service and the Aluminum Company of America. What he did was buy several small contiguous farms. If you spend time at his resort, you might stay in one of the four old farmhouses still standing. Or, if that doesn't appeal to you, you can stay in the lodge. If you need to go to church, an old church building still stands on resort property. Luke's rates for all these lodging places are low to moderate. You can eat brunch and supper at the lodge for a total of $12, or $6 if you're three to seven years old and for nothing if you're still younger.

Nine horses and a pony live at the resort. You can rent them to ride on Luke's 40 miles of hiking and riding trails. You can fish in the resort's private lake, or go to Tellico or Chilhowee Lakes. Citico Creek, in the state's Tellico Wildlife Management Area in Cherokee National Forest, is near. Rainbow trout wait there to be caught. In season, guests can hunt turkeys, deer, boar and bear on Luke's property.

If you hang onto your teeth, you can go back to Citico Creek and follow the rough road up the creek to a junction with the new scenic highway that someday may be finished between Tellico Plains, Tenn., and Robbinsville, N. C. The Tennessee part is finished. Up there on Sassafras Ridge is Rattlesnake Rock, where the rattlers used to sun in spring just after they crawled out of their winter dens. Mountaineer Bill Stratton and some of his buddies went there each spring and killed snakes until the stench repelled them.

Not so far away is Stratton Gap, where one of Bill's ancestors is buried. According to the story handed down, he liked Tennessee and North Carolina equally well. So he asked to be buried with his feet in one state and his head in the other. His family complied.

From Stratton Gap (sometimes called Stratton Meadow), you can take a road down North River to the road along Tellico River. Follow the Tellico River Road down to Bald River Falls, which is just above the confluence of the two rivers. It's a beautiful waterfall, like a herd of white horses galloping down a cliff.

If you've a mind to do so, you can hike a fine trail from the road up to the top of the falls and then 5.6 miles upriver to Bald River Road at Holly Flats. There, unless somebody is waiting for you in a car, you turn around and walk back. I did that not long ago. It's a good hike. You're nearly always

Turkey Pen Resort, Vonore

in sight and sound of the river. Sometimes the sound is a whisper, sometimes a roar. You walk past three or four more waterfalls, but none as pretty as the first one. Lots of laurel, rhododendron, dog hobble, trailing arbutus and galax along the trail. This area down in Bald River Gorge is a National Wilderness Area. No more logging, no motorized vehicles, please.

This is just a sample of the hundreds of miles of hiking trails in the Cherokee National Forest. There also are separate trails for motorcycles and still others for horses.

Lots of miles of fishing streams, too. North River and Bald River and the North and South forks of Citico Creek, plus all their tributaries, are wild trout streams. Creel limit on these is three fish. Minimum size limit for rainbows is nine inches and for brook trout, six inches. Ask about other regulations.

Citico Creek and Tellico River are stocked with fish. You need a special daily fishing permit for them. Creel limit is seven fish. You can use just about any kind of lure or bait.

Drive on down the Tellico to Tellico Plains. Then take State 68 to Ducktown and Copperhill — the Copper Basin. The first time I saw the basin, about 40 years ago, it looked like nothing else I'd ever seen, in Tennessee or elsewhere. Thousands of acres of brown and red barren land. No tree or blade of grass. No topsoil. Even the mineral soil was eroded, hard, with no protection or nutrition for any plant that might sprout.

In 1843, somebody thought he had discovered gold here in this out-of-the-way corner of Tennessee, just west of North Carolina and right on top of the Georgia line. But it wasn't gold; it was copper, to the finder's disappointment. So the copper was mined. The first mine, the Hiwassee Mine, opened in 1850. The reconstructed mine chimney still stands. Mining ceased for the Civil War and resumed a few years later.

Miners cut trees by the millions, fanning out as far as 20 miles, to get fuel for the smelting. Wood became so scarce that even the stumps were pulled and burned. Workmen laid alternate layers of wood and ore

on roasting piles several feet high and up to 200 feet long. Sulfur dioxide fumes from the roasting are said to have been so dense that mules hauling ore had to be belled to keep them from colliding in the murky atmosphere.

This caused what may have been the first major acid rain problem in the nation. The fumes killed every weed and tree sprout missed by the stump pullers.

At its worst, late last century and early in this one, the barren area covered about 35,000 acres. Sediment and minerals drained into the Ocoee River and killed every fish and spring lizard in it. Only in relatively recent years have fish come back to the river and fishing is still not good above Parksville Lake to Copperhill. But good fishing now is reported in Parksville Lake.

The damage spilled into North Georgia, and Georgia asked the U. S. Supreme Court to make the Tennessee miners stop what they were doing to Georgia. Justice Oliver Wendell Holmes replied for the court. He said Georgia didn't have to put up with that kind of treatment from Tennesseans.

That decision coincided with the mining company's discovery that it could reclaim sulfuric acid from the fumes and make money doing it. That put a stop to the spread of the environmental damage. But it did nothing to restore vegetation and fertility to the land already bare. Rains beat upon it and dug gullies deep enough to hide elephants. Scientists estimate that an average of four feet of soil washed from the basin after it was laid bare.

Nothing much good happened until TVA was born in 1933. Land reclamation and reforestation were among the jobs Congress and the President gave it. TVA asked a sister New Deal agency, the Civilian Conservation Corps, to start planting pine trees in the basin. The U. S. Forest Service, the University of Georgia and other agencies later joined the effort.

TVA still works there, now in conjunction with the Tennessee Chemical Co., present owner of the chemical operation. The company is doing the greater part of the work now. Mining is being phased out and only the chemical operation will remain after this summer.

The results have been slow, steady and amazing.

From 35,000 acres, the great scar has receded to about 2500 acres still almost totally bare.

So successful has been the reclamation that some oldtimers of the Copper Basin want to put a stop to it. All their lives they've lived in this barren basin. When it was nearly reclaimed, they discovered they loved it and didn't want it to be covered completely with green grass and trees.

If you stop at the Ducktown Basin Museum and watch a movie of the area's history, you will hear the narrator speak of the need to preserve part of the "beloved red scar."

Yes, the woman said, this is a Swiss community. And the Swiss still live in this section of Grundy County.

People with such names as Suter, Schild, Schlageter, Stampfli ("Rose Stampfli still makes cottage cheese"), Scholer.

"He still uses coal oil lamps," the woman said of one person. "He don't want any electricity. He farmed with a mule till she died."

Alberta and I had stopped to make certain we were on the right road. If we were, we should be approaching a place called Laager, according to our map. The man who answered our question at a service station said we were already in Laager.

As I got back into the car, I noticed a street marker that said "65th Ave."

Sixty-fifth Avenue? In a place so small it barely got on the map?

But it turned out to be bigger than we first thought. And it's not just Laager; it's also Gruetli. And the two of them together are stretched along State Highway 208. They now are one town, we later learned, and the Laager-Gruetli population is about 2000.

We went past 64th Avenue and were going on down the list when we passed a marker bearing information about the Swiss Memorial School. Then we decided to stop again. We found a woman who gave us

names of several Swiss families. The names all started with "S." She said she knew Swiss names starting with other letters; she just couldn't remember them.

I never heard of Laager and Gruetli before I found them, and that's a sample of my ignorance of the whole South Cumberland region. The part of the South Cumberlands I'm talking about is in Warren, Van Buren, Bledsoe, Grundy and Sequatchie counties. All interesting country, some of it spectacular, much of it beautiful, nearly all of it a little strange.

Several years earlier, I had been to Fall Creek Falls State Park. But that was before it became a resort park and the Cadillac of the Tennessee park system. And, way back in 1972, I had been to Savage Gulf. But that was before it became the Savage Gulf State Natural Area. In fact, my guides on that trip were Herman Baggenstoss, whose idea it was to make that wild country a state natural area, and Roger Bollinger of TVA. TVA was plugging the same idea.

This time, Alberta and I were on a two-day trip, looking for places and things you might find interesting, worth a trip of a few days or a week.

Our first stop was Crossville. You know Crossville. It's where you go to see performances at Cumberland County Playhouse Friday, Saturday and Sunday, March through November. The late author-director-actor-playwright Paul Crabtree led the movement to establish that theater in the middle 1960s. It's been a success ever since.

South of Crossville are remnants of an unusual New Deal project called Cumberland Homesteads. We turned in that direction, on US 127.

Before you reach the intersection of 127 and State 68, you see sandstone cottages, and at the intersection you see an 80-foot-high octagonal sandstone tower. The tower housed administrative offices of Cumberland Homesteads a half-century ago. It now houses a museum related to this project that Franklin D. Roosevelt's wife, Eleanor, visited twice in the 1930s.

The project was on 10,000 acres of land the federal government bought from the Missouri Land Co. The government divided the land into 250 homesteads. The 250 lucky families who got them were chosen from more than 4000 applicants. Homesteaders lived in the sandstone cottages, all made of the material commonly called Crab Orchard stone. Many of the cottages and the tower still stand and are still used.

Across Highway 68 from the tower is Cumberland General Store. It's interesting but its merchandise is selected more for tourists than for rural Cumberland Countians. One item we found was what looked at first like an oldtime wood-burning kitchen range, but it plugs into an electric outlet and the price tag was $2595.

We continued a mile southeast on 68 and came to the J & J Factory Outlet, where Alberta thought we should stop. I have no expertise or much interest in outlet shopping. Miss Alberta is my consultant in such matters. She looked a bit and said the merchandise was good and so were the prices.

If you want to see a *real* general store, drive a few miles down Highway 68 into Grassy Cove and you'll soon reach the general store of J. A. Kemmer & Son. J. A., who started the store in 1930, is gone now. George, the son, and his wife Emily run it.

Grassy Cove is one of the loveliest places in the Cumberlands. It's not a park. As far as I know, no government owns so much as an acre of it. But the farmers who own the cove land have managed it in such manner that it has never lost its beauty. The cove is about five miles long and two miles wide. You see cattle, sheep, hogs out on the rolling grassland. You see a meandering creek.

This is Grassy Cove Creek. It runs into Mill Cave 400 or 500 yards behind the Kemmer store.

But we haven't seen the last of this water. Years ago, someone told me the stream rambles through the innards of Brady Mountain and then emerges at the base of the mountain on the other side as the Sequatchie River. The story told was that somebody put dye and wood chips in the creek and then waited for them to appear on the other side. Sure enough, after about two days, the dye and chips showed up.

Emily Kemmer confirmed that the creek provides most of the water for the beginning of the Sequatchie River. She said it rises at what some call the Big Spring. On a quadrangle map, it's called Head of Sequatchie. How to get there?

Go back to 127 and turn south, Emily Kemmer said. Go past the entrance (on the right) of Cumberland Mountain State Rustic Park. Then go about a mile farther south and turn onto a road that slants left just beyond a gasoline station.

This road was on no map we carried. It bore no name, no number. But we learned later that it's a section of the old Alvin C. York Highway. (In Fentress County, 127 is marked as the Alvin C. York Highway.) We followed it six or eight miles down into the upper valley of the Sequatchie.

I wish the state years ago had bought the Big Spring, the Head of Sequatchie. But this beautiful spot is privately owned. The owners aren't home all the time. So you can't blame them for leaving the gate locked and posting a "keep out" sign.

The old highway and the river stay close together for several miles. The highway eventually takes you back to 127, north of Pikeville. But, since this old road and most of those it intersects bear no names or numbers, you're not always sure you're on the right road. Stop and ask somebody.

We got back to 127 and headed on down Sequatchie Valley. With Walden Ridge as the eastern boundary of the valley and the Cumberland Plateau the western boundary, this is one of the prettiest valleys in Tennessee.

We followed 127 to State 30, just north of Pikeville. Then we took 30 westward up onto the Cumberland Plateau and on to the northern entrance to Fall Creek Falls State Resort Park.

It's quite a park. More than 16,000 acres of forest, lake, streams, waterfalls, golf course, tennis courts, trails.

A magazine, Sports Digest, rated the 18-hole golf course in the top 25 public courses in the nation. Fishermen have taken two state-record fish from the 345-acre lake. One was a bluegill that weighed more than three pounds and the other was a channel catfish that jolted the scale at 41 pounds. Naturally, a fee is charged for fishing such a fine lake.

If fishing is the main interest of a big family or a group, they may want to rent one of the 10 plush two-story fishermen's cabins. Each has two bedrooms and sleeps up to eight persons. Each has a fireplace, television set, phone and all linens and utensils for cooking and eating. Each cabin has a private porch extending over the lake. It can be used for cooking and sunbathing. And if the fish are biting there, you can fish from the porch and never leave home. Ten inland cabins are similarly equipped, except you can't fish from them. People who use boats on the lake aren't allowed to use their own. You rent a boat or canoe from the park and use an electric motor. This is to minimize noise. It's OK to bring your own electric motor.

You can bring your own bicycle or your own horse to ride on the bike and equestrian trails. Or you can rent a bike or a horse. For those who'd rather swim, there's an Olympic-sized pool. Then there's tennis, badminton, horseshoe pitching, and you might even find a basketball and a hoop to shoot at.

Though this is a resort park with a touch of luxury, it also is one of the wildest of the state parks. It has about 12 miles of hiking trails for day hikers and 25 miles for overnight backpackers. It has some virgin forest down in Cane Creek Gorge, which is so rugged that loggers never bothered to try to cut it and take it out. Most of the park acres are forested.

It has the most magnificent waterfall I've seen since I looked at those in Yosemite National Park. The falls is 256 feet high, and Park Manager A. J. Anderson said it's America's highest waterfall east of the Rockies. "The World Almanac" agrees. Except for a few feet of cascading water at the top, all this comes down in a straight drop, a lovely column of shining water.

When you tire of looking at this waterfall, go look at Cane Creek Falls, 85 feet high. Then, from the same overlook, you can stay in your tracks but make a half turn to the right and see 95-foot Rock House Branch Falls. There's another, Piney Creek Falls, but we saved it for the next trip. You can overdo looking at waterfalls.

I stop short of calling rooms at the park's inn luxurious. On the other hand, somebody accustomed to luxury would not think he's roughing it in one of them. Each has a phone, a television and a back porch looking out on the lake. Fourteen Canada geese spent about half their time in the water and on the shore just outside our room. These 14 like the place well enough to stay throughout the year. Winter migrants sometimes stop and swell the population to about 200.

Rates for a double room are in the medium range April 1-Oct. 31 and in the low range the rest of the year. If you're 62 or older, you get a 10 percent discount from May 1 to Labor Day and 20 percent the rest of the year. For more information and for reservations, call 800-421-6683.

If you don't want a room at the inn or a cabin, maybe one of the park's 228 campsites would be more to your liking. There is a small charge for these.

Eating is not a problem. The restaurant menu shows considerable variety and reasonable prices. There are at least two snack bars. And if you're camping or in a housekeeping cabin, you can buy the makings of your meals at the park store.

The park has a wildflower festival in May. Autumn leaves are best in the second half of October and sometimes into November.

After more waffles and sausage and bacon and coffee than we should have eaten the next morning, we left the park by the south exit and started looking for State Highway 111. We followed it a dozen or more miles south and then turned west on State 399.

It was on 111 and 399 that we became aware of how thinly populated this region is. We drove for stretches of two or three miles without seeing a house. We met few cars.

We turned right off 399 onto 108 and pretty soon started seeing more houses, including those of Laager and Gruetli. Soon after Gruetli, we reached State Highway 56 and turned south on it toward Tracy City. We went through Tracy City and almost to Monteagle before reaching the headquarters of the South Cumberland State Recreation Area (SCSRA).

Nothing else in Tennessee is quite like SCSRA. It has a good visitors center, and it's the administrative center for eight separate state recreation units in the South Cumberlands.

We met Randy Hedgepath, bearded ranger-naturalist of SCSRA, who seems to be able to answer all questions about nearly anything in Grundy County. I asked him about the Swiss. He said John Henry Scholer is the man who still uses coal oil lamps. He said most of the colony arrived about 1876-78. They thought they were coming to cleared land. They found it uncleared. So they named it Gruetli, a Swiss word meaning to root out, clear away.

He also said the Swiss have an annual festival the last weekend of July. If you attend, somebody may give you samples of Swiss cheese and wine.

The newest of the eight areas under SCSRA administration was set aside in 1986. It's Hawkins Cove. The main reason for state protection of the cove is to preserve a rare plant which, as far as botanists know, grows only in the South Cumberlands. It's the Cumberland rosin weed. Randy said it grows to be five or six feet tall, has small yellow flowers and its leaves feel like sandpaper.

The jewel of the eight is the 11,500-acre Savage Gulf State Natural Area. It's "Savage" because of Samuel Savage, an early settler. And it's "Gulf" because that's what Grundy Countians call a gorge.

Though accommodations at Fall Creek Falls State Resort Park border on luxury, the amenities at Savage Gulf are meager. The closest thing to luxury here are flush toilets at the ranger stations at the two area entrances.

One entrance is off Highway 399. It's near Savage Creek and Savage Falls. The other is just north of Beersheba Springs and is called the Stone Door entrance.

On the earlier trip, Herman Baggenstoss had taken Roger Bollinger and me into the area at Savage Creek. We stood on the lip of the gorge above the creek and watched a red-tailed hawk glide down the gorge, wings motionless, red tail glistening in the sunshine of a perfect May morning.

We went down to Savage Falls, first of about 75 falls in the creek as it races down the gulf to meet the Collins River. Savage Creek, Big Creek and the Collins are the three major streams in the area. All have cut deep gulfs into Cumberland Plateau. So rugged is this gorge region that an estimated 500 acres of virgin forest escaped loggers' saws and axes. Laurel was blooming and warblers were warbling that May morning.

So this time, we decided to use the other entrance. I wanted to see that geological freak called the Stone Door. It's an easy two-mile roundtrip hike from the parking area at the ranger station. Take time for good gorge views along the way.

Nature opened the Stone Door nobody knows how many thousand years ago. A 150-foot-high chunk of the gorge wall broke away above Laurel Creek near where it joins Big Creek. But it didn't go far. It stopped after a move of only a yard or two. On the right side, between the gorge wall and the stone section that broke away, is the door opening, a steep, rough route down into the gorge. This is the beginning of the 10-mile Stone Door Connector Trail. A few yards down that trail, I watched three rock-climbers practicing their skills.

Then back to Miss Alberta and the car.

How you get back home is your choice. We went north on 56, past what seemed like hundreds of tree and shrub nurseries, to McMinnville. Then we found State 30 again and went east on it through Spencer and back to Sequatchie Valley.

Just before you reach the rim of the plateau and start down into the valley, you may notice a small sign some thoughtful person erected. It says:

"Sequatchie Valley, a view to remember."

It is.

N early anybody with a grain of affinity for the outdoors — for natural land not much changed by humans, for wildlife, for solitude, for hiking far from the smell of exhaust fumes — wants to get into Great Smoky Mountains National Park.

With more than a half-million acres, it's the biggest national park in the East. More visitors come to it each year than to any other national park. It has the largest mixed deciduous-evergreen virgin forest in the nation, about 200,000 acres, or nearly two-fifths of the park.

A treasure of trees and smaller plants grow in it. It probably has more plant species than any other area of equal size in the country. At least 131 species of trees grow there, about as many as in all Europe.

Great Smokies animal life ranges from tiny insects — "no-seeums," the local name for a tiny biting gnat — to black bears, deer and the exotic European wild boar, which has become a destructive pest in the park. There have been reliable sightings of mountain lions in the park, but nobody is sure whether these are permanent residents. It's possible that someone occasionally secretly releases Western cougars in the park. Another possibility is that a remnant population of the native Eastern cougar remains there and was never exterminated, as was generally believed.

For people in this region, there are three regular routes for getting into the park. Gatlinburg traditionally has been the door most used. But Pigeon Forge comes before Gatlinburg on that conventional route, and since Dollywood opened in Pigeon Forge, the traffic jam there has frustrated motorists. But Dollywood shuts down during the winter, and there are at least a couple of reasons for stopping in Pigeon Forge — three, if you like shopping at the outlet malls there.

The two I have in mind are the Old Mill and Pigeon Forge Pottery, just across the road from each other. Douglas Ferguson opened the pottery 41 years ago. It's the oldest and largest pottery in Sevier County. The Old Mill is far older. The Little Pigeon River has been powering that operation since 1830. It's one of the oldest water-powered mills in Tennessee. You might like a tour of the mill and a bag of its product.

However, you can get to Gatlinburg from the Knoxville area without going through Pigeon Forge. At Sevierville, take US 411 northeast, as if you were going to Newport. But you'll soon come to State 416

and markers for Pittman Center. Take 416. You'll like it. It wanders for miles in amiable companionship with a fork of the Little Pigeon River, through good Sevier County country. Eventually, the river and the road part company, with the river wandering to the left. Pretty soon, you part company with 416, at a point where it turns abruptly left. You continue in the same direction, but now on Bird's Creek Road. Follow it several miles.

You're coming up on Gatlinburg's back side. Maybe its best side. Pretty soon, you'll be into a nest of craftsmen, a group called Great Smoky Arts & Crafts Community. It has nearly 50 members. Not all are craftsmen. The Wild Plum Tea Room isn't a craft shop, but it's a member of the community. It serves very nice soups, sandwiches, desserts and the like. But it's open irregularly during the off season. So don't go there then without first checking by phone.

Buckhorn Inn isn't a craft shop. It's a fine place to sleep and dine. Yes, dine; not just eat. Look south at Mt. Le Conte as you dine. On a clear day, the people far up at Le Conte Lodge can look down and see Buckhorn Inn, but few others can. It's mostly hidden in the woods, on Tudor Mountain Road, off Buckhorn Road.

It's not a big place. With five rooms in the main building and more in four cottages, it can accommodate about 20 guests. Breakfast is served from 8:30 to 9:30. If you wish you can stay at the inn on a bed-and-breakfast basis. Rates are moderate to high. Dinner is at 7 and costs $15. Sometimes you can get dinner at the inn without being an overnight guest; it depends how many are spending the night. To be sure, phone for reservations.

The first member of the craft community you reach on Bird's Creek Road is John Cowden. He's been making a living since 1947 carving lovely objects from wood.

When you reach the intersection of Glades Road and Buckhorn Road, you can go either way. But you should travel both roads on your trip, for the community craftsmen are on both, as well as on State Highway 321 (the road between Gatlinburg and Cosby).

Buckhorn Inn, Gatlinburg

Henry Morton is not a member of the crafts community, but if you need an apple tree, stop and see him. He and his mother live at the intersection of Glades Road and Proffitt Road. Though she has an electric range, she prefers to cook on her old wood-burning range. Henry's specialty is producing old-fashioned apple trees. He has more than 100 varieties, including nearly a dozen Limbertwigs. I like Limbertwigs, perhaps because a big Limbertwig tree stood behind the barn on the farm of my childhood.

I stopped at the Potter's Mark and visited with potter Wally Smith, who has been in business on Buckhorn Road for 16 years. He said he's the only potter in East Tennessee who salt glazes. His wife, Jean, works in the same building. She weaves women's garments, no two alike. She makes about 300 a year, he makes about 6000 pottery articles. She learned weaving at the Arrowmont School of Arts and Crafts in Gatlinburg. So have lots of others.

The school's history goes back to 1912, when a national women's fraternity, Pi Beta Phi, established the Settlement School in Gatlinburg. It was kind of a missionary project. Public education in the mountains of East Tennessee was not the best then. School terms lasted only a few months.

The school became involved in the total community — to the point that some of the teachers from afar married local young men. The fraternity provided nursing service. Oldtimers still talk of Marjorie Chalmers, a nurse who came in 1936 and stayed on the job 26 years. The school staff urged adults in the community to continue the native crafts — weaving, basketry, woodworking, broom making.

In 1926, the fraternity established Arrowcraft Shop as a retail outlet for the craftspeople. It's the oldest gift shop in Gatlinburg. It now markets craft articles for more than 60 weavers and other craftsmen.

Over the years, public education improved in East Tennessee and the regular public school system gradually took over the work of the Settlement School. By 1968, Sevier County had completed the school takeover.

Meanwhile, Pi Beta Phi had become involved in craft education. There had been some craft teaching in the high school part of the Settlement School. But a formal craft school started in 1945, when about 50 students attended the first summer crafts workshop. With help from the University of Tennessee, Pi Beta Phi put the courses on college level. Some students took them for college credit. The next year, Marian Heard, craft professor in home economics at UT, became director of Arrowmont.

The school now offers courses in a great variety of crafts: spinning, blacksmithing, weaving, basket making, woodworking, pottery, jewelry, metal work, drawing, quilting, paper making, vegetable dyeing, silk screening and others. About 1000 students per year attend. Some come for a week or two, others for longer.

If you're in Gatlinburg at breakfast time, consider the Burning Bush Restaurant, far south on the Parkway, within a rabbit hop of the park boundary. I've eaten breakfast at lots of places. None I can remember surpasses the Bush, especially not in variety. If you listed in a single column all the items on that breakfast menu, it would be close to a yard long. You can order everything from two varieties of quail (bobwhite and Pharoah) to ordinary scrambled eggs. If you'd rather have your eggs fancied up, try several types of *frittates* (Mexican omelets). Or eggs Benedict. Or eggs Gatlinburg. You'll like the beginner, Le Conte Sunrise, a blend of six or seven fruit juices. You might like the rainbow trout. Or the filet mignon. I ate much too much of the waffles topped with whipped cream. I like to eat in the glassed-in porch where I can see the birds at the feeders outside.

It's not a place to eat breakfast before going on a long hike. You don't want to carry all that food to Mt. Le Conte. So we'll just go up to the top of the mountain at Newfound Gap and then go west on the Clingmans Dome Road to Indian Gap. We're going to walk from the gap down the Old Indian Road. It's only 3.5 miles, mostly down hill. It was a route across the mountains for the Indians far back in the dim past. White settlers came and widened the old Indian trail into a road for sleds and droves of livestock. Then it became a toll road for drovers, walkers, horsemen and vehicles drawn by mules, oxen and horses. At Indian Gap, it veered eastward and went down Oconaluftee Valley on the North Carolina side.

This old road continued to be the only route over the middle of the mountain until the late 1920s, when a new road was built across the mountain at Newfound Gap.

Since it was never paved, the old road quickly reverted to a trail, probably much like it was when only Indians used it. Not far down the mountain, the trail crosses Road Prong of the West Prong of Little Pigeon River. Road and stream intersect several times in their routes down the valley. The last crossing can be a problem after heavy rain. Flowers bloom along the way. I particularly remember sweet-smelling purple-fringed orchids in June or early July.

You usually meet few other people on this trail, not until your trail intersects the Chimneys Trail and the two become one the rest of the way to the Chimneys Parking Area, on US Highway 441. It's best to have a car waiting there, for there's not much point in walking back to Indian Gap.

Some day when you eat less breakfast, put a lunch and some liquid and whatever else you need in a day pack and go back to the same general starting point. Except this time follow the Clingmans Dome Road a little farther west to a parking area on the south side of the highway at the trailhead for the Fork Ridge Trail. You're not going down that trail, though. You cross the highway and go a few yards to the Appalachian Trail. Go west on it to the intersection with the Sugarland Mountain Trail. That's where you're going this time — about 13 wonderful miles down the crest of the Sugarlands. It's beautiful in spring when the laurel blooms, even better in fall when the colors flame. You may see deer, bear, hawks, the little red squirrels mountain folks call boomers, lots of songbirds. One thing you'll see in the high country is not so good: lots of dead Fraser fir trees, killed by balsam woolly aphids, possibly aided in their work by air pollution.

On your way down, you'll pass the Rough Creek Trail, to your left down to Rough Creek and then to Little River. Farther down, your trail will intersect the Huskey Gap Trail, which links US 441 with the old road along Little River. At Huskey Gap, you have about three more miles to go. The worst part is in this final three miles, a steep climb up a ridge before you go down the other side of the ridge to the car that better be waiting for you at Fighting Creek Gap, on State 73. Chances are you won't encounter many other hikers on the Sugarland Trail.

But on this next trail you may want to walk, you'll meet lots of people. For it's to Mt. Le Conte, probably the most popular year-round destination for long hikers in the Great Smokies. The ideal way to do Le Conte is to hike up one day, spend the night and walk back on a different trail the next day. You can spend a night in a shelter that's similar to the Appalachian Trail shelters. It sleeps a dozen people. But be sure you get a permit to stay there. Or you can enjoy more amenities at Le Conte Lodge.

Though the lodge is 5.2 miles from the nearest paved road by way of the shortest trail, the demand for lodging there is amazing. It's better to make a reservation the year before you want to stay there. But you can always try for a current-year reservation. You usually can get reservations for some night during the week, but most weekends are filled.

Oct. 1 is the earliest you can make a reservation any year for a time the following year. The best weekends usually are taken the first week or two of October. The number to call is 615-436-4473. If it's busy, be patient. The mailing address is P. O. Box 350, Gatlinburg, Tennessee 37738.

You can eat dinner and breakfast at the lodge. The meals are not fancy but they're ample, wholesome and tasty.

At more than 6300 feet above sea level, the lodge is the highest resort in Eastern America. The highest point of the mountain is 6593 feet, making Le Conte only the third highest peak in the park. But that's a minor matter. When people think of what's lovely and spectacular in the park, they don't often think of those two higher places, Clingmans Dome and Mt. Guyot. Both are

Le Conte Lodge, Great Smoky Mountains National Park

rounded, unspectacular domes.

Le Conte has craggy natural platforms for long looks down over the mountains. A Le Conte tradition is to go after supper to Cliff Top to watch the sunset. If the clouds are right, it can be an experience of grandeur. A tradition less followed is to get up long before breakfast and walk to Myrtle Point for the sunrise.

Five major trails lead to Le Conte. If I could go only once, I'd walk 6.75 miles up the Rainbow Falls Trail and then seven miles back down the Bullhead Trail. Those two start at the same place, in Cherokee Orchard, near Gatlinburg. You can leave your car in the parking area and come back to it the next day. Be sure to lock it and leave nothing visible to tempt burglars. If you can't arrange to spend the night on top, you can do this hike in one long day, but you may be weary at day's end.

Rainbow Falls Trail has, of course, Rainbow Falls. In some rare times of prolonged cold, the falls freeze into a spectacular hourglass shape. In spring, laurel and rhododendron bloom on Rocky Spur, on the

trail beyond the waterfall. The Bullhead has lots of wildflowers and it's a great place to see October colors. The lodge usually opens in late March and closes about the middle of November.

A longer route into the Smokies is through Cosby. Travel I-40 to Newport and then State 32 to Cosby. Or, if you have time to spare, go on south on 40 through Newport to the Foothills Parkway and follow the parkway to 32 and it to Cosby. The parkway is a rewarding drive, especially in autumn.

A short distance from Cosby is Cosby Campground. A good short hike out of the campground is to Henwallow Falls, about two miles.

It's a peaceful place, down below the falls, where one can listen to water music and watch the little stream gliding and splashing down the wrinkled rock ledge. One of my good experiences in the Smokies was at Henwallow Falls. I walked there alone one morning, while Alberta attended a dulcimer workshop in Cosby. On this particular morning, Henwallow Falls was covered with salamanders. Hundreds of salamanders. They were everywhere on the moist cliff. I suppose some mating urge caused this great salamander congregation. I've been back later to Henwallow and never saw even two salamanders. Nor have I seen such a salamander convention anywhere else. But someone once told me about seeing a great salamander migration on Little River. These at Henwallow weren't migrating. They just lay there on their bellies in the wet coolness, while I marveled.

You can drive south from Cosby on 32 to Davenport Gap at the North Carolina border and hike from there westward on the Appalachian Trail to Mt. Cammerer and one of the best long-range views in the mountains. But you'll earn your reward. For it's nearly all uphill from Davenport to Cammerer. The altitude gain is from 1975 feet at the gap to 4928 at the tower. The round trip is about 11.5 miles. Cammerer is at the end of a spur trail a little more than a half-mile to the north off the AT. The view from Cammerer is so good the Park Service many years ago erected a fire observation building here and didn't bother to put it atop a tower. The little wood-and-stone building still stands, though it's no longer used for its original purpose. It suffers from vandalism. Catawba rhododendron grows on Cammerer's rocky face and the scene is magnificent when it blooms in June.

If you're in a group that has two cars, you can leave one of them at Cosby Campground. And, instead of hiking back to Davenport, you can continue west on the AT to Low Gap and go from there down to the campground and the car. That'll make your total hike about 11 miles, maybe slightly less.

If you're hungry when you get back to Cosby, you can eat good trout at the restaurant at the Cub Motel, except in winter when it's closed. The waitresses debone the fish for you if you're unskilled at that task. If you're lucky, you'll get a table near the long rear windows and be able to look down on Cosby Creek and across the creek to the pool where the trout live.

Cosby each springtime is the scene of the Cosby Ramp Festival, sponsored by the local Ruritan Club. A ramp is a wild onion-like plant. Its offensive odor lingers for days on the breath of those who eat it. But mountain people used to eat it — and many still do — because it was one of the first edible plants that poked green leaves up through the forest litter in March and April. The last Sunday in April usually — but not always — is the date for the ramp festival. Admission is charged.

The Folk Life Center of the Smokies holds festivals in June and September, attracting folk musicians from many states to a hilltop above Cosby.

Another route into the Smokies is through Maryville and Townsend. All kinds of good things are in this western end of the park: Cades Cove, Abrams Creek, Gregory Bald, the Parson Branch Road. Townsend is a quiet entrance to the Smokies. No Dollywood. No crowded streets and sidewalks.

The Smoky Mountain Passion Play Association presents "The Smoky Mountain Passion Play" in Townsend each year from near the middle of June to late August. Performances are at 8:30 p.m. Monday, Wednesday, Friday and Saturday. Another Biblical play, "Damascus Road," is performed at the same hour in the same amphitheater on Tuesdays and Thursdays.

If you need breakfast, stop in Townsend at the Carriage House Restaurant for sausage and eggs. If you want to hike on a trail where you're unlikely to meet many other hikers, drive a mile or two on up to the Y, at the intersection of the Little River Road and the Laurel Creek Road to Cades Cove and where Little River collects its West Prong at that big swimmin' hole. You'll walk the Chestnut Top Trail. It starts a few yards north of the intersection and angles up a cliff back in the direction of Townsend.

This moist north-facing cliff is fine wildflower habitat. Among the flowers you see there from March into May are wild iris, laurel, dogwood, redbud, serviceberry, hepatica, spring beauty, bloodroot, trailing arbutus, bishop's cap, two varieties of trillium, at least four of violets and seven or eight other wildflower species. If you want only to see the flowers, you can walk about three-fourths of a mile, to where the trail swings abruptly from northwest to southeast, and turn back.

But you may want to continue on into a different habitat — dry, instead of moist, not many wildflowers, lots of pines and oaks. You may see an occasional birdfoot violet and halberd violet, some laurel bloom.

Eventually, you reach the old Schoolhouse Gap Trail, about 4.5 miles from where you started. Here you can turn back. Or you can turn left on the Schoolhouse Gap Trail (actually an old, old road) and follow it about 2.5 miles to the Laurel Creek Road. You should have a car waiting there, for you probably don't want to walk the highway back to the Y.

Everyone physically able should hike to Gregory Bald when the wild azaleas bloom. But not everyone on the same day. Gregory is one of the Great Smokies "grassy" balds. Other balds in the park are "heath" balds, which contain a thick cover of such heath plants as laurel, rhododendron and blueberries. When sheep and cattle grazed on Gregory more than 50 years ago, it was mostly grass. Since then, some heath plants and other plants have invaded. Gregory's wild azalea display, usually in the second half of June, is the finest I've ever seen. Bloom colors range from red-orange through orange, yellow, sand, pink and white. The white blooms have a pleasant fragrance.

I know of a man, a former University of Tennessee student, who was doing his master's thesis on the Gregory azaleas. He had nearly finished his research. He had a great mass of notes stored in the old Moore Spring Shelter (no longer standing). While he was out one day, a bear came into the shelter and ate his notes. He never finished the thesis.

To get to Gregory, follow the Cades Cove Loop Road just past the Cable Mill entrance to the Forge Creek Road. Follow that road to an intersection where the Parsons Branch Road splits to the right and the Forge Creek Road goes left. Take the left fork and continue to where the road dead-ends at a turnaround. Start walking. You'll

go up little Forge Creek Valley, through a magnificent forest of tulip poplars and hemlocks. The trail eventually climbs out of the valley and goes up Gregory Ridge. One-way distance is a little more than five miles.

If you don't want to hike, if all you want is an intimate drive through the forest, you'd like the Parson Branch Road. Same route as to the Gregory trailhead, except you keep to the right at the fork of the road. You'll go over Hannah Mountain and then down along Parson Branch to US 129. It's a one-way road; so you can't go back the way you came. You might like to follow crooked old 129 down the mountain above Calderwood Lake, then down beside Chilhowee Lake until you reach the Foothills Parkway. Then follow the Parkway back to the Maryville-Townsend Road. Parson Branch and Forge Creek Roads are closed in winter. (For a fuller account of these and similar roads in the park, read "Mountain Roads and Quiet Places," on sale at visitors centers in the park.)

Abrams Creek produces more pounds of trout per mile than any other stream in the park. This is mostly because the stream flows through limestone country. Limestone water produces lots of insects and other creatures trout like to eat. No other major stream in the park has this limestone advantage. But Abrams has one disadvantage: The rocky creekbed is very slippery. Lots of trouters take a spill. Just don't break anything.

L et's go trout fishing, museum hopping, hiking, birding and then have a look at Norris Dam, the first one TVA built. You can do it all within five or six miles of the dam.

When John Rice Irwin was a boy, he sometimes chopped corn for an uncle who usually paid him 25 cents a day. But one day, the uncle told John Rice he could take the usual quarter or he could take an old-time coffee grinder, no longer used. To the derision of some young friends, John Rice immediately chose the coffee grinder.

That was an early indication of Irwin's

love for old and discarded household and farm objects. He also liked to listen for hours to stories his grandparents told about life long ago in rural East Tennessee.

What all this eventually led to was his forsaking more conventional ways of making a living in favor of owning and operating a museum. The Museum of Appalachia, it's called. Some who are versed in that field say it's the most remarkable museum of its type in America.

Over the past 25 years, Irwin has roamed the Southern Appalachians in search of tools and farm and household implements that bring to light long-forgotten customs and methods of living and working. His quest has taken him into Cumberland Mountain coal mines so shallow he couldn't stand erect and to the region's loneliest hollows.

To reach his place, our first stop on this trip, go north on I-75 to Exit 122 and turn northeast on State 61. You'll have no trouble finding the museum.

You may notice first the rail fence surrounding the place. Or the two big work steers in a field. Or the flock of fainting goats. (A peculiar strain of goats; when badly frightened, they drop to the ground, briefly immobilized.) Or his herd of sheep. Or a mama hen clucking to her little ones.

For this place is more than the collection of the approximately 250,000 old inanimate objects Irwin has collected and put on display in 25 buildings scattered over a 65-acre farm. It's a place that lives, where somebody plants and cultivates a garden, occasionally splits rails, makes sorghum molasses.

Nobody is going to look at all those 250,000 items in one visit. Irwin has displayed them in about 40 groupings. But there are a few items that are so different they won't be grouped. Look at what interests you most and save some for another visit.

If you're interested in bits, the things that fit into the mouths of horses and mules, Irwin has more than you ever thought you'd see in one place — thousands.

He doesn't have quite that many traps. But you never thought there were so many kinds. Some of the great number of steel traps must be at least very similar to some of the others. But surely there are not many others, anywhere, like the self-setting mousetrap that dumps one victim after another into a glass jar while it keeps right on re-setting itself without human help.

Irwin says steel traps affected "the course of American history." It was the trapper, and after him, the fur buyer, who always plunged ahead of the others into the unknown wilderness.

Fly traps didn't affect history nearly so much. But Irwin has a fly trap made by a man who knew something about flies. He knew they wouldn't fly downward to get out of the trap after they had entered the opening at the bottom and flown up to the top of the trap.

Another old example of the trapmaker's art is a quail trap of a type Irwin says was used in the Middle Ages. It's about 30 feet long. Quail follow a trail of grain into it and keep going to the end. Like those flies that won't fly down, quail don't turn back.

He has snare traps and deadfall traps. One simple gadget, made a long time ago by Enoch Williams of Grainger County, drops a rock on the head of a rat or rabbit when the creature pulls at a bait. Well, it might not have worked *every* time but it likely worked some of the time.

But Enoch Williams, who couldn't read, was capable of more technical work. The museum has Williams' telescope. He made it from scrap glass and metal. The machine he made for grinding the lens also is there.

Irwin thinks the most historic item in his collection is a "goosewing" axe found near old Fort Loudoun on the Little Tennessee River. It's believed to have been used by English soldiers at the fort, and it may have been used in the fort's construction in the middle 1750s.

The museum has huge old meat troughs made from tulip poplar trees, fashioned much the same way Indians made dugout canoes. One thing Irwin wants and doesn't have is such a canoe. One of the big meat troughs is from the Sharp family of Big Valley of Union County, where Irwin was born and where his ancestors lived for generations.

Museum of Appalachia, Norris

Look at the auger display. Irwin says people 100 years and more ago *had* to have augers. They used one kind of auger to bore a hole to make a rifle, other kinds to bore holes for pegs used in building houses, still others for making looms, spinning wheels and stringed musical instruments. The largest auger in the collection was used for boring through logs to make wooden water pipes. Irwin says that auger is 2600 times larger than his smallest boring tool, a gimlet.

He has two oldtime bark grinders, used for grinding tanbark from which was extracted tannic acid for tanning hides for leather.

There are noise-making items — fox horns, stage coach horns, bells of many sounds and uses, noisemakers called rattletraps. You may hear a loud bonging from the big clock that used to be on the Anderson County Courthouse in Clinton. Paul Evans of Norris keeps the clock in working order.

Every October, on a three- or four-day weekend, the museum is the scene of the annual Museum of Appalachia Tennessee Fall Homecoming. Thousands come from many states to listen to oldtime music and good-natured joking that goes on on stage for hours each day. Tennessee's governor usually shows up one day, along with movie and television stars. "Roots" author Alex Haley, who lives close to the museum (as a result of John Rice's friendship with him) attends and autographs his books. Old-timers — or youngsters who have learned oldtimer ways — make lye soap, hammer hot iron in a blacksmith shop, rive roofing shingles, dye yarn, spin flax, brew sassafras tea.

The Museum of Appalachia charges admission.

Nowhere else that I know will you find two such similar museums so near each other as the Museum of Appalachia and the Lenoir Museum, which is on US 441, in Norris Dam State Park. They're five miles apart.

At 96, Will G. Lenoir is the state's oldest

employee. He never intended to work for the state. But after he turned over to the state his vast collection of memorabilia a dozen years ago, the state could find no person more qualified to tell visitors about it. He's at the museum on weekends during the winter and through the week in summer.

Doesn't he ever miss, maybe because of illness?

"I don't get sick," he said, only half in jest. He's healthy.

He shows off an odd-looking circular saw with very short teeth. Earl Olson of Norris found it far up Clear Creek, Lenoir said. Earl is an authority on the Clear Creek area. He knew this saw blade was part of the water-powered cotton gin that George Taylor operated long ago on the creek. The creek passes within a few yards of the museum on its way to Clinch River. Beside the creek is the Old Mill, an 18th century grist mill that was operated long ago by John Rice Irwin's ancestors.

In the Lenoir collection is a rare barrel organ with 44 moveable figures. No one here has seen another like it. When the organ is wound, it plays 10 tunes. Tiny dancers dance, horses gallop, a clown clowns and a woman churns. When Lenoir bought the organ from a woman in Bulls Gap for $2000, it was in sad condition — a jumble of separate parts, many of them broken, in three boxes. Paul Evans (same one who helps with the old clock at the Museum of Appalachia) and Reg Lovell of Norris and Joe Diehl of Knox County did the restoration. Paul did the mechanical work. Reg worked on the music, and Joe made new legs for the broken ones on the horses. Lenoir said Joe carved the crooked legs of the running horses from hickory bark. Making the legs, with the sharp crooks, from regular wood would have been difficult to impossible, he said. Joe's wife, Anna, painted them. Evans thinks skilled German craftsmen made the barrel organ and that they made only this one. He found inside it, used for padding, a German newspaper dated May 13, 1826.

A crowd usually is on hand when the barrel organ is wound, and its little people perform at 10:30 a.m. each Saturday.

A cobbler's bench and all kinds of tools for working leather will give you some idea of how people made shoes long ago. Those early shoes were made the same for both feet, Lenoir says. He will show you the tiny wooden pegs, more than 100 years old, used to peg on the soles. And a "pain reliever," used to stretch a shoe where it pressed too hard on a corn.

Hearing aids were different long ago. In the Lenoir Museum is one with a speaking end, a hearing end and a yard-long tube between them. The person with poor hearing put the hearing end in his better ear and handed the other end to the speaker.

There's a 150-year old stage coach horn. One of its uses, Lenoir says, was to signal ahead to an inn how many passengers wanted lunch.

This museum has lots of animal yokes. Lenoir shows a spiked yoke. You put that on a cow to keep her from sucking herself. Another way to stop her, Lenoir said, was to split her tongue. Then there's the spiked calf weaner that causes the cow to kick the calf when it tries to suck.

Lenoir is proud of the entire set of stone-working tools once owned by B. A. Vess, who cut the stones used in the stone houses, walls and bridges of the town of Norris.

Not every article in this collection is from humble origins. Take a look at the Chinese porcelain piece from the Ming Dynasty.

There's a 1500-year-old Indian burial urn found in a Georgia cave.

Oldtimers from Knoxville may want to pull out one of the four swinging stools at a table from Peter Kern's Ice Cream Parlor.

Admission to Lenoir Museum is free.

Within sight of the museum is an odd-looking low-water dam TVA built across the Clinch River at Hibbs Island. Its purpose is to improve trout fishing downstream. TVA sometimes shuts off the flow from Norris Dam for many hours at a time. This formerly caused much of the downstream riverbed to become so dry that many aquatic insects died. These little creatures are trout food. Their death was bad for trout. The low dam — called a weir dam — traps a considerable volume of water which is released slowly downstream, keeping the riverbed wet.

Lots of fishermen try for trout in the Clinch. Fishing there is as good as the state trout stocking program, and that's been pretty good recently. Fishing on Norris Lake, on the other hand, is only as good as the natural reproduction. For the lake gets no stocking. But fishing often is good, especially in spring.

Norris Dam, started in 1933 and completed in 1936, was TVA's first. On the 50th anniversary of its completion, TVA said the dam had generated 19 billion kilowatt-hours of electricity. TVA cannot provide an exact figure for the worth of that much power. But retail rates averaged close to 3.5 cents a kilowatt-hour over the 50 years. That amounts to $665 million. The cost of the dam and related projects — such as Norris Freeway and all the land bought for the lake — was $32.2 million. Three spinoffs from the project are Big Ridge, Norris Dam and Cove Lake State Parks. Though it's only one of more than a dozen TVA dams above Chattanooga, Norris provides about one-fourth of the flood control for Chattanooga, most critical point on the Tennessee River for flooding.

TVA maintains two excellent trails along the Clinch River below the dam, one on each side. One is the Song Bird Trail. It's one of the Tennessee Wildlife Resources Agency's designated Wildlife Observation Areas. Because it has several different kinds of habitat — river, old fields, bottomland hardwoods, grassy areas, as well as dense thickets — it has wide bird variety. It has a large population of Eastern bluebirds, partly because of the bluebird nesting boxes placed years ago in the meadow near the river. It also has wrens, screech owls, goldfinches, several kinds of sparrows, orchard orioles and others. Several years ago, a pair of Baltimore orioles nested in a tree beside the river. You often can see great blue herons flying above the river or wading when the water is low. The Canada goose population on the river and on Melton Hill Lake is growing, expanding upriver from the lake. In 1986, for the first time, geese were on the river only a few yards below Norris Dam. Birds aren't the only wildlife along the river. When you walk the Song Bird Trail, you often see rabbits and groundhogs and, infrequently, a deer. The trail is only eight-tenths of a mile long. A section of it is paved for wheelchair travelers.

On the other side of the river is the Riverbluff Trail. It's as good for wildflowers as the other is for birds. It has hepatica, several varieties of violets, two kinds of trillium, twin-leaf, Dutchman's-breeches, toothwort, celandine poppies, spring beauties, rue anemone, purple phacelia, wild ginger and others. But what it's famous for is trout lilies. Acres of the steep hillside are yellow and green with the blooms and spotted green leaves of this small flower. Best bloom time is in April. Many walk only far enough along the river to see the wildflowers. But the trail turns away from the river, climbs the hill and goes back along the ridgecrest, making a loop. The entire trail is 3.2 miles long.

Some might want to look around the city of Norris, the town TVA built when it built the dam. It was to house TVA workers and officials. But it was to be a permanent model city, not just a temporary work camp. In the old part of the city, streets usually — but not always — curve at intersections, instead of turning at precise angles. So far, there are no traffic lights. On portions of some streets, houses are grouped in semi-circles around small green commons. There is a lovely large commons opposite the building that now houses Norris Middle School. Sidewalks don't run right beside the streets. Actually, they are paved pedestrian paths that in some instances aren't close to streets. In some areas, attractive open stone gutters drain surface water into storm sewers.

The first three TVA chairmen (A. E. Morgan, David Lilienthal and Gordon Clapp) lived in Norris.

In 1948, TVA sold the town to the highest bidder, which in turn sold the houses to individuals. Norris was incorporated in 1949. The first mayor was R. G. "Buddy" Crossno, owner of the town dairy, called the Norris Creamery. At dawn, Norrisonians could look out their windows and see the mayor delivering their milk.

Introduction to the tables

Following each chapter of this book are lists of attractions, lodging places and parks in the region covered by the text. These lists, arranged alphabetically by towns, are intended to give readers an idea of what is available in the area; they are not endorsements by either Carson Brewer or The Knoxville News-Sentinel, nor do they list every attraction and place to spend the night.

In the lists of attractions, we aimed to include those places of an historical or educational nature.

In the list of lodging places, we tried to include interesting and unusual places to stay. We did not list any chain-owned hotels or motels.

We suggest you call and verify the information given in these listings when planning a trip or making reservations. While a park may allow leashed pets on the premises, for instance, it may not permit them in the lodge or cabins. While it may not have a pool, as listed on our tables, it may have swimming available in a lake. A few of the higher-priced inns include lunch and/or dinner as well as breakfast in the price of a room. And while some inns may not permit children to stay, they may make exceptions for those over 12.

We also have included the mailing addresses and phone numbers of chambers of commerce in the region. They can be helpful in learning more about services available.

Tennessee Attractions

McMinn County Living Heritage Museum Athens, Tenn. 37303 615-745-0329	Nine rooms of exhibits with more than 2000 items reflecting life in the region from the time of the Cherokee Indians to the Great Depression. Open Tuesday-Sunday. Admission.
The Ole Brown Museum Beersheba Springs, Tenn. 37305 615-692-3522	Formerly a country store, this is a good place to browse through photos, scrapbooks and early history books about the region. Open May-September. Located on Hwy. 56.
Bristol Caverns Bristol, Tenn. 37621 615-878-2011	Spectacular dripstone cave which was used by Indians in their raids upon settlers. Open daily. Admission.
Bristol International Raceway Thunder Valley Dragway Bristol, Tenn. 37625 615-764-1161	World's fastest half-mile track is home of major NASCAR events. Call for racing schedules.
Grand Guitar Museum Bristol, Tenn. 37620 615-968-1719	A guitar-shaped museum containing more than 200 guitars and other string instruments from around the world. Open March-December. Free.
Cordell Hull Birthplace Byrdstown, Tenn. 38549 615-864-3247	Log cabin birthplace of the "Father of the United Nations" and Secretary of State under Franklin D.Roosevelt. Open Thursday-Monday, June-August. Free.
The Alpine Slide Chattanooga, Tenn. 37419 615-825-5666	Take a "bobsled" ride down Raccoon Mountain on a 2350-foot track. Open daily during summer, weekends in spring and fall. Admission.
Audubon Acres Chattanooga, Tenn. 37402 615-892-1499	130-acre park has hiking trails, wildlife to observe and the Spring Frog Cabin, built by Indians in 1754. Open weekends March-November. Free.

Chattanooga Choo-Choo Chattanooga, Tenn. 37402 615-266-5000	Complex of restaurants, shops and gardens, as well as antique trolley car rides, an ice skating rink and one of the largest model train displays in the world. Open daily. Charges for trolley car and model train displays.
Chickamauga-Chattanooga National Military Park Chattanooga, Tenn. 30742 404-866-9241	This is the nation's largest and oldest national military park and is located in 17 park units. Open daily. Free.
High Adventure Sports Chattanooga, Tenn. 37409 615-825-0444	Guide service for hot air ballooning, hang gliding, caving, rafting and other sports. Open daily. Fees.
Houston Antique Museum Chattanooga, Tenn. 37403 615-267-7176	Features 15,000 glass pitchers, Toby jugs, mustache cups, whale oil lamps and music boxes. Open Tuesday-Sunday. Admission.
Hunter Museum of Art Chattanooga, Tenn. 37403 615-267-0968	A 1904 mansion and contemporary gallery house a permanent collection of American art and special exhibits throughout the year. Open Tuesday-Sunday. Donations.
Lake Winnepesaukah Chattanooga, Tenn. 30741 404-866-5681	Family amusement park with more than 30 rides and picnic facilities. Open Thursday-Sunday, May-Labor Day. Admission.
Lookout Mountain Incline Railway Chattanooga, Tenn. 37350 615-821-4224	The world's steepest and safest incline reaches a grade of 72.7 percent. Open daily. Admission.
Lookout Mountain Museum Chattanooga, Tenn. 37350 404-820-2531	Life-size dioramas of Indian history and other events. Artifacts include Civil War equipment and Indian ceremonial axes and tools. Open daily. Admission.
Lookout Mtn. Caverns/Ruby Falls Chattanooga, Tenn. 37409 615-821-2544	145-foot waterfall flows 1120 feet below Lookout Mountain. Guided tours descend to cave by elevator then continue on foot. Observation deck atop outside tower. Open daily. Admission.
National Knife Museum Chattanooga, Tenn. 37421 615-892-5007	Over 5000 cutlery items, including many one-of-a-kind pieces, valued in excess of three million dollars. Open Monday-Saturday year round. Free.
Raccoon Mountain Caverns Chattanooga, Tenn. 37409 615-821-9403	Guided tours through beautiful formations. Tours through undeveloped sections available. Aerial tramway and campground. Open daily. Admission.
Raccoon Mountain Flight Park Chattanooga, Tenn. 37409 615-821-9403	Serves both novice and expert hang gliders and features the world's only hang gliding simulator. Open daily April-December. Fee for simulator and lessons.
Reflection Riding Chattanooga, Tenn. 37409 615-821-1160	350-acre arboretum is patterned after an English garden and features more than 1000 species of wildflowers, trees and shrubs. Open daily. Admission.
Rock City Gardens Chattanooga, Tenn. 37350 404-820-2531	Beautiful rock gardens and scenic vistas. See seven states from Lover's Leap. Open daily. Admission.

Tennessee Valley Railroad Musm. Chattanooga, Tenn. 37421 615-894-8028	Second-largest railroad museum in the country. Working steam and diesel locomotives, rail cars and equipment. Steam locomotive takes passengers on six-mile excursion through a tunnel cut prior to the Civil War. Open June-Labor Day. Admission.
Primitive Settlement Cleveland, Tenn. 37311 615-476-5096	A collection of log cabins restored and furnished with items used by early Americans. Open daily April-October. Admission.
Red Clay State Historic Area Cleveland, Tenn. 37311 615-472-2627	Final council ground of the Cherokee Nation. Replica of Indian farm and council house. Visitors center/museum and picnic grounds. Open daily. Free.
Hidden Hollow Park Cookeville, Tenn. 38501 615-526-4038	86-acre park features waterfalls, lakes, covered bridges and many plants and animals. Picnicking, swimming, fishing, hiking. Open daily. Admission.
Folklife Center of the Smokies Cosby, Tenn. 37722 615-487-5543	Rustic center preserves mountain music, crafts and folklife. Open daily. Free. Admission for special events.
Cudjo Caverns Cumberland Gap, Tenn. 24248 703-861-2203	Walk under two states and see the world's largest stalagmite formation on a 45-minute tour. Open daily April-October. Admission.
Renegade Mountain Crossville, Tenn. 37723 615-484-5285	Snow skiing, including rental equipment and instruction. Restaurants and lounges open year round.
Cumberland County Playhouse Crossville, Tenn. 38555 615-484-5000	An indoor stage theater offers musicals and plays March through November. Admission
Jefferson County Museum Dandridge, Tenn. No Phone	Self-guided walking tour of 30 buildings on the National Historic Register. Free.
Rhea County Courthouse Dayton, Tenn. 37321 615-775-0187	Scene of the famous Scopes Monkey Trial, restored to its 1925 appearance. Museum in basement. Open Monday-Saturday. Free.
Doe River Covered Bridge Elizabethton, Tenn. 37643 No phone	The most photographed structure in Carter County. Originally built for $3,000, it spans the river for 134 feet. Located off Hwy. 19E.
Unicoi County Heritage Museum Erwin, Tenn. 37650 615-743-9449	This community-supported museum is housed in a restored turn-of-the-century home and offers exhibits of Blue Ridge pottery, railroad memorabilia, antique dolls and toys, and items from general stores, apothecaries, doctor's offices and barbershops of days gone by. A nature trail is at the rear of the grounds. Open May-October. Local crafts for sale in community room.
National Fish Hatchery Erwin, Tenn. 37650 615-743-4712	Outdoor water raceways and indoor tanks show development of thousands of rainbow trout. 42-acre complex includes visitors center, museum and picnic area.

Arrowmont School of Arts & Crafts Gatlinburg, Tenn. 37738 615-436-4604	Pi Beta Phi Sorority started this school in 1926 to educate mountain children. Now it attracts arts and crafts students from around the country. Their crafts, as well as those of the staff members and local craftspeople, are sold in the Arrowcraft Shop.
Gatlinburg Sky Lift Gatlinburg, Tenn. 37738 615-436-4307	See the Smokies from the off-season ski lift. Open daily April-October. Admission.
Gatlinburg Space Needle Gatlinburg, Tenn. 37738 615-436-4629	Glass-enclosed elevator goes up 342 ft. to observation deck. Open daily. Admission.
Great Smoky Arts and Crafts Community Gatlinburg, Tenn. 37738 615-436-5497	This community is composed of more than 50 shops and studios, some open all year. Largest group of crafts shops in the south. Two large craft shows are held in April and November.
McCarter's Riding Stables Gatlinburg, Tenn. 37738 615-436-5354	Guided trips through the Smokies. Open daily March-November. Fee.
Mountaineer Museum Gatlinburg, Tenn. 37738 615-436-9535	Artifacts of early Gatlinburg. Open April-October. Admission.
Ober Gatlinburg Resort Gatlinburg, Tenn. 37738 615-436-5423	Aerial tramway from downtown Gatlinburg goes two miles to Ober Gatlinburg's shops, skating rink, alpine slide, skiing, black bear museum and Old Heidelberg Castle restaurant. All activities year round. Open daily. Admission.
Smoky Mountain Winery Gatlinburg, Tenn. 37738 615-436-7551	Sample 15 Gatlinburg-made wines. Open daily March-December. Free.
Samuel W. Doak House Greeneville, Tenn 37743 615-639-4681	Federal style brick farmhouse on Tusculum College campus. Built in 1818, it is filled with period furniture and contains craft demonstration studios. Open March-December. Free.
Andrew Johnson Nat'l Historic Site Greeneville, Tenn. 37743 615-638-3503	Tour Johnson's tailor shop and one of his two homes in the town, as well as his gravesite. Open daily. Admission for house tour.
Abraham Lincoln Museum Lincoln Memorial University Harrogate, Tenn. 37752 615-869-3611	One of the largest groupings of Lincoln and Civil War materials in the world. Open daily except during December and January. Admission.
Cumberland General Store Homesteads, Tenn. 38555 615-484-8481	This re-creation of a turn-of-the-century general store offers "Goods in Endless Variety for Man & Beast." Open year round.
Homesteads Tower Museum Homesteads, Tenn. 38555 615-484-2697	Tells the story of the region's development during the New Deal. Open March-December.
Alvin York's Grist Mill and Park Jamestown, Tenn. 38556 615-879-9948	Sgt. York, hero of WWI and Congressional Medal of Honor honoree, operated this grist mill in later years. Designated as a State Historical Area. Open daily. Free.

Highland Manor Winery Jamestown, Tenn. 38556 615-879-9519	Open for tours and tastings. Reservations recommended. No charge. Open Monday-Saturday.
Glenmore Mansion Jefferson City, Tenn. 37760 615-397-9642	A near-perfect example of Victorian architecture. Five-story, 27-room house. Open weekends May-October, by appointment other times. Admission.
Tipton-Haynes Farm Johnson City, Tenn. 37605 615-926-3631	A restored farm of the 1800s and site of the "Battle of the Lost State of Franklin." The farm includes a log barn, granary, the former law office of David Haynes, and a visitors center/museum. Open April-October. Admission.
Christopher Taylor House Jonesborough, Tenn. 37659 No phone	A 200-year-old log house in which young Andrew Jackson boarded while living in Tennessee's oldest town. Free.
The Mail Pouch Jonesborough, Tenn. 37659 615-753-5971	The town's only remaining saloon building, boasting a near-perfect Mail Pouch Tobacco sign of turn-of-the-century vintage. The building is located on Courthouse Square and houses fine crafts. Open Monday-Friday.
Visitor's Center and Museum Jonesborough, Tenn. 37659 615-753-5961	The story of Jonesborough from the 1770s has been preserved in permanent exhibit. Open year round. Admission to museum.
Mauk's Jonesborough Pharmacy Jonesborough, Tenn. 37659 615-753-4648	Continuous pharmaceutical service since 1891 and a good place to browse through antiques, too.
The Exchange Place Kingsport, Tenn. 37664 615-288-6071	A restored 19th-century farm and crafts center. Once served as a place to exchange horses and Virginia currency for Tennessee. Open weekends May-October. Free.
The Netherland Inn Kingsport, Tenn. 36772 615-247-3211, 246-2662	Early tavern and boatyard complex on the Holston River. The three-story wooden hotel is restored and filled with period furniture. Open Friday-Sunday, May-October. Admission.
Armstrong-Lockett House Knoxville, Tenn. 37919 615-637-3163	This 1834-vintage home features the late Buck Toms' collection of Federal period furniture and English silver. Open Tuesday-Sunday. Admission.
Beck Cultural Exchange Center Knoxville, Tenn. 37915 615-524-8461	Museum recording the achievements of Knoxville's black community from the early 1800s. Open Tuesday-Saturday, Sunday by appointment. Free.
Bijou Theater Knoxville, Tenn. 37901 615-522-0832	This old-time theater house, built in 1817, now houses concerts, plays and special productions. Call for schedules and ticket information.
Blount Mansion Knoxville, Tenn. 37901 615-525-2375	This 1792 home was where Tennessee had its beginnings. It was the home of Gov. William Blount and contains furnishings from the frontier era. Open Tuesday-Sunday. Admission.
Confederate Memorial Hall Knoxville, Tenn. 37919 615-522-2371	Antebellum mansion museum served as Confederate General Longstreet's headquarters during the Civil War. Open daily. Admission.

Dulin Gallery of Art
Knoxville, Tenn. 37919
615-525-6101

Contemporary art, the Thorne Miniature Rooms and traveling exhibits. Open Tuesday-Sunday. Admission, except on Sundays.

East Tennessee Historical Society
Knoxville, Tenn. 37902
615-523-0781

The U.S. Customs House, built in 1874, houses Tennessee archives, including the public library's collection. Open Monday-Friday. Free.

James White Fort
Knoxville, Tenn. 37915
615-525-6514

In 1786 the founder of Knoxville built this home and stockade in the Tennessee wilderness. Now it is located on the outskirts of downtown. Open daily, except January. Admission.

John Sevier Historic Site
Knoxville, Tenn. 37920
615-573-5508

Log cabin home and farm of Tennessee's first governor, filled with period furnishings, including some that were used by the Sevier family. Open Tuesday-Saturday, March-October. Also shown by appointment. Admission.

Knoxville Zoological Park
Knoxville, Tenn. 37914
615-637-5331

Famous for its large cats, reptile complex and new marine animal complex, home to polar bears, seals, sea lions and penguins. Open daily. Admission.

The McClung Museum
Knoxville, Tenn. 37996
615-974-2144

Exhibits on anthropology, archaeology, arts, science and history. On University of Tennessee campus. Open Monday-Friday or by appointment. Free.

Ramsey House
Knoxville, Tenn. 37917
615-546-0745

Built in 1797, this was the first stone house in the territory. Open Tuesday-Sunday, April-October. Admission.

Speedwell Manor
Knoxville, Tenn. 37920
615-577-2757

This mansion was originally built in another town and moved to its present location. Furnished with 18th and 19th-century furniture and art. Open Tuesday, Thursday and Sunday. Admission.

Students' Museum and Akima
Planetarium
Knoxville, Tenn. 37914
615-637-1121

History, culture and art with special activities for children during school holidays. Open daily. Admission.

The Tennessee Theatre
Knoxville, Tenn. 37901
615-525-1840

This 1928 movie palace was one of the last built with a theater organ, which is still used to entertain movie audiences before and after shows. The theater has been restored to its original condition. It is now the home of the Knoxville Symphony Orchestra and Knoxville Opera Company. Call for ticket information.

Iron Mountain Stoneware
Laurel Bloomery, Tenn. 37680
800-437-4901

This company produces dinnerware sold in fine stores nationwide. It operates an on-site store which sells seconds and twice a year offers discount sales on first-quality merchandise. Free admission.

Sam Houston Schoolhouse
Maryville, Tenn. 37801
615-983-1550

Tennessee's oldest rural schoolhouse. Houston taught in the school in 1812. Open daily. Free.

Thompson-Brown House
Maryville, Tenn. 37801
615-984-6200

This two-story log house now serves as the Smoky Mountain Visitors Center. Open Monday-Saturday, April-October. Free.

Cumberland Caverns Park McMinnville, Tenn. 37110 615-668-4396	90-minute tours of the second largest cave in the nation. Underground dining room and theater. Open daily June-August, weekends in May, September and October; by appointment November-April. Admission.
Davy Crockett Tavern & Museum Morristown, Tenn. 37815 615-586-6382	A reproduction of the Crockett tavern which Davy's father operated in the 1790s. Open Monday-Sunday, March 15 - Nov. 15. Admission.
Rose Center Morristown, Tenn. 37816 615-581-4330	A cultural center, historical museum, art gallery, children's "touch" museum and crafts shop. Open Monday-Saturday. Free.
Newport/Cocke County Museum Newport, Tenn. 37821 615-623-7304	Indian artifacts, historical documents, pioneer implements are displayed in the community museum. Open Monday-Friday by appointment. Free.
Museum of Appalachia Norris, Tenn. 37828 615-494-7680	65-acre Appalachian village contains more than 250,000 pioneer relics, 25 log structures and crafts shop. Considered by many to be the most complete collection of mountain culture. Open daily. Admission.
Lenoir Museum Norris, Tenn. 37769 615-494-9688	This museum in Norris Dam State Park contains pioneer artifacts. An 18th century grist mill operates daily during the summer. Open daily May-October, weekends November-April. Free.
American Museum of Science and Energy Oak Ridge, Tenn. 37830 615-576-3200	Movies, models, demonstrations and gadgets tell the story of energy and its uses for man. Operated by the U.S. Department of Energy. Open daily. Free.
Children's Museum of Oak Ridge Oak Ridge, Tenn. 37830 615-482-1074	"Hands on" learning center with 20 major exhibit areas. Open daily. Admission.
Museum of Fine Arts Oak Ridge, Tenn. 37830 615-482-1182	Home of the Gomez collection of 60 works by contemporary artists. Open daily. Admission.
Oak Ridge Energy Tour Oak Ridge, Tenn. 37831 615-482-7821	38-mile, self-guided auto tour of nine energy resources, including the Bull Run Steam Plant, the Graphite Reactor, Oak Ridge Gaseous Diffusion Plant, Oak Ridge National Laboratory and UT Forestry Experiment Station and Arboretum. Open daily. Free.
Dollywood Pigeon Forge, Tenn. 37863 615-428-9400	A re-created 1880s mountain village. Much of singer Dolly Parton's background can be seen throughout the park in restaurants, crafts, rides and musical entertainment. Open daily Memorial Day-Labor Day, and from Friday-Tuesday in May and September. Admission.
Flyaway Pigeon Forge, Tenn. 37863 615-453-7777	Man-made winds set at 100 m.p.h. allow visitors to fly inside a padded vertical wind tunnel. One of three such facilities in the world. Open daily in summer, call for openings during the rest of the year. Admission.
Helicopter Rides Pigeon Forge, Tenn. 37863 615-453-2997	A bird's eye view of Pigeon Forge and the Smokies. Late May-October. Fee.

Mill Creek Park Pigeon Forge, Tenn. 37863 615-453-1100	Picnic on the river, fish, wade, visit the petting zoo and playground. Open daily May-October. Admission.
The Old Mill Pigeon Forge, Tenn. 37863 615-453-4628	Water-powered mill, built in 1830, offers 15 varieties of flour, meal and grits. A National Historic Site. Open Monday-Saturday year round. Tours of mill April-October. Admission for tours.
Ogle's Water Park Pigeon Forge, Tenn. 37863 615-453-8741	A giant water playground: wave pool, water slide, sunning area, playground, miniature golf. Open daily June-September, weekends in May. Admission.
Pigeon Forge Pottery Pigeon Forge, Tenn. 37863 615-453-3883 or 453-3704	Watch pottery being made by local craftspeople. Open daily.
Smoky Mountain Car Museum Pigeon Forge, Tenn. 37863 No phone	Antique, vintage and classic cars on display. Open daily spring through fall. Admission.
Rocky Mount Piney Flats, Tenn. 37686 615-538-7396	The oldest original territorial capitol in the U.S. and one of the oldest buildings in Tennessee. Governor William Blount made his home there with the William Cobb family, who built the large log house in 1770. Costumed guides will lead visitors on a trip through the restored house and demonstrate the skills of a typical pioneer family of the 18th century.
Hawkins County Courthouse Rogersville, Tenn. 37857 615-272-7165	The oldest courthouse in Tennessee (1836). The main courtroom is said to be copied from Independence Hall in Philadelphia.
The Amis House Rogersville, Tenn. 37857 No phone	Three miles southeast of town on Burem Road, this stone house was built as a defense against Indians. May be viewed from the outside only. No admission.
The Kyle House Rogersville, Tenn. 37857 No phone	Built in 1830, this was Confederate headquarters during the Civil War. May be viewed from the outside only. No admission.
Historic Rugby Visitors Center Rugby, Tenn. 37733 615-628-2441	Pictures and other exhibitry will take viewers through Rugby's first century. Open March-December 15. Admission includes walking tours of nearby buildings.
Historic Rugby Rugby, Tenn. 37733 615-628-2441	Seventeen original Victorian buildings still stand in this rural English colony founded by author Thomas Hughes in the 1880s. The public library contains one of the finest collections of Victorian literature in America. Tours of the town available daily from March till mid-November. Admission.
Forbidden Caverns Sevierville, Tenn. 37862 615-453-5972	See sparkling formations, waterfalls and natural chimneys. Open daily April-October. Admission.
Rock House Sparta, Tenn. 38583 615-738-8830 or 836-3552	An 1840s stagecoach stop frequented by Andrew Jackson while in route to Washington, D.C. Open by appointment. Free.

Old Mountain Village Sweetwater, Tenn. 37303 615-745-2602	A large collection of authentic log buildings, each re-stored to its original condition. Open daily Memorial Day-Labor Day. Admission.
The Lost Sea Sweetwater, Tenn. 37874 615-337-6616	Offers guided tours and a boat ride on the "World's Largest Underground Lake." It is a Tennessee Historic Site and is open year round. Admission.
Grape Patch Winery Telford, Tenn. 37690 615-257-3776	Sample wine or take a leisurely walk through the vine-yard. Tours may be arranged by phone.
Cades Cove Riding Stables Townsend, Tenn. 37886 615-448-6286	Hourly trips in the Smokies. Free guide with tours. Open daily April-October. Rental fee.
Davy Crockett Stables Townsend, Tenn. 37882 615-448-6411	Hour, half-day or overnight trips in the Smokies. Open daily year round. Rental fee.
Tuckaleechee Caverns Townsend, Tenn. 37882 615-448-2274 or 448-2422	One-hour and 15-minute guided tours of the caverns every 30 minutes. Open daily April-October. Admission.
Smoky Mountain Passion Play Townsend, Tenn. 37882 615-984-4111 or 984-2244	Outdoor drama depicting the life of Christ four nights a week and the story of the Apostle Paul on two more. Closed Sundays. June 12-Aug. 22. Admission.
Fort Loudoun State Historic Area Vonore, Tenn. 37885 615-884-6217	Offers museum and reconstructed fort of one of Tennes-see's oldest historic sites. Open year round. Free.
Sequoyah Birthplace Museum Vonore, Tenn. 37885 615-884-6246	Tennessee's only tribally-owned historic attraction, this museum tells the story of the Cherokee people and one of their most famous leaders. Also includes Cherokee Memorial and museum gift shop. Open March-Decem-ber. Admission.

Tennessee Lodging Places

	Dates open	Rooms	Cabins	Private bath	Breakfast offered	Lunch offered	Dinner offered	Pool	Tennis court	Children welcome	Pets welcome	Rates: L - Low, less than $30; M - Moderate, $31-$60; H - High, $61 and up
Timberfell Lodge Baileyton, Tenn. 37743 615-234-9272	Year round	✓		✓	✓*	✓	✓					M-H
Chanticleer Lodge Chattanooga, Tenn. 37350 404-820-2015	Year round	✓	✓	✓	✓*				✓	✓	✓	M
Chattanooga Choo-Choo Hilton Chattanooga, Tenn. 37402 615-266-5000	Year round	✓		✓	✓	✓	✓	✓	✓	✓		H
Johnson's Scenic Court Chattanooga, Tenn. 37350 404-820-2000	April - Dec. 25	✓		✓	✓*				✓		✓	M
Read House Chattanooga, Tenn. 37402 615-266-4121	Year round	✓		✓	✓*	✓	✓	✓		✓		H
Southern Inn Chattanooga, Tenn. 37412 615-894-0440	Year round	✓		✓	✓	✓	✓	✓	✓	✓		M
Fairfield Glade Resort Crossville, Tenn. 38555 1-800-262-6702	Year round	✓	✓	✓	✓	✓	✓	✓	✓	✓		L-H
Bent Creek Mountain Inn Gatlinburg, Tenn. 37738 615-436-2875	Year round	✓		✓	✓	✓	✓	✓	✓	✓		H
Brookside Resort Gatlinburg, Tenn. 37738 615-436-5611	Year round	✓	✓	✓					✓		✓	M-H
Buckhorn Inn Gatlinburg, Tenn. 37738 615-436-4668	Year round	✓	✓	✓	✓*		✓					M-H
Carr's Northside Cottages/Motel Gatlinburg, Tenn. 37738 615-436-4836	Year round	✓	✓	✓					✓		✓	✓	M
The Edgewater Hotel Gatlinburg, Tenn. 37738 615-436-4151	Year round	✓		✓	✓	✓	✓	✓		✓		H
Glenstone Lodge Gatlinburg, Tenn. 37738 615-436-9361	Year round	✓		✓		✓	✓	✓		✓		M-H
Homestead House Gatlinburg, Tenn. 37738 615-436-6166	Year round	✓		✓	✓			✓	✓			M-H

* Included in room charge

	Dates open	Rooms	Cabins	Private bath	Breakfast offered	Lunch offered	Dinner offered	Pool	Tennis court	Children welcome	Pets welcome	Rates
River Terrace Motel Gatlinburg, Tenn. 37738 615-436-5161	Year round	√		√	√	√		√		√		M-H
Rocky Waters Motor Inn Gatlinburg, Tenn. 37738 615-436-7861	Year round	√	√	√				√		√		M-H
Steiner Bell Gatlinburg, Tenn. 37738 615-436-6561	Year round	√		√	√	√	√	√	√			M
LeConte Lodge Great Smoky Mtns Nat'l Park 615-436-4473 37738	March-November		√		√*	√				√		H
Big Spring Inn Greeneville, Tenn. 37743 615-638-2917	Year round	√			√*	√	√	√				M-H
Jonesborough B&B Jonesborough, Tenn. 37659 615-753-9223	Year round	√			√*					√		M
The Blakely House Knoxville, Tenn. 37902 615-523-6500	Year round	√		√	√*					√		M-H
The Graustein Inn Knoxville, Tenn. 37923 615-690-7007	Year round	√		√	√*							M-H
The Middleton Knoxville, Tenn. 37902 615-524-8100	Year round	√		√	√*					√		M-H
Mountain Breeze B&B Knoxville, Tenn. 37922 615-966-3917	Year round	√		√	√*	√	√					M
Three Chimneys of Knoxville Knoxville, Tenn. 37916 615-521-4970	Year round	√		√	√*					√		M
Windy Hill B&B Knoxville, Tenn. 37909 615-690-1488	Year round	√		√	√*					√	√	M
Snapp Inn B&B Limestone, Tenn. 37681 615-257-2482	Year round	√			√*					√		M
The Grand Hotel Pigeon Forge, Tenn. 37863 615-453-1000	Year round	√		√				√	√	√		M-H

Rooms · Cabins · Private bath · Breakfast offered · * Included in room charge · Lunch offered · Dinner offered · Pool · Tennis court · Children welcome · Pets welcome · Rates: L - Low, less than $30, M - Moderate, $31-$60, H - High, $61 and up

	Dates open	Rooms	Cabins	Private bath	Breakfast offered	* Included in room charge	Lunch offered	Dinner offered	Pool	Tennis court	Children welcome	Pets welcome	Rates: L - Low, less than $30; M - Moderate, $31-$60; H - High, $61 and up
Mountain Home Inn Pigeon Forge, Tenn. 37863 615-453-1605	Year round	√									√		M-H
Riverchase Pigeon Forge, Tenn. 37863 615-428-1299	Year round	√		√					√		√		L-M
Hale Springs Inn Rogersville, Tenn. 37857 615-272-5171	Year round	√		√	√*	√	√				√	√	M-H
Newbury House Rugby, Tenn. 37733 615-628-2441	March 1 - Dec. 15	√											M
Pioneer Cottage Rugby, Tenn. 37733 615-628-2441	March 1 - Dec. 15			√									M
Highland Manor Motel Townsend, Tenn. 37882 615-448-2211	Year round	√		√					√		√		L-H
Talley-Ho Motel Townsend, Tenn. 37882 615-448-2465	Year round	√		√	√	√	√	√	√	√	√		L-M
Wear's Motel & Cottages Townsend, Tenn. 37882 615-448-2296	Year round	√	√	√					√	√	√		L
Turkey Pen Resort Vonore, Tenn. 37885 615-295-2400	Year round	√	√	√	√				√	√	√	√	M

Tennessee Parks

	Lodge	Campsites	Dumping station	Hook-ups	Cabins	Pool	Picnicking	Boating: R-Public ramp, M-Marina, L-Horsepower limits	Boats to rent: C-canoe, P-paddleboat, F-fishing boat	Hiking trails	Fishing	Water skiing	Primitive camping	Supply store	Museum	Leashed pets welcome
Observation Knob Park Bristol, Tenn. 37620 615-878-5561		188	√	√		√		R		√	√	√	√			√
Cove Lake State Recreational Park Caryville, Tenn. 37714 615-562-8355		99	√	√		√	√	ML	PF	√	√		√			√

	Lodge	Campsites	Dumping station	Hook-ups	Cabins	Pool	Picnicking	Boating: R-Public ramp, M-Marina, L-Horsepower limits	Boats to rent: C-canoe, P-paddleboat, F-fishing boat	Hiking trails	Fishing	Water skiing	Primitive camping	Supply store	Museum	Leashed pets welcome
Booker T. Washington State Recreational Park, Chattanooga, Tenn. 37418, 615-894-4955	✓					✓	✓	R	P	✓	✓	✓				✓
Cherokee National Forest, Cleveland, Tenn. 37311, 615-476-9700		685	✓				✓	RM	C	✓	✓	✓	✓	✓		✓
Red Clay State Historic Park, Cleveland, Tenn. 37311, 615-472-2627							✓			✓					✓	✓
Cumberland Mountain State Rustic Park, Crossville, Tenn. 38555, 615-484-6138		147	✓	✓ 37	✓	✓		ML	CPF	✓	✓		✓	✓		✓
Sycamore Shoals State Historical Area, Elizabethton, Tenn. 37643, 615-543-5808							✓			✓					✓	✓
Great Smoky Mountains National Park, Gatlinburg, Tenn. 37738, 615-436-5615	✓	926	✓				✓			✓	✓		✓	✓	✓	✓
Harrison Bay State Park, Harrison, Tenn. 37341, 615-344-6214		115	✓	✓			✓	RM	F	✓	✓	✓	✓	✓		✓
Pickett State Rustic Park, Jamestown, Tenn. 38556, 615-879-5821	✓	32	✓	✓ 15				L	C F	✓	✓		✓		✓	✓
Indian Mountain State Park, Jellico, Tenn. 37762, 615-784-7958		50	✓	✓			✓	M	P	✓	✓		✓			✓
Bays Mountain Park, Kingsport, Tenn. 37660, 615-229-9447							✓			✓	✓				✓	
Warrior's Path State Park, Kingsport, Tenn. 37663, 615-239-8531		134	✓	✓		✓	✓	RM	PF	✓	✓	✓	✓	✓		✓
Norris Dam State Park, Lake City, Tenn. 37769, 615-426-7461		50	✓	✓ 10	✓		✓	RM	F	✓	✓	✓	✓		✓	✓
Davy Crockett Birthplace State Park, Limestone, Tenn. 37681, 615-257-2061		75	✓	✓		✓	✓	R		✓	✓				✓	✓

	Lodge	Campsites	Dumping station	Hook-ups	Cabins	Pool	Picnicking	Boating: R-Public ramp, M-Marina, L-Horsepower limits	Boats to rent: C-canoe, P-paddleboat, F-fishing boat	Hiking trails	Fishing	Water skiing	Primitive camping	Supply store	Museum	Leashed pets welcome
Standing Stone State Rustic Park, Livingston, Tenn. 38570, 615-823-6347		35	√	√	24	√	√	ML	PF	√	√		√			√
Big Ridge State Park, Maynardville, Tenn. 37807, 615-992-5523		52	√	√	19	√	√	ML	C F	√	√		√	√		
Panther Creek State Recreational Park, Morristown, Tenn. 37814, 615-581-2623		50	√	√		√	√	R		√	√	√				√
Big South Fork National River & Rec. Area, Oneida, Tenn. 37841, 615-569-6963		229	√	√	2		√	R L		√	√		√		√	√
Fall Creek Falls State Resort Park, Pikeville, Tenn. 37367, 615-881-3241	√	227	√	√	20	√	√	ML	CPF	√	√		√	√	√	√
Roan Mountain State Resort Park, Roan Mountain, Tenn. 37687, 615-772-3303		107	√	√	20	√	√			√					√	√
Rock Island State Park, Rock Island, Tenn. 38581, 615-686-2471		50	√	√		√	√	R	C	√	√	√	√	√		√
Edgar Evins State Rustic Park, Silver Point, Tenn. 38582, 615-858-2446		60	√	√	34	√	√	R		√	√	√	√		√	√
Burgess Falls State Natural Area, Sparta, Tenn. 38583, 615-761-2299							√				√					√
South Cumberland Recreation Area, Tracy City, Tenn. 37387, 615-924-2980					1		√	L		√	√		√		√	√
Grundy Forest State Natural Area, Tracy City, Tenn. 37387, 615-924-2980							√				√		√		√	√
Savage Gulf State Natural Area, Tracy City, Tenn. 37387, 615-924-2080										√	√		√		√	√
Grundy Lakes State Park, Tracy City, Tenn. 37387, 615-924-2980							√	L		√	√				√	√

	Lodge	Campsites	Dumping station	Hook-ups	Cabins	Pool	Picnicking	Boating: R-Public ramp	M-Marina	L-Horsepower limits	Boats to rent: C-canoe	P-paddleboat	F-fishing boat	Hiking trails	Fishing	Water skiing	Primitive camping	Supply store	Museum	Leashed pets welcome
Fort Loudoun State Historic Area Vonore, Tenn. 37885 615-884-6217							✓							✓	✓	✓			✓	✓
Frozen Head State Natural Area Wartburg, Tenn. 37887 615-346-3318							✓							✓			✓			✓
Cumberland Gap National Historical Park Middlesboro, Ky. 40965 606-248-2817		160	✓		1		✓							✓			✓		✓	✓

Tennessee
Chambers of Commerce

Athens
13 N. Jackson St.
Athens, Tenn. 37303
615-745-0334

Bristol
20 Volunteer Pkwy.
P.O. Box 519
Bristol, Tenn. 37620
615-968-4399

Chattanooga
1001 Market St.
Chattanooga, Tenn. 37402
615-756-2121

Cleveland
2100 Keith St.
P.O. Box 2275
Cleveland, Tenn. 37320
615-472-6587

Cookeville
302 S. Jefferson Ave.
Cookeville, Tenn. 38501
615-526-2211

Crossville
Corner 2nd & Main Sts.
P.O. Box 453
Crossville, Tenn. 38555
615-484-8444

Dayton
305 E. Main Ave.
Dayton, Tenn. 37321
615-775-0361

Elizabethton
Hwy 19E Stateline Road
P.O. Box 190
Elizabethton, Tenn. 37643
615-543-2122

Erwin
South Main Ave.
P.O. Box 713
Erwin, Tenn. 37650
615-743-3000

Etowah
P.O. Box 458
Etowah, Tenn. 37331
615-263-2228

Gatlinburg
520 Parkway
P.O. Box 527
Gatlinburg, Tenn. 37738
615-436-4178

Jamestown
Courthouse Square
P.O. Box 496
Jamestown, Tenn. 38556
615-879-9948

Jefferson City
P.O. Box 428
Jefferson City, Tenn. 37760
615-397-9642

Johnson City
603 E. Market St.
P.O. Box 180
Johnson City, Tenn. 37605
615-926-2141

Jonesborough
P.O. Box 636
Jonesborough, Tenn. 37659
615-753-9021

Kingsport
408 Clay St.
P.O. Box 1403
Kingsport, Tenn. 37662
615-246-2010

Kingston
501 N. Kentucky St.
P.O. Box 666
Kingston, Tenn. 37763
615-376-5572

Knoxville
301 Church Ave. S.E.
P.O. Box 2688
Knoxville, Tenn. 37901
615-637-4550

Lenoir City
200 Depot St.
P.O. Box 445
Lenoir City, Tenn. 37771
615-986-2715

Loudon
Depot Square
P.O. Box K
Loudon, Tenn. 37774
615-458-4378

Madisonville
110 Locust St.
Madisonville, Tenn. 37453
615-442-4588

Maryville
309 S. Washington St.
Maryville, Tenn. 37801
615-983-2241

McMinnville
110 S. Court Square
P.O. Box 574
McMinnville, Tenn. 37110
615-473-6611

Morristown
825 W. First North St.
P.O. Box 9
Morristown, Tenn. 37815
615-586-6382

Newport
803 Prospect Ave.
Newport, Tenn. 37821
615-623-7201

Oak Ridge
1400 Oak Ridge Turnpike
Oak Ridge, Tenn. 37830
615-483-1321

Oneida
P.O. Box 442
Oneida, Tenn. 37841
615-569-6900

Pigeon Forge
1159 N. Parkway
P.O. Box 209
Pigeon Forge, Tenn. 37863
615-453-8574

Rogersville
403 E. Main St.
Rogersville, Tenn. 37857
615-272-2186

Sevierville
200 High St.
P.O. Box 285
Sevierville, Tenn. 37862
615-453-6411

Spring City
Hwy. 27 S.
P.O. Box 355
Spring City, Tenn. 37381
615-365-5210

Tazewell
P.O. Box 332
Tazewell, Tenn. 37879
615-626-4149 or 626-4844

Kentucky

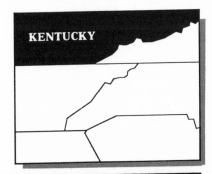

KENTUCKY

Chapter Two

L et us dwell and feast and travel for a day or two in Kentucky's region of bluegrass, black barns and the earliest history of this 15th state of the Union. It also is where marijuana once was a major crop.

We drive for miles through apparent agrarian richness — wide, rolling grassy fields, herds of cattle and horses, and great houses resting like forts on the high ground.

First stop is Harrodsburg, the Mother Town of Kentucky, which Kentuckians claim is the oldest permanent English settlement west of the Allegheny Mountains. Daniel Boone, George Rogers Clark and James Harrod walked and talked and planned here more than 200 years ago. Naturally, Harrodsburg people are strong on history.

Near the center of town is Old Fort Harrod State Park, where stands an exact replica of the old fort, along with the re-created log cabin in which Abraham Lincoln's parents were married, an avenue of Kentucky coffee trees, an

63

Beaumont Inn, Harrodsburg

exceptionally large osage orange (hedge apple) tree, planted in 1870, and the Old Fort Harrod Amphitheater. From mid-June through Labor Day, two outdoor dramas, "The Legend of Daniel Boone" and "Lincoln," are performed in the amphitheater on alternate nights except Sunday.

In this town of fewer than 4000 citizens, you can take a driving tour of nearly 50 places of historic interest. One that is particularly romantic is the grave of the Unknown Girl. In this grave are the remains of a young woman (or as she is called in the literature, "a beautiful Southern belle") who visited the old Harrodsburg Springs resort before the Civil War. She and a young man arrived at about the same time, at the peak of the social season. She went to a ball. All the young men clamored to dance with her. Suddenly, unexpectedly, she crumpled to the floor while dancing. She was dead. The young man who had arrived when she did left during the excitement and was not seen there again. The name the girl had given was fictitious. Her identity was never learned. Harrodsburg people buried her under a spreading tree on the grounds of Harrodsburg Springs. To this day, the city tends her grave.

Only yards from the grave is a marker for two locally bred Kentucky Derby winners, George Smith, in 1916 and Leonidas, in 1883.

Could the horse have been named for Confederate General Leonidas K. Polk? For on still another marker is that general's prayer, made in St. Philip's Episcopal Church following the bloody battle of Perryville: "Peace to the land and blessing on friend and foe alike."

Another piece of history you may like is the old Mud Meeting House, the first Dutch-Reformed Church west of the Alleghenies. It stands on a low hill near silvery little Salt River. Alberta and I followed the tour directions to the church, where we were surprised to see a "no trespassing" sign. After driving that far, I decided I was going to see that unusual building. So I walked around the gate for a closer look. It — at least, the exterior — is mostly of mud. It is framed in oak, and the spaces between the framework are packed with clay mixed with straw. The Harrodsburg Historical Society has restored it to its 1800s appearance. I trust the "no trespassing" sign will be down by the time you arrive.

One marker indicates the site where Daniel Boone and Evan Hinton built a double log cabin in 1774. Boone used it occasionally on visits until the Shawnees burned it in 1777.

Still another place you don't want to miss — you even may want to eat and sleep there — is Beaumont Inn, which is on the National Register of Historic Places. The main building has stood since 1845. It was the home of various schools in its earlier years. It's been an inn for the past 68 years, operated by four generations of the same family.

We ate lunch there. Fried chicken. Good. The very special specialties of the house are two-year-old country ham and corn pudding, the latter served as a vegetable. Luncheon prices range from about $7.25 to $8.95, and you can eat dinner for $10.50 to $15.50 and breakfast for $4.95. Included in breakfast, if you want them, are cornmeal batter cakes with brown-sugar syrup. However, only overnight guests can buy breakfast. Room rates are moderate to high. The inn has 17 rooms in the main building and 12 others in three nearby buildings. It opens near the middle of March and closes about the middle of December. Make reservations for both food and lodging. Phone 606-734-3381.

We had already decided not to nestle the night in Old South luxury at the Beaumont. Luxury is more or less the norm now, be it old or new. We headed up US 68 for what we visualized as something different, a Spartan night at the Shaker Village of Pleasant Hill, eight or nine miles northeast of Harrodsburg.

More bluegrass, more black barns, some of them with white doors. Some black wooden fences and some white ones. Many stone fences wrapped around green fields where horses and cattle nibbled in livestock heaven. I'd guess most of those stone fences were built 75 to more than 100 years ago when labor was easier to come by. They were built well, and most of them have survived with timely maintenance, but there are gaps in some that didn't get the maintenance.

The Shakers were great fence builders. They once owned about 7000 acres of this rich Kentucky Bluegrass country, and it was surrounded and crisscrossed by 50 miles of stone fences.

A woman who some think was not overly enamored with her blacksmith husband brought a band of Shakers from England to New York in 1774. They didn't call themselves Shakers. Not at first, anyway. They were the United Society of Believers in Christ's Second Appearing. Among their beliefs was that Christ would return as a woman. In fact, some apparently thought their leader, Mother Ann Lee, formerly married to the blacksmith, was Christ reincarnated. They believed in celibacy, equality of the sexes and races, full confession of sins, the dissolution of marriage vows, and owning property in common. For some reason, they also believed people should eat in absolute silence. Some who took a dim view of the Believers called them the Shaking Quakers, because of their physical gyrations during worship and because the sect originated as a dissident group of Quakers. They've been called Shakers ever since.

One might think a group that forbade men and women to sleep together wouldn't last another generation. But they stayed around well into the 20th century. They established 19 communities in America, and this one in Mercer County, Ky., was among the largest. It lasted from frontier times in 1805 until 1910. They lasted so long without procreation because they kept attracting converts and because they adopted lots of orphans. Orphans were plentiful then.

At the height of the Shakers' success at Pleasant Hill, they had nearly 500 members. Their hogs, cattle and sheep won prizes. They grew corn, wheat, rye, hemp, tobacco and flax. They were considered to be among the best farmers in Kentucky, and they owned some of the richest land. They had the largest herd of registered Durham shorthorn cattle in America. They imported Leicester sheep from England, and today you may see a herd of about 20 of that same breed grazing on Shakertown land. Though the community generally had little to do with non-believers, they sold to outsiders and bought from them. But they sold far more than they bought, and the balance of payments must have been similar to that of Japan and the U. S. today.

However, they had their troubles, and the Civil War probably was the greatest of these. Clashing armies surged into the peaceful community. Soldiers ate most of the Shaker food and never paid a penny. After the war, the community sometimes was plagued with "Winter Shakers," who came and filled their bellies during winter and then left without helping with the crops of summer. Some Shakers weakened in their faith. Forsaking the belief in communal property, some became acquisitive and stole from others. Some leaders made disastrous investments of community assets. The Shakers lost much of their property in lawsuits. By September 1910, only a dozen aged Shakers remained. They deeded the rest of the property to a Harrodsburg man who agreed to care for them the rest of their lives. The last Mercer County Shaker died in 1923.

In 1961 a group of private citizens began restoring the village. They had left 27 of the original buildings. They now have 2252 acres of the Shaker land. Shakertown is said to be America's only National Historic Landmark to have all services, including touring, dining, lodging and shopping, situated in original historic structures.

This non-profit Shaker Village of Pleasant Hill has not one true Shaker believer. But they believe in restoring the village and saving its history. They rent 72 rooms in 14 different buildings at moderate to high rates. They feed guests lunch and dinner for moderate sums. A "country buffet breakfast" so big that any reasonable human could survive on it until breakfast the next day costs $5.25. One dessert specialty is lemon pie, which includes the rind and is delicious. It's unlike any other lemon pie you've tasted. For $5 an adult can buy a ticket that entitles him to roam through those interesting old buildings, learn their former uses and see the old Shaker crafts performed again. Costs range from nothing to $2.50 for young visitors. For $4, $2.50

Centre Family Dwelling, Shaker Village of Pleasant Hill

and $1, depending on how old you are, you can go down to the Kentucky River and ride a Shaker paddlewheel riverboat. It's mainly from these cash sources that the organization keeps the village going and continues its restoration.

I talked with Denise Perkins, who was spinning wool shorn from the village's 20 sheep; with cooper Maurice Lester, who was making noggins, piggins and churns just as the Shakers did; and with Garnett Ashford, who was making flat brooms that a New York Shaker invented in 1798. Back in the 1800s, Shakers made a lot of money from these brooms. Earlier brooms were round. You can buy Garnett's brooms in the village gift shop, $10 for short-handled brooms and $12.50 for long-handled ones. If the Shakers had been able to sell brooms for so much, they might still be in business.

Garnett said he didn't take up broommaking until he retired from farming at the age of 70. He said the broomcorn he uses comes from Mexico, the broomsticks from the Fiji Islands and the hemp for tying the brooms was grown in India. In the old days, the Shakers grew it all in Pleasant Hill.

Odd thing about the hemp: It once was a major crop of Mercer County. The Shakers grew 100 to 150 acres of it most years. Garnett said he grew hemp on a contract with the U. S. Government during World War II. It went into ropes for the Navy. That was before people started calling the hemp plant by its other name, marijuana, and smoking the leaves. Growing it now is illegal.

I asked Garnett why some Kentucky farmers have black barns. They're black because they're painted with coal tar, he said. And they're painted with coal tar because that by-product of coal costs only about one-fifth as much as regular paint and lasts as long.

Something else Garnett said is that lots of the grass you see in Bluegrass country is

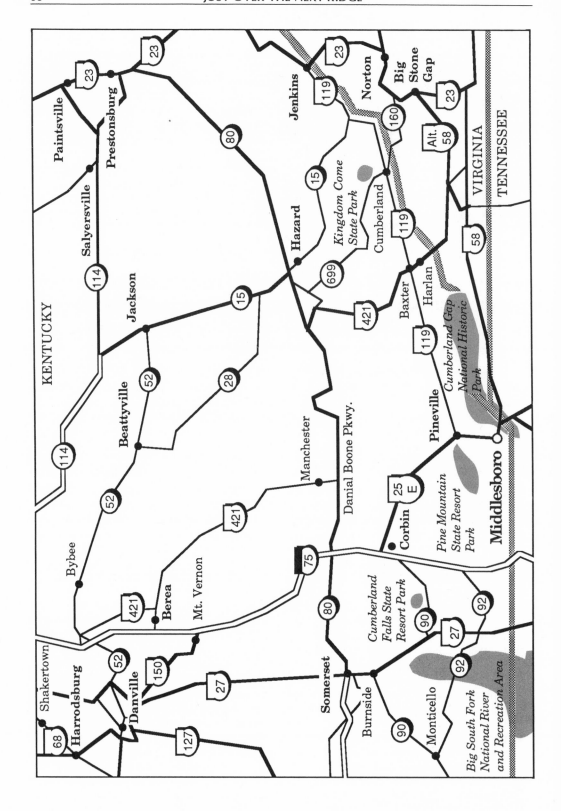

not bluegrass. It's fescue and orchard grass. These two, especially fescue, stay green longer than bluegrass.

After dinner that evening, Alberta and I walked along lanes lighted by small electric bulbs in copper lanterns on wooden posts. Quiet, peaceful.

Everyone who spends a night at Shakertown sleeps in one of the old Shaker buildings. Alberta and I stayed in one of the four rooms of the little two-story Ministry's Workshop. It wasn't Spartan to the point of being uncomfortable, but it wasn't luxury. For instance, no closets. You do as the Shakers did — hang your clothes on wall pegs. These pegs, spaced about a foot apart and a little more than six feet above the floor, are available for hanging nearly anything. The Shakers sometimes hung their chairs on the wall when they weren't sitting in them. The combination tub-shower was fine for my shower but cramped for Alberta's tub bath. The bed was plain but comfortable. We slept well.

Next morning, after filling ourselves with the Shakertown buffet breakfast, we headed southeast across the Bluegrass to Berea, home of Berea College and that school's Boone Tavern.

You can buy excellent food in Boone Tavern's spacious dining room. You can sleep in one of the tavern's 57 air-conditioned rooms, furnished with reproduced early American furniture crafted by the college students. But you cannot buy an alcoholic drink in Boone Tavern. For that matter, neither can you buy a drink in Harrodsburg or Shakertown. All of these places are in dry counties. If you need a pick-me-up before dinner, bring your own. Also, men should bring jackets and women should bring dresses or well-tailored pantsuits to Boone Tavern, for they won't let you into the dining room without them for dinner and for the Sunday midday meal.

Berea people are fond of saying their town is "where the mountains meet the Bluegrass." But more of Berea College's 1500 students come from the mountains than from the wealthier Bluegrass country. Officials of the college say theirs is the only college in the nation that charges no tuition, admits only low-income students,

makes all of them work in a college job and is committed to serving Southern Appalachia. It is nearly impossible for a wealthy student to gain admission to the college, no matter how well-qualified the person otherwise may be.

Students work 10 to 15 hours a week in addition to carrying a full academic load. Their earnings are applied to their school expenses. But this is not enough. Much of the $7100 cost for each student comes from gifts and endowment income. Your waiter or waitress will be a student. The bed you sleep in was made by students. Articles you buy in the tavern gift shop probably were made by students.

Don't tip the students who serve you in the dining room, not if you expect that specific student to keep the money. Tipping is discouraged, partly because tips would enable servers to make considerably more money than other students. If someone unknowingly violates the no-tipping custom, the money goes into a fund which benefits all students.

Berea College, an independent, non-denominational school, was founded in 1855. The idea for Boone Tavern was born in the mind of Nellie Frost, wife of the college president, in 1908. That was the year she had to provide meals and lodging in their home for about 300 guests. She told her husband the college needed a guest house. So Boone Tavern was opened the next year. It has since grown considerably.

Meal prices are reasonable. And you get flowers on the table, art on the walls and fine food, including such specialties as spoonbread, Jefferson Davis pie and Boone Tavern cornsticks.

Room rates are moderate. For reservations, phone 606-986-9358, or write to Boone Tavern Hotel, College P. O. Box 2345, Berea, Ky. 40404.

You may want to take a free student-guided tour of the campus. During the academic year, tours start at 9 a.m. and 2 p.m. Monday through Friday and at 9 a.m. Saturday. Summer tours start at 9 and 10:30 a.m. and 1:30 and 3 p.m. Monday through Friday and 9 a.m. and 1:30 p.m. Saturday. Tours start at the tavern.

An Alabama girl, a chemistry major,

guided my group. One of the stories she told was about the chapel. A wealthy woman friend of the college, Miss Olivia Phelps-Stokes, gave the money to build it early this century. Two stipulations went with the gift: The donor's name must not be on the building until she died and it was to be built entirely with student labor. Since the students were not experienced in construction, they first erected a practice brick building. It was finished in 1902, still stands and is still used. You can see how the workmanship improved as you follow the results upward story by story. The Phelps-Stokes Chapel, also still standing, was finished two years later.

Berea, a community of about 8300, is an outstanding craft center. The craft tradition began with the college in the mid-19th century. Students still do excellent craft work, but the town also has fine craftspeople and craft shops not directly connected with the school. Several crooked rural-road miles to the northeast is the small community of Bybee where stands the old, old Bybee Pottery. Unlike most modern-day potteries, this one does not specialize in fancy artistic work. It produces serviceable dinnerware and bakeware at reasonable prices. It's been doing that since pioneer days. Legend says it was established in 1809. Actual sales records go back to 1845. It has been owned by five generations of the Cornelison family, and members of the sixth generation now work in it.

Don't miss the college's Appalachian Museum, only a few yards from Boone Tavern, where you can step a century back into an Appalachian life of old-time farm tools, banjos, hand-made play-pretties for children and a slideshow of an era before store-bought goods and modern ways.

Berea, about 130 miles north of Knoxville and 40 miles south of Lexington, is just off I-75.

If you haven't had enough of Kentucky when you leave Berea, stop for a meal or a night or for just a short hike at Cumberland Falls State Resort Park. If you spend the night during a full moon, you may see the only moonbow in the nation. It's formed in the mist caused by the 68-foot drop of the 125-foot wide Cumberland River.

Room rates at the park's Dupont Lodge are moderate. Rates are lower from Nov. 1 to April 1 than during the rest of the year. Those 62 and older benefit from a 15 percent discount. Phone 800-325-0063 for reservations. If you're interested in one of the park's 11 efficiency cottages, ask about rates. A buffet meal in the lodge dining room costs about $8. Ordering dinner from a menu will cost from about $5 to about $16. The buffet is available daily Memorial Day through Labor Day and irregularly the rest of the year.

The park is on the west side of I-75 opposite Corbin.

After we get back into Tennessee, headed down 75 above Caryville, you will notice a series of peculiar high rock formations on your left. Lots of people ask if this has a name. It does; it's the Devil's Race Track. The maker of mountains was in a playful mood when he made the Devil's Race Track.

For a look at a different face of Kentucky, let's go up State 33 to Tazewell, then northwest on US 25E to Cumberland Gap National Historical Park and then explore some of the coal country of Kentucky's eastern mountains.

Cumberland Gap is where Tennessee, Virginia and Kentucky join. The national park is in all three states. Just inside Virginia, I turned eastward on US 58, heading for Ewing, Va., and a walk to Sand Cave and White Rocks, both in the national park.

When you reach Peoples Bank, turn left on State Road 734. Follow it a mile or two to a small park maintained by the Thomas Walker Civitan Club. I had an old map which showed you could go either of two routes for the first mile or so before the two join to become one.

A fellow parked there in a truck said he was Ike Harper. He said he brought the mail early each morning from Bristol to Ewing. Then he had nothing to do until 4 in the afternoon, when he took mail back to Bristol. So he spent most of the day parked in this quiet place.

I asked him which trail most people

used. He said the one to the left, the one that goes past the club shelter. I invited him to go with me. He looked at the sky and declined. Said it might rain.

I put on my day pack and headed up the mountain. This trail is steep and rocky. I think I missed a right turn which would have taken me to a junction with the other trail. I kept straight up the mountain on a route others obviously had walked before me. And I reached the regular trail higher on the mountain side. This trail — actually, an old road that Jeeps traveled in pre-park days — provided easier walking. However, people ride horses on it and make it muddy in places. It wasn't too bad this time, but I don't recommend it during rainy weather.

I came to a marker for a trail to White Rocks. Horses aren't allowed on it, the marker says. Since my main objective was Sand Cave, I didn't take the White Rocks Trail. (Later, at the park visitors center, I got a new map which shows I could have taken the White Rocks Trail and also reached Sand Cave.)

White Rocks was plainly visible above me and had been since I turned north in Ewing. It's a high bare-rock cliff about a mile long on the crest of Cumberland Mountain above Ewing. It looks more gray than white.

I reached the crest of the mountain about a half-mile beyond the White Rocks Trail intersection. Two deer hurried out of my way. Old snow lay on the mountaintop. Lots of deer tracks and some turkey tracks.

The old Ewing Trail plunges downhill to a meeting with the Ridge Trail, where a marker says the Hensley Settlement is only about 4½ miles west on the Ridge Trail. I didn't have time for the settlement this time. But I remembered the last time I was there. It was in early August 1970 and blueberries and huckleberries were ripe. I must have eaten a pint. And I met Jesse Gibbons.

Jesse was the park's farm demonstration man at Hensley Settlement. He was born in the settlement and had never lived far from it.

But I'd better tell you first what Hens-ley Settlement was and is. If you're familiar with Cades Cove in the Great Smokies, think of it as being much smaller and on a mountaintop and you have an approximation of Hensley Settlement.

Jesse Gibbons told me the first Hensley ever to go up to the mountaintop was Ceph Hensley. He said Ceph was having a misunderstanding with some law enforcement people down in the lowlands, and he thought this flat place on the mountaintop would be a good place to stay until the lawmen were more inclined to see things his way.

Ceph liked the place so much and talked about it so much when he went back to the lowland that one of his listening nephews, Burton Hensley, bought the place. He bought 500 acres there in 1903. Jesse said Burton was one of his great-grandfathers.

Burton divided his 500 acres into 16 parts and gave one part to each of his 16 children. One of them was Nicey Ann, who married Sherman Hensley. (Yes, same name, but I don't know whether they were kin.) I think Sherman and Nicey Ann were the first people to live in the settlement on a permanent basis. Sherman bought additional land from some of the others who did not move there. He and Nicey Ann moved up in 1903. They had 19 children. The graves of nine of them stand in a straight line in the graveyard.

Several others followed the Sherman Hensleys to the mountaintop. Nobody seems to know exactly how many people lived there at the peak of the settlement's population. Estimates range from 40 to 100. They built about 40 structures — dwellings, barns, corncribs, smokehouses and so on. One building served as school house and church.

Nobody ever built a road to Hensley Settlement. Nor a phone line or power line. Only trails led there. People walked them, rode horses over them and sometimes had mules or oxen pull crude sleds over them. Sometimes when they bought pieces of farm equipment, they had to take them apart and carry them up a piece at a time.

They grew corn and fed some of it to their hogs, ground it into meal for bread and made it into moonshine liquor. They also grew cabbage, potatoes, beans, parsnips, onions, oats, sorghum. They had apple trees and made apple brandy. A man could carry a gallon of liquor off the mountain and sell it for $10. If he took the same amount of corn off the mountain as it took to make the liquor, he would have received less than one-fourth as much for it.

People on the mountain raised cattle, sheep and lots of hogs. Hogs and sheep ran wild most of the time. Hogs ate chestnuts and grew fat in the fall. They were finished on corn (to make the meat better flavored) shortly before hog-killing time — late November to early February.

Liquor and livestock were the cash crops. Jesse said law enforcers didn't bother the moonshiners much. One man became a little too brazen in toting his products down to a mining camp and got into trouble, Jesse said. A story is told about a Kentucky sheriff who climbed the mountain and was so overwhelmed by hospitality that he forgot why he came.

The Hensley Settlement people lived hard lives. Most of them apparently decided that life in the lowlands was better. They left the settlement within a half-century after it was started. Sherman Hensley was the last to leave. Nicey Ann had died. Their children had left or died. He lived alone the last two years before moving down to nearby Caylor, Va., in 1951. When he died in 1979, at the age of 98, they took his body up to the settlement and buried it in the Hensley graveyard.

Hensley Settlement was somewhat like many Appalachian pioneer settlements. The differences were that this one was on a mountaintop, and it was in the 20th century instead of the 18th or early 19th.

The National Park Service preserves the settlement. It keeps the remaining buildings in good repair. It maintains some of the fields. You cannot drive to it. You have to walk, just as the Hensleys did.

Instead of going to the settlement on this recent trip, I turned right at the intersection of the Ewing and Ridge trails and walked east on the Ridge Trail until I came to a spur trail to Sand Cave.

You first reach Sand Cave Branch, which tumbles down a high ledge near the cave opening and goes meandering down the Kentucky side of Cumberland Mountain. Along its sides are pretty pebbles the size of marbles down to the size of sand grains.

Sand Cave is not a cave, not a dark tunnel reaching far underground. It's a "rock house." There are hundreds of rock houses in the Cumberlands but Sand Cave is the biggest I've seen. This is a huge "room" tucked back into the mountainside. I believe 1000 persons could find shelter in it.

The opening is about 150 feet wide and 40 feet high. The ceiling — with colors ranging from off-white to tan, yellow, blue, green and a pinkish red — tapers to the ground about 100 feet back into the mountain. Unlike in a true cave, you're never in darkness in Sand Cave, not unless you spend the night.

Walking is difficult inside the cave because the powdery sand is many inches deep. It's harder to walk in than beach sand. The sand comes from slow weathering of the sandstone above. Virginians and Kentuckians have been going to Sand Cave for generations.

Go back to the Ridge Trail and continue eastward on it about a mile to White Rocks. The trail leads you around to the back side of the cliff and then to the top for a look south across Virginia into Tennessee. Immediately below is beautiful Powell Valley. This is one of the better views in the Southern Appalachians. The wide bare rock you stand on is pocked with depressions. One, the size of a bathtub, was filled with water overlaid with ice. Imbedded in some of the sandstone are pretty quartz pebbles.

I went back down the mountain, said hello and goodbye to Ike Harper and then went west on 58 toward Cumberland Gap.

Beautiful drive. This stretch of 58 is the approximate route Daniel Boone and 30 axmen blazed in 1775. This was part of what came to be know as the Wilderness Road. It ran from the Long Island of the Holston (now Kingsport) north and then west to Cumberland Gap.

Earlier, Boone had gone through the gap into Kentucky at least five times. A marker on 58 near Indian Creek says Shawnee Indians killed Boone's son James and four

Sand Cave, Cumberland Gap National Historical Park

others there in 1773. Dr. Thomas Walker of Virginia and five companions probably were the first white men to see the gap. That was in 1750.

Nobody lived there then. The Cherokees, who lived to the south, followed buffalo trails northward through the gap to hunting grounds in Kentucky. The Shawnees lived to the north and came south and contested with the Cherokees over whose hunting grounds these were.

But after Boone and his axmen blazed the Wilderness Road, a flood of pioneers — nearly 200,000 in the next 25 years — poured through the gap en route to the Bluegrass of Kentucky, to Indiana, Illinois and points westward.

Some carried their belongings in crude wagons, others walked and led horses on whose backs rested all their plunder. Others had no horses. They carried their possessions in bundles tied to the ends of sticks on their shoulders.

One story is handed down about a woman no longer young who grew tired of being asked where she was from and where she was going. She began anticipating the questions. Before asked, she said, "From Buncombe County, North Carolina, bound for Indiana, by gum." Then she would add, "Say, mister, give me a chaw of terbaccer."

Millions now speed through the gap on US 25E. That's supposed to end by the middle 1990s. By then, twin tunnels are scheduled to be finished under the mountain about one-half mile west of the gap. One 4500-foot tunnel will carry two lanes of northbound traffic, and the other will carry southbound traffic. A stone column about 45 feet thick will be left between the tunnels. At their deepest, the tunnels will be 750 feet below the surface.

The latest target date for use of the tunnels is 1994.

After that, the gap is to be restored to a

condition more like it was when Daniel Boone traveled it.

It wasn't that Boone needed to find the easiest route over the mountains for his personal convenience. That long-winded long hunter could cross the highest mountains. But when whole families moved and took horses, cattle, pigs, and seeds to plant in new lands, they needed the easiest routes across mountain barriers.

New Englanders call them "notches." People in the Rocky Mountains call them "passes." But in the Southern Appalachians they are "gaps." And Cumberland Gap is the most notable of them all.

Stand in the gap and look up at the Cumberland Mountains on either side and realize how much easier it was to walk through the gap than to climb over the mountain.

Geologists say Cumberland Gap is a water gap, though no water flows through it now. But a long time ago, when this area was relatively flat, a stream now called Yellow Creek flowed southward into Powell River. Then Cumberland Mountain began to rise in the path of the creek. For more years than anybody knows exactly, the stream cut into the rising mountain, just as a saw will cut into a log raised under it. But the mountain finally rose faster than the stream could cut. The mountain eventually changed the course of Yellow Creek from south to north. So it now flows into the Cumberland River. But, thank goodness, it didn't change directions until after it had carved the gap.

Cumberland Gap usually gets all the credit for making it easier for the pioneers to move through the mountains. But it's not that simple. Cumberland was just one mountain to cross. There were others. If Boone and his axmen had blazed the route across Cumberland Mountain at some gap east of Cumberland Gap, they'd have run into other mountains — Black Mountain and Pine Mountain. Black Mountain is the highest mountain in Kentucky, but it is not nearly as long as either Cumberland or Pine Mountain.

However, the Cumberland Gap route offered a happy combination of geographic circumstances. Black Mountain dwindled to insignificance at that point. And Cumberland River had cut a route through Pine Mountain.

So the westward travelers walked through Cumberland Gap and then moved northward into what's called the Middlesboro Basin. Two theories exist on what caused the basin: A meteor landed there or an underground cavern collapsed under it. Whatever the cause, the basin was easy to travel. Then the travelers followed Yellow Creek Valley most of the way north to the Cumberland River. They followed the northwest bank of the river through Pine Mountain. They crossed the river at Cumberland Ford, at the present Pineville. After that, it was fairly easy going northwest to the Bluegrass County.

I didn't go to the Bluegrass this time. Instead, I turned left off US 25E south of Pineville and drove up to Pine Mountain State Resort Park.

I like Kentucky parks. And this one high on Pine Mountain is the oldest of them all and one of the best. After a Kentucky State Park Commission was established in 1924, people in Pineville started working to get the first park. Citizens and Bell County donated 2500 acres of land for it in 1925. Not much was done with it at first. But with the coming of President Franklin D. Roosevelt's New Deal and the Civilian Conservation Corps, things started to move. The young CCC men built hiking trails, roads, shelters, log cabins.

Ten of those cabins are still used. They've been renovated. They're comfortable. They look great. The lodge the CCC built of sandstone and chestnut logs still stands as part of the present larger lodge.

After I checked into the lodge, I decided some walking was in order before supper. I'd already walked only about 10 miles that day. So I headed for the Chained Rock. The Chained Rock is a delightful spoof, a monument to the sense of humor of Bell Countians.

You cannot get a 100 percent straight story on the chaining of the rock. Accounts don't jibe. But you can walk a half-mile from the parking area to it. You can see that great chain bound to that mighty boulder that seems about to topple off the cliff into Pineville, more than 1000 feet below. Here's the account you read on the marker:

"Chained Rock is a boulder formation of Pine Mountain, 2200 feet above sea level. The chain, 101 feet long, with seven-pound links, was carried here by a four-mule team in two trips. It is anchored to the rock with pegs 1½ by 24 inches concreted into holes star-drilled by hand. In 1933, the Pineville Chained Rock Club, assisted by the Boy Scouts and the CCC, replaced an old chain with this chain to hold the rock, which by tradition is to protect the city of Pineville."

Despite what the marker says, some officials of Pine Mountain State Park will tell you the present chain is the first one. For this belief, they depend on the word of Fred Chappell, who helped plan and execute the chaining of the rock. In an account he wrote decades later (in 1977) Chappell, an engineer, leaves the strong impression that the present chain is the only one that's ever been there.

The first time he ever saw the rock, Chappell wrote, was when he visited in the home of his Aunt Ellen Galloway in 1909, just after the Chappell family had moved to Pineville.

"I walked out on the porch and looked across town and up at the crest of Pine Mountain. There on the crest, looking like it was . . . about ready to slide off and roll down on Old Town was a great big rock and what appeared to be a crack between it and the bigger, more solid-looking rock just to the west of it.

"I went back into the apartment and made some remark to Aunt Ellen that that big rock looked like it was just about ready to roll off onto the town. She said, 'It can't. It's chained.' Being six and a half years old, I accepted that as a fact."

When Chappell grew up, he learned that travelers passing through Pineville had been looking up at that rock and saying the same thing he'd said. And Pineville people, tongue in cheek, had been giving the same reply his aunt gave him.

Chappell went on to tell of the time in 1933 when he and some friends were sitting on a curb at the southwest corner of the Courthouse Square. They were sitting there talking because it was in the middle of the Great Depression and there wasn't much else to do.

One of the group, Headley Card, said he wished someone really would chain that rock up there on the mountain. He said he'd been called a liar and had lied more about it than anything else.

Almost immediately, the Chained Rock Club was formed, with just three members at first. They sought and got the sponsorship of the Kiwanis Club. One reason for this was that they needed protection by local business leaders in case somebody on the chaining job was injured. They also needed to scrounge materials from Kiwanians.

They got the huge chain from the owner of a Southwest Virginia stone quarry. The owner gave it to them because it was so big he knew of no practical use for it.

They got two two-mule teams to haul the chain up the mountain in two sections. Once on top, the sections were joined.

They borrowed sledgehammers, chisels and diamond-point drills from the State Highway Department and used them to drill the holes to anchor the chain. They drilled holes in the Chained Rock and also in Turtle Back Rock behind it. Turtle Back is called that because erosion has patterned it to look like the shell of a giant turtle. It's the higher rock and the stable rock. In theory, Chained Rock cannot fall as long as it's chained to Turtle Back Rock.

One club member persuaded a Kentucky Utilities machinist to make 30-inch-long bolts to drive into the holes. After this was done, workers poured hot melted stick sulfur (donated by a hardware store) into the holes around the bolts to within three inches of the top. They filled the top three inches with cement grout. (The cement topping prevents anyone from setting fire to the sulfur.) As the sulfur cools and recrystalizes, it expands, Chappell says, exerting pressure on the bolts and sides of the holes. The bolts can't be extracted — at least not easily.

Stretching the heavy chain from Turtle Back to Chained Rock was a problem because there is a wide, deep chasm between them. To accomplish this, they borrowed a block and tackle and other equipment from the phone company.

All that work by men and mules and Boy Scouts, all those donated and borrowed materials and equipment. Just for a spoof, just to make true a tall tale Bell Countians had been telling travelers for generations.

Back at the lodge, I hurried to dinner with good appetite. Restaurants at all Kentucky state resort parks have the same menu. Over the years, a favorite selection of mine has been something they call hot brown. It consists of slices of turkey breast and country ham, topped with cheese sauce, bacon and tomato. This time, though, I passed up the hot brown in favor of chopped beef steak imperial, covered with sauteed mushrooms; I thought I'd get more food that route. I got enough. For dessert I ate a Kentucky parks special, bread pudding topped with bourbon sauce. (This is the only form of bourbon you can ingest legally at this place.)

Next morning after breakfast, Park Manager Steve Metts took me down the steep trail to his favorite spot, Hemlock Garden. Little Bear Wallow Creek gurgles and glides among great boulders down in this gorge where a small virgin hemlock forest flourishes. Laurel, rhododendron, galax, partridge berry and other wildflowers bloom here in season. At the bottom of the gorge, looming like a small Mayan temple in a Central American jungle, is a stone picnic shelter built by the CCC men a half-century ago.

Several annual entertainments occur at the park. Toward the end of April is a photography weekend timed for the peak of the wildflower bloom. The Mountain Laurel Festival starts on Thursday night of Memorial Day weekend and lasts through Sunday. Lots of music. Crowning of a queen and a visit by the Kentucky governor. Most of this is in the natural Laurel Cove Amphitheater. The Great American Dulcimer Convention is on the last weekend of September.

Room rates at the park's 30-room Herndon Evans Lodge are low to moderate. Those 62 and older get discounts. For $75 a day, you can rent a modern two-bedroom cabin, with kitchen and equipment, central heat and air conditioning, cable TV, and sleeping space for 10 (two double beds in each bedroom and a living room couch that opens into a double bed).

The CCC-built rustic one-bedroom cabins rent for $65 a day.

Steve Metts thought I might like to visit another state park, Kingdom Come, 45 miles away on top of Pine Mountain at Cumberland. Way to get there: North on US 25E to intersection of US 119, east on 119 to Cumberland, then up a steep little road of switchbacks to the park.

Kingdom Come is not a resort park. If you want to eat there, bring your own sandwich. It's a wild little park of scenic views, odd sandstone formations and history. Barry Howard is the manager.

Barry gave me a short lesson on Pine Mountain. It's a long ridge, extending southwestward from Elkhorn City, Ky., 125 miles to near Jellico, Tenn. There are only three major breaks in it: at Pineville, where the Cumberland River passes through it; at Breaks of the Sandy, where the Russell Fork cuts through it; and near Jellico, where Clear Fork has cut a rocky gorge through it.

At the park's 2760-foot Creech Overlook, you can look down and see Kingdom Come School, about two miles away. In a roundabout way, the park gets its name from the community. But if John Fox Jr. had not written a novel called "The Little Shepherd of Kingdom Come," the park probably would have another name. (We'll see more John Fox tracks in Virginia.) Part of the setting of that novel was in the little Kingdom Come community. Howard thinks Fox must have been sitting atop the mountain when some of the scenery in the novel was imprinted on his mind.

How did the community of Kingdom Come get its name? One story is that one of a group of early settlers asked if they were the first to live there. And someone answered, "No, King done come," referring to a man named King who had arrived earlier.

Another piece of the John Fox novel title lives in the Little Shepherd Trail through the park. This 38-mile trail runs along the mountain crest from US 421 at Harlan to 119 near Whitesburg. It's not a good trail for hikers because it's primarily for four-wheel-drive recreation vehicles. It offers a jolting ride and countless views.

Part of Kingdom Come Park once had another name, Raven's Rock. Barry and I walked to the rock, a big area of bare sandstone. According to stories handed down from early visitors, so many ravens roosted here they blackened the sky at dusk. Barry says he's seen no ravens roosting in recent years, but he has seen them flying nearby. Ravens nested two or three years ago at Bad Branch, not far northeast of the park, he said.

The park has a rock-house amphitheater. It's not nearly as large as Sand Cave, but up to 300 people gather in it. One annual event there is a story-telling festival called "Tales from here to Kingdom Come." It's usually scheduled for the first weekend of June. Another annual event is for Masons only. They come from all over Kentucky for a confirming ceremony in early August. Legend has it that this rock house was the last lair of Simon Benge, an early-day outlaw of mixed Indian-white ancestry.

Nearly all this Southeastern Kentucky region is coal country. From Creech Overlook you can see the opening of an operating deep mine and the scars of old strip mines.

Driving back westward on 119, I thought of this as I met 18-wheel coal trucks, one after another. I passed under coal conveyors and saw little mining communities in the valley of Poor Fork of Cumberland River. Poor Fork joins the main Cumberland just downstream from Baxter.

I turned off 119 and onto 421 to reach Baxter, a tiny town that has a coal monument in the center of its major intersection. It stands 20 or more feet tall and is peaked at the top.

Allan Howard, owner of the Harlan Retreading Co., a few feet from the monument, says the fortunes of Harlan Countians rise and fall with the ups and downs of the coal industry. Coal means much to them. That's why they erected the monu-

ment years ago. He said the original idea was for all the coal companies in the county to contribute coal for the monument. But most Harlan County coal proved to be too soft for that use. So the monument builders used unusually hard bituminous coal which then was produced by only one company. Harlan County does not produce anthracite (hard) coal.

Allan said I should talk with his son Steve, a past president of the Harlan Jaycees and a member of a Jaycee committee responsible for erecting a coal memorial on the lawn of the Harlan County Courthouse. The memorial is to all those killed in Harlan County coal mine accidents since the first carload of coal was shipped out of the county in 1911. Steve said the memorial monument will bear the names of about 1400 victims. This figure is much larger than the combined total of Harlan Countians listed on other courthouse lawn memorials as having died in World War II and the conflicts in Korea and Vietnam.

Harlan once was called "Bloody Harlan" because it was the scene of sporadic violence from 1937 to 1941. The conflict was between John L. Lewis' United Mine Workers and the coal operators.

I once knew a former Harlan woman who claimed to have been born in a corner behind the kitchen range during one of those skirmishes. The house was in the line of fire between the two sides. The mother was alone at home. When time came to birth, she crept behind the stove, a shield from bullets from one direction.

Structures of coal are not unique to Harlan County. Bell County has one, too. It's the building that houses the Middlesboro Chamber of Commerce. It was built of 40 tons of coal in 1926.

Middlesboro was a boom town. Scottish engineer Alexander A. Arthur came there in 1886 and thought he saw a great future in coal and iron. He got $20 million in English capital and poured it into his venture over a two-year period. Middlesboro was founded and grew to a population of 10,000 within two years. The magnificent 700-room Four Seasons Hotel was built nearby in Tennessee.

But financial panic followed in 1893.

Middlesboro's population shrank to 2000. The Four Seasons was razed and sold for salvage.

Recovery was gradual but slow. Lincoln Memorial University now stands on the site of the Four Seasons. And Middlesboro,

with about 12,200 people, has grown larger than it was before the panic.

As you return to Tennessee, you may want to stop at Lincoln Memorial University and the Lincoln Museum, which houses outstanding collections related to Lincoln and the Civil War.

Kentucky Attractions*

Dr. Thomas Walker State Shrine Barbourville, Ky. 40906 606-546-4400	Small park and picnic grounds on the site of the first residence in Kentucky. Dr. Walker, the first white man to enter Kentucky, led a small survey party here in the early 1750s. Open year round. Free.
Appalachian Museum Berea, Ky. 40404 606-986-9341	Exhibits of farming tools, utensils, handmade goods, in addition to a slide program. Open year round. Admission.
Churchill Weavers Berea, Ky. 40403 606-986-3126	This handweaving facility, founded in 1922, offers self-guided tours of the loom house and artisan demonstrations. Open year round. Free.
Bybee Pottery Bybee, Ky. 40385 606-369-5350	This pottery has been operating since 1845. Some geologists consider the clay the purest in the world. Open year round. Free.
Col. Sanders Original Restaurant Corbin, Ky. 40701 606-528-2163	Col. Harland Sanders developed his famous recipe in this restaurant in the 1940s. Open year round.
Tombstone Junction Corbin, Ky. 42634 606-376-5087	Re-created western frontier town features country and western entertainers. Open Memorial Day through Labor Day. Admission.
Constitution Square State Shrine Danville, Ky. 40422 606-236-5089	A reproduction of Kentucky's first courthouse square. The first post office west of the Alleghenies still stands. The jail, meeting house and courthouse are replicated. Open year round. Free.
McDowell House & Apothecary Danville, Ky. 40422 606-236-2804	Built about 1795, this was the home and office of Dr. Ephraim McDowell, who performed the first successful abdominal surgery in 1809. Tours give a sense of the life of an early Kentucky physician. Open year round. Admission.
Ward Hall Georgetown, Ky. 40324 502-863-1619	One of the finest examples of Greek Revival architecture in the south. Built in 1853, it is furnished with period pieces and sits on 152 acres of prime bluegrass land. Open May-October. Admission.

* We suggest you call and verify the information given in these listings when planning a trip or making reservations. See introduction to the tables on page 45 for further explanation.

Dixie Belle Riverboat
Harrodsburg, Ky. 40330
606-734-5411

View beautiful Kentucky River palisades from this paddlewheeler, operated by the Shaker Village from May - October. Admission.

Old Harrodsburg Pottery
Harrodsburg, Ky. 40330
606-734-9991

Collection of pottery and hand-dipped candles made on sight. Open March - December. Free.

Shaker Village of Pleasant Hill
Harrodsburg, Ky. 40330
606-734-5411

This restored village on 2700 acres offers exhibition buildings furnished with original Shaker furnishings and shops in which workers demonstrate their crafts. Dining and lodging available. Open all year. Admission.

Austin Nichols Distillery
Lawrenceburg, Ky. 40632
502-839-4544

The home of Wild Turkey bourbon. The distillery has been operating since 1855. Tours of the facility offered Monday-Friday at no charge.

Ashland Henry Clay Estate
Lexington, Ky. 40502
606-266-8581

The home of Henry Clay from 1811 until 1852. It is furnished with Clay family heirlooms. Open February - December. Admission.

Headley-Whitney Museum
Lexington, Ky. 40510
606-255-6653

Lexington's art museum offers jeweled ornaments, paintings and Oriental porcelains. Open year round. Admission.

Hunt-Morgan House
Lexington, Ky. 40508
606-253-0362

Built in 1814 by Lexington's first millionaire, this is a Federal masterpiece and the former home of some of Kentucky's premier citizens. Open February-December. Admission.

Keeneland Race Course
Lexington, Ky. 40592
606-254-3412

Internationally known for fine Thoroughbred racing in April and October. The April meet is highlighted by the Blue Grass Stakes. Workouts are held from 6 to 10 a.m. April through October. Admission for races.

Kentucky Horse Park
Lexington, Ky. 40511
606-233-4303

This working horse farm features the International Museum of the Horse, carriage rides, other exhibitions and competitions. Open mid-March-January. Admission.

Lexington Cemetery
Lexington, Ky. 40508
606-255-5522

This cemetery, chartered in 1848, is considered one of the country's most beautiful. Henry Clay, Mary Todd Lincoln's family and other notables are buried here. Year round.

Mary Todd Lincoln House
Lexington, Ky. 40511
606-233-9999

Abraham Lincoln visited this home three times. It was built in 1803 and was his wife's home for 17 years. Contains many personal articles of the Lincoln and Todd families. Open April - December. Admission.

Raven Run Nature Sanctuary
Lexington, Ky. 40515
606-272-6105

274 acres are dedicated to the preservation of Kentucky River palisades. Seven miles of hiking trails wander through meadows and woodlands. Open year round Wednesday-Sunday. Free.

Red Mile Harness Track
Lexington, Ky. 40585
606-255-0752

More world records in trotting have been set here than at any other track in the world. Open April - June and September-October. Admission.

Spendthrift Farm Lexington, Ky. 40507 606-293-1994	Home to over 400 Thoroughbreds. Tour includes the farm, training center and multimedia presentation. Monday-Friday year round. Admission.
Renfro Valley Country Music Ctr. Renfro Valley, Ky. 40473 606-256-2664	This has been a country music home since 1930s. Weekend shows include gospel, country and bluegrass performers. Open March-November. Admission.
White Hall State Shrine Richmond, Ky. 40475 606-623-9178	Home of Cassius Marcellus Clay, an abolitionist, newspaper publisher and friend of Abraham Lincoln. One of the two buildings was built in 1798 and the other building had central heating and indoor plumbing in the mid-19th century. Open April-October. Admission.
Big South Fork Scenic Railway Stearns, Ky. 42647 606-376-5330	Excursions into the Big South Fork National River and Recreation Area. May-October. Fee.
Buckley Wildlife Sanctuary Versailles, Ky. 40383 606-873-5711	This sanctuary offers 285 acres of trails, a museum and a birdblind for observation. Open Wednesday-Sunday year round. Admission.
"Jack" Jouett House Versailles, Ky. 40383 606-783-7902	The home of Revolutionary War hero Captain Jack, who saved Thomas Jefferson, Patrick Henry and others of the Virginia Assembly from British capture. Open Tuesday-Saturday, April-October. Free.
Old Taylor Distillery Versailles, Ky.40383 606-873-3171	The oldest bonded warehouse in the world (1879) offers distillery tours, antique bottle collection and barrel-making display. Open Monday-Friday year round. Admission.

Kentucky Lodging Places

	Dates open	Rooms	Cabins	Private bath	Breakfast offered	Lunch offered	* Included in room charge	Dinner offered	Pool	Tennis court	Children welcome	Pets welcome	Rates: L - Low, less than $30 M - Moderate, $31-$60 H - High, $61 and up
Boone Tavern Berea, Ky. 40404 606-986-9358	Year round	√		√	√	√	√				√	√	M
Beaumont Inn Harrodsburg, Ky. 40330 606-734-3381	March 12 - Dec. 12	√		√	√	√	√	√	√		√		M-H
Bryan Station Inn Lexington, Ky. 40505 606-299-4162	Year round	√		√							√		L
Campbell House Inn Lexington, Ky. 40504 606-255-4281	Year round	√		√	√	√	√	√	√		√		M-H
Grenelefe Inn Lexington, Ky. 40505 606-277-1191	Year round	√		√				√			√	√	M

	Dates open	Rooms	Cabins	Private bath	Breakfast offered	* Included in room charge	Lunch offered	Dinner offered	Pool	Tennis court	Children welcome	Pets welcome	Rates: L - Low, less than $30; M - Moderate, $31-$60; H - High, $61 and up
Carriage House Motor Hotel Paintsville, Ky. 41240 606-789-4242	Year round	✓		✓	✓	✓	✓	✓			✓	✓	M
Hawkeye Farm B&B Paris, Ky. 40361 606-987-5487	Year round		✓	✓	✓*								H
Shaker Village at Pleasant Hill Pleasant Hill, Ky. 40330 606-734-5411	Year round	✓		✓	✓	✓	✓				✓	✓	M-H

Kentucky Parks

	Lodge	Campsites	Dumping station	Hook-ups	Cabins	Pool	Picnicking	Boating: R-Public ramp, M-Marina, L-Horsepower limits	Boats to rent: C-canoe, P-paddleboat, F-fishing boat	Hiking trails	Fishing	Water skiing	Primitive camping	Supply store	Museum	Leashed pets welcome
Fort Boonesborough State Park Richmond, Ky. 40475 606-527-3328		173	✓	✓			✓	RM	C	✓	✓	✓	✓	✓	✓	✓
Buckhorn Lake State Resort Park Buckhorn, Ky. 41721 606-398-7510	✓				1	✓	✓	RM	F	✓	✓	✓				✓
General Burnside State Park Burnside, Ky. 42519 606-561-4104		110	✓	✓		✓	✓	R		✓	✓	✓	✓			✓
Cumberland Falls State Resort Park Corbin, Ky. 40701 606-528-4121	✓	30	✓	✓	27	✓	✓			✓	✓		✓	✓	✓	
Kingdom Come State Park Cumberland, Ky. 40823 606-589-2479							✓	L	P	✓	✓		✓			✓
Greenbo Lake State Resort Park Greenup, Ky. 41144 606-473-7324	✓	63	✓	✓		✓	✓	RML	CPF	✓	✓	✓	✓	✓		✓
Old Fort Harrod State Park Harrodsburg, Ky. 40330 606-734-3314							✓								✓	✓

	Lodge	Campsites	Dumping station	Hook-ups	Cabins	Pool	Picnicking	Boating: R-Public ramp M-Marina L-Horsepower limits	Boats to rent: C-canoe P-paddleboat F-fishing boat	Hiking trails	Fishing	Water skiing	Primitive camping	Supply store	Museum	Leashed pets welcome
Lake Cumberland State Resort Park Jamestown, Ky. 42629 502-343-3111	✓	150	✓	✓	30	✓	✓	RM	C F	✓	✓	✓	✓	✓	✓	✓
Levi Jackson Wilderness Road State Park London, Ky. 40741 606-878-8000		185	✓	✓		✓	✓			✓				✓		✓
Cumberland Gap National Historical Park Middlesboro, Ky. 40965 606-248-2817		160	✓		1		✓			✓			✓		✓	✓
Pine Mountain State Resort Park Pineville, Ky. 40977 606-337-3066	✓	32	✓	✓	20	✓	✓			✓			✓		✓	
Jenny Wiley State Resort Park Prestonsburg, Ky. 41653 606-886-2711	✓	128	✓	✓	17	✓	✓	RML	P F	✓	✓	✓	✓	✓		
Natural Bridge State Resort Park Slade, Ky. 40376 606-663-2214	✓	90	✓	✓	10	✓	✓			✓			✓		✓	✓
Daniel Boone National Forest Winchester, Ky. 40391 606-745-3100		931	✓	✓			✓	RM	F	✓	✓	✓	✓	✓	✓	✓

Kentucky Chambers of Commerce

Berea
105 Boone St.
P.O. Box 318
Berea, Ky. 40403
606-986-9760

Corbin
401 S. Lynn Ave.
Corbin, Ky. 40701
606-341-9500

Georgetown
100 S. Broadway
Georgetown, Ky. 40324
502-863-5424

Harlan
105 S. Main St.
P.O. Box 268
Harlan, Ky. 40831
606-573-4717

Harrodsburg
222 S. Chiles St.
In Historic Morgan Row
Harrodsburg, Ky. 40330
606-734-2365

Lexington
P.O. Box 781
Lexington, Ky. 40507
606-254-4447

Middlesboro
North 20th St.
P.O. Box 788
Middlesboro, Ky. 40965
606-248-1075

Pikeville
P.O. Box 897
Pikeville, Ky. 41501
606-432-5504

Richmond
Richmond Bank Plaza
P.O. Box 876
Richmond, Ky. 40475
606-623-1720

Virginia

VIRGINIA

Chapter Three

A bingdon, an old city of about 4500 permanent residents and lots of visitors, is a good place to sleep and eat and find entertainment while you explore the richly varied region of Southwest Virginia that offers everything from culture to coal mines.

It's about 140 miles northeast of Knoxville if you go the simplest route —I-40 and I-81. But stay away from interstates after you arrive. The narrow, crooked roads are more fun.

As soon as Alberta and I arrived and unpacked at the old Martha Washington Inn, I went back to the car and headed for hiking country. Alberta went for a cultural-historical browse in Abingdon.

I headed southeast on US 58, down across the Middle Fork of Holston River, then across the South Fork, both lovely streams rippling over stone beds. I hoped to find an office of the Mount Rogers National Recreation Area at Damascus, where someone could suggest a good hike for the time I had before supper.

No such office there. Go to the Post

Office, somebody in the library suggested. I did and someone there said to phone Charles H. Trivett, who knows all about such matters and is willing to share. Trivett said to continue through Damascus on 58 and go several miles beyond to where 58 swings sharply right and local road 603 goes left. Follow 603 to its junction with 600 and take 600 up to Elk Garden. At Elk Garden I would find the Appalachian Trail. Then, he said, I should have enough time for a 5-mile roundtrip hike on the AT to Whitetop Mountain.

That sounded familiar. Alberta and I had been to Elk Garden on a cold spring morning several years ago. We had hiked, not to Whitetop, but in the opposite direction, to Mt. Rogers, which at 5729 feet is the highest mountain in Virginia. That was a nine-mile round-trip. I recalled that at Elk Garden, we had walked across a wide grassy-bald area, similar to Gregory Bald and Spence Field in the Great Smokies. I suppose the bald area *is* Elk Garden. Nothing much else is there except a parking area and trail markers. No houses, no people except hikers or hunters. Early May snowflakes had swirled around us as we started walking. After we crossed the grassy area and entered the woods, we came upon the largest ramp patch I'd ever seen.

We hiked through good mountain country to the top of Mt. Rogers. One of the tree species growing there is the Fraser fir. You know the Fraser fir. It's that evergreen that was so lovely in the Great Smokies high country until the balsam woolly aphid wiped out nearly every adult tree except a few at Clingmans Dome, where the National Park Service is trying to save them. Aphids also killed most of the other Fraser firs in other parts of the Southern Appalachians.

There is an exception: Mt. Rogers. For some reason, the aphids have done far less damage there. Officials of Jefferson National Forest (of which the recreation area is a part) say that the extreme dry weather of the middle 1980s combined with the aphids to kill a few firs. But they believe the trees would have withstood the aphids if the dry weather hadn't come. At any rate, more Fraser firs remain in good health at Mt.

Rogers than at any other place in their range. Be glad. For these are the loveliest trees of the Southern Appalachian high country. Why have these on Mt. Rogers survived? Nobody knows for sure. I once heard a forestry professor speculate that the Mt. Rogers firs might be of a slightly different strain, and part of the difference might include stronger natural resistance to the aphids.

Small Fraser firs are beautiful Christmas trees. Colin Campbell, a lawyer who practices in Independence, Va., tells how people used to get more than one Christmas tree from the same fir in the Mt. Rogers area. They cut the first Christmas tree well up the trunk, above the first branches. The stump and the remaining branches continued to live. Gradually, one of those branches became dominant. The other branches were cut, allowing the one left to grow up straight. Soon, they had another Christmas tree.

This time, darkness was too near for me to go and look at the Mt. Rogers firs. I would go the other direction, to Whitetop. The trail to Whitetop ascends most of the way. But it's never excessively steep. I wasn't sure what I'd find at Whitetop, but the name led me to expect a huge grayish-white rock. Wrong.

I walked out onto another bald, a big grassy area, with almost no trees. The top of it is 5520 feet above sea level. The view is for miles. But why is it Whitetop? Fearing Alberta would start getting nervous if I didn't get back to Abingdon by dark, I didn't linger to ponder that puzzle.

However, before we went to dinner, I phoned Charles Trivett and asked for an explanation. He said that if I were standing down in the snowless lowlands and looking up at a snow-covered Whitetop, I wouldn't have to ask.

With that question answered, I began appreciating the Martha Washington Inn. This was our first stay there since United Coal Co. of Bristol bought it in 1984 and spent more than $5 million restoring it. It needed restoring. The last time we'd been there, the infirmities of age were outnumbering the charms of age.

No more. When I took a shower, I no-

Martha Washington Inn, Abingdon

ticed the shower rod was polished brass. Same for the faucets, the clothes rod in the closet. In the bedroom proper, period furniture glowed from good care.

Everywhere you look in the public portions of the hotel you see fireplaces, which in cool weather are gas-lighted. The bell captain said there are 14 of them, including four in the bar.

The three-story red-brick building which houses the hotel has stood since 1832, when General Francis Preston and his wife, Sara Buchanan Preston, built it as their home. (She was a niece of Patrick Henry.) It has since served as the home of a women's college and, starting in 1935, as a hotel.

Hanging on the wall in one of the second-floor lobbies is a printed account of how a large oak outside the dining room got there. On orders of the Prestons, 100 slaves and 40 yoke of oxen transplanted it from nearby Fruit Hill. But when I looked for the oak it wasn't there. Maybe it was a victim of the restoration.

Alberta had eaten lunch at the Hard-

ware Company Restaurant and liked it well enough to want to go back for dinner. ("The deep-dish apple pie, with walnuts and raisins, was sooooo good.") But we both also wanted to try the First Lady's Table at the Martha Washington. We compromised by going to the Hardware Company for a drink (bourbon and water for me, straight water for Alberta) and then back to the hotel for dinner.

Operators of the Hardware Company serve moderately priced food — unless you order lobster tails — and they have a sense of humor. In this town of dozens of historic markers, a marker on the front door of the Hardware Company says, "On this site in 1897 nothing happened." Though nothing happened there in '97, some interesting stories probably were told around pot-bellied stoves on long-ago winter days when the building actually did house a hardware store. The moveable ladder clerks used to reach items on high shelves is still on its track behind the bar.

Dinner at the First Lady's Table was good. Good service, good decor — though the lights are too dim to suit me — and food cooked by somebody who knew exactly how to do it.

It's expensive but it's worth the money if you aren't skating close to the edge of your budget. At least three or four other good restaurants serve less expensive food. In addition to the Hardware Company, there are the Plum Alley Eatery, an open-courtyard place between Plum Alley and Main Street, open from May to October; and the Tavern. Though I haven't eaten in the Tavern, friends whose taste I trust say it's good. Also, I haven't eaten at Shoney's in Abingdon. But it must be good because it was packed, and the line was long when I stopped there intending to grab a quick lunch before the hike. I looked at the line and skipped lunch.

Abingdon is famed for several reasons. One reason is that it's an old town. Not old by Virginia Tidewater standards, but old in the west-of-the-mountains part of the state. It claims to be the first English-speaking town incorporated in the water-shed of the Mississippi. The community was first called Wolf Hill. Wolves denned in a cave in the hill. Their howling disturbed Daniel Boone's dogs when he and Nathaniel Gist camped there, causing Boone to give the place its first name. When Black's Fort was built in 1776, the name was changed to that. Then the name was changed to Abingdon when the town was incorporated in 1778.

Abingdon has produced more than its share of leaders. At one time, three former Virginia governors — Wyndham Robertson, David Campbell and John B. Floyd Jr. — lived there within a mile of each other. U. S. Secretary of War John B. Floyd, Secretary of the Treasury John Campbell and Virginia Supreme Court Chief Justice Preston W. Campbell were from Abingdon.

The town is a regional arts and crafts center. One shop, a cooperative owned by craftspeople, is called Cave House because it's at the cave where the wolves lived.

But it was none of these things that brought the most fame to Abingdon. The fellow who did that was Robert Porterfield, from nearby Glade Spring. The young man wanted to be an actor. He went to New York, to Broadway. But in 1932, the heart of the Great Depression, Broadway actors were going hungry.

So he came back to the family farm at Glade Spring, bringing with him 24 other hungry actors and an idea. The idea was that actors hungry for food should trade their talents for food grown by Southwest Virginians hungry for entertainment.

They opened Barter Theater in 1933. That first season one could sit in the orchestra seats for 35 cents or "the equivalent in produce." Canned green beans, chickens, eggs, hams, watermelons, milk, butter and lots of other farm-grown food poured into the box office, and the people who brought them filled the theater. When the season ended, the actors' collective weight was 305 pounds greater than at the beginning, and they were $4.30 and quantities of jams and jellies in the black.

The theater's fame and success grew. It became the official State Theater of Virginia. Abingdon is the only small U. S. city, far from a large metropolitan center, that is home to a regional Actors Equity company. The box office long ago stopped accepting produce for admission. Porterfield died in 1971. A Southwest Virginia highway bears his name, but he will be remembered longest by those who love vibrant, live regional theater.

The theater opens in late April and closes near the middle of October. Admission prices for 1987 are $10 for Friday and Saturday evenings and $7.50 for all other times. Matinee performances are at 2 p.m. Wednesdays, Thursdays, Saturdays and Sundays. No performances on Monday. Phone 800-368-3240 for reservations.

At breakfast at the Martha Washington the next morning, Alberta ordered French toast. She tasted it and declared it was the best she'd ever eaten. She gave me a sample and I agreed. The extra little something was bits of crushed almonds coating the toast.

After breakfast, we pointed the car generally north. Our destination was Breaks Interstate Park, far up on the Virginia-Kentucky border. But there were many crooked, interesting miles between us and the park. Northwest on US 19 and 58 to

Breaks Interstate Park, Breaks

Hansonville, then northeast on 19 to its intersection with US 460, then northwest on 460 through the Virginia coal country.

The day before, I'd hiked in the Blue Ridge — high mountains, mostly forested, sloping down to farming and grazing land to the north. Now, we were leaving that pleasant, prosperous-looking farm country and entering a disorderly jumble of steep foothills of the Cumberlands.

We drove down a narrow valley, past little communities called Cedar Bluff, Red Ash, Keen Mountain, Oakwood, Deel, Vansant, and then Grundy, somewhat larger. Most of the way, a stream was on our left, with tracks of the Norfolk & Western Railroad just across the stream. Great numbers of filled coal cars stood still on the tracks. In the little communities, a row or two of houses rested on flat places dug out of the hillside. Some of the houses are large and attractive.

Everywhere there was evidence of coal mining. We passed towering metal-sided structures which someone said are coal-washing towers. We came to a bridge where a marker said we were crossing Dismal Creek, entering from the right into Louisa Fork. Another marker warned us to watch out for steam on the road. None on the road this time, but we looked up Dismal Creek and saw a great column of steam rising straight up from a towering building. A coke oven, we were told. We turned right on local road 638, paralleling the creek. We drove under wide metal shields which protect motorists from coal that might drop from small coal cars riding high-wire tracks over the road. We went past the coke oven, marveling at the monster, then went back to 460.

This is not scenic beauty. But what you see in this narrow valley is impressive. From just yards away, you are looking at a huge coal-industry operation.

A few miles north of Grundy, we turned west on local road 609 which at first passes more coal-mining operations. Then, by an unusually steep and crooked route, it climbs a mountain to Breaks Interstate Park. I was glad we met no coal trucks on that road.

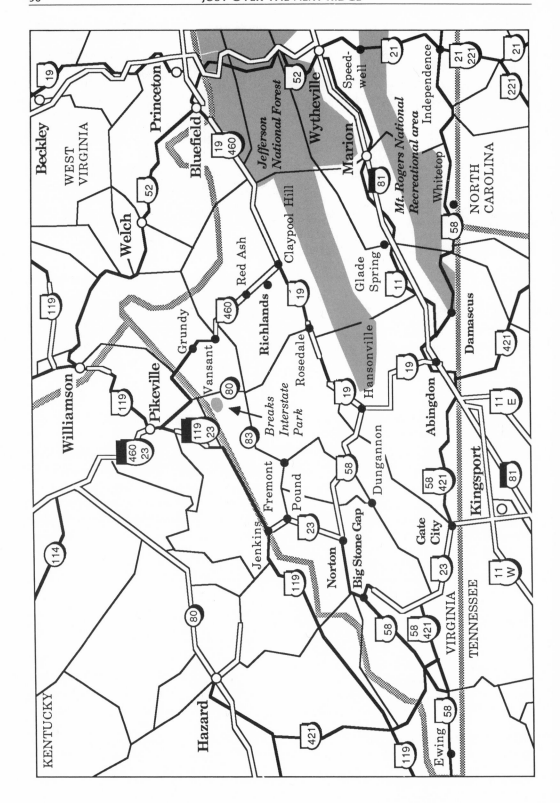

As state parks go, this one is big. And spectacular. "The Grand Canyon of the South," some call it. After entering the park, you quickly come to an overlook where you look far down at the Russell Fork of Big Sandy River. You stand at the outer rim of a horseshoe-shaped bend in the river and its canyon. Across the river, inside the horseshoe, stands a tree-clad mountain called the Towers. This gorge is about five miles long and park boosters claim it is "the deepest gorge east of the Mississippi."

How deep? Some of the literature says 1600 feet. That probably is wrong. Park Supt. James L. Childress said about 1000 feet.

Childress said the park contains 4600 acres, with 3450 of them in Virginia and the rest in Kentucky. It has two small lakes and about 10 miles of hiking trails. The motor lodge, campground and park visitors center are closed from the end of October to April 1. But the rest of the park, including the park office, housekeeping cottages and other facilities, remains open all year.

We left the park and followed State 80 and 83 to US 23 at Pound. Then we turned south on 23 through more coal country — Wise, Norton, Appalachia, Big Stone Gap.

Big Stone Gap is a coal mining center and the town to which author John Fox Jr. brought his Austrian opera-star bride, Fritzi Scheff, in 1908. Fritzi had never seen the raw coal mining country in the hills of Southwest Virginia. And Southwest Virginians had never seen the likes of Fritzi. You remember John Fox; we met him in Kentucky in Kingdom Come State Park, which is not far from Virginia. Fox used this border country as settings for his novels and short stories.

Fritzi brought 40 trunks of fine clothes. It took nearly a week to unload and unpack them. She also brought five maids and a lap dog. Fritzi was successful, spoiled and talented. She was a native of Vienna. Her mother was a prima donna of Wagnerian opera, her father a successful physician-scientist. Fritzi followed her mother into grand opera. She became well- enough known that she appeared before Queen Victoria. She made her American debut at the Metropolitan Opera in 1900. She turned to comic opera in America and was equally successful. She traveled in her own private railcar. Theater people called her "the little devil" because of her temper tantrums. One story handed down is that Fox and Fritzi met after she sent him a congratulatory note about one of his stories, "Hellfer-Sartin." They married a few months later. Fox by then was a successful newspaper writer and novelist. He had covered the Spanish-American War and the Russo-Japanese War. "The Little Shepherd of Kingdome Come" had become a best-seller and "The Trail of the Lonesome Pine," published only months before the marriage, would do even better.

Fox had grown up in Bourbon County, Ky., heart of the Bluegrass. Two of his half-brothers had gone into coal mining in Jellico, the little town on the Tennessee-Kentucky border. John Jr. mined coal there in 1882 and again in 1886. He had begun writing by then, and his first published story, "A Mountain Europa," was set in the Jellico area. It involved an out-of-area sophisticate who first saw his country-girl sweetheart as she rode a bull down a country lane.

The coal-mining Foxes moved from Jellico to Big Stone Gap in 1888. Their father and mother followed two years later. John Jr. and Fritzi had agreed she would follow her career and he his. This meant she was on the road much of the time. So Big Stone Gap was never her home, but she and he had long visits there in the Fox home. She played golf, tennis, rode horseback and helped finance a Big Stone Gap baseball team.

The two-career marriage that now works for many couples didn't work then for John and Fritzi. They were divorced in 1913. He died in 1919.

Some Big Stone Gap oldtimers think that some members of the Fox family were not overly fond of Fritzi.

One thing is certain: Fritzi is not the woman people remember first in the life of John Fox Jr. That woman, part real and part fiction, was June Tolliver.

She was the heroine of "The Trail of the

Lonesome Pine." Big Stone Gap people say her real name was Elizabeth Morris. Elizabeth, it is said, came to Big Stone Gap and lived as a paying guest in the home of Mrs. Jerome Hill Duff, a widow, and attended school at Duff Academy. Fox became acquainted with her, and she was his model for June Tolliver.

What was the Duff home now is the June Tolliver House. It's on the National Register of Historic Places. The Lonesome Pine Arts and Crafts Association owns it, keeps it open to the public and operates a gift shop in part of it. When we were there, Sarah Broadwater, a retired teacher, was one of those on voluntary duty. She showed us the room where Elizabeth Morris (June Tolliver) lived, some pieces of

furniture from the Fox home, and various pictures, including Fritzi Scheff's.

"The Trail of the Lonesome Pine" lives as an outdoor drama produced Thursday, Friday, Saturday and Sunday evenings during July and August. It is staged in the June Tolliver Playhouse, on the grounds of the June Tolliver Home.

When you go to Big Stone Gap, you can also see the Fox home. You can walk through the study where John Fox Jr. wrote and you can even see the old typewriter he used. You also can see the Southwest Virginia Museum, a collection of turn-of-the-century articles, and the Westmoreland Coal Museum, which shows the history of coal mining in that region.

Virginia Attractions*

Barter Theater Abingdon, Va. 24210 703-628-3991 800-572-2081,368-3240	Founded in 1933 as a theater where performers traded theater tickets for food and other supplies, the Barter is the State Theater of Virginia. Its season runs April-October. Call for show schedule and ticket information.
White's Mill Abingdon, Va. 24210 703-628-5383	A National Historic Landmark. Has been in operation for over 100 years and is still working today. Tours. Small charge for fishing. Open year round.
John Fox Jr. Museum Big Stone Gap, Va. 24219 703-523-2747	This was the home in which Fox wrote "The Trail of the Lonesome Pine" and 14 other novels. Built in 1888, it houses family furnishings and mementos. Tours daily except Monday. Admission.
June Tolliver House & Craft Shop Big Stone Gap, Va. 24219 703-523-1235	The heroine of "The Trail of the Lonesome Pine" lived in this restored 19th-century home. The craft shop features mountain crafts, including coal jewelry and corn shuck dolls. Open May 17-Dec. 20. Free.
Southwest Virginia Museum Big Stone Gap, Va. 24219 703-523-1322	This 1880s building was the home of some of the area's prominent citizens and now houses furnishings, costumes, portraits and books by local authors. Open March-December. Admission.
Trail of the Lonesome Pine Big Stone Gap, Va. 24219 703-523-2060 or 523-1235	An outdoor drama tells the story of the coming of the coal mines to the Virginia mountains. Folk music, some original, is interspersed throughout the play, which is in its 24th season. May - Dec. 15. Admission.

* We suggest you call and verify the information given in these listings when planning a trip or making reservations. See introduction to the tables on page 45 for further explanation.

Westmoreland Coal Museum
Big Stone Gap, Va. 24219
703-523-4950

This museum, owned by Westmoreland Coal Co, captures the coal industry in Virginia from its beginnings in the 1890s through modern day operations. Closed Mondays and Tuesdays. Free.

Trainstation Marketplace
Bristol, Va. 24201
703-466-2000

Renovated train depot contains unusual shops and restaurants. Open daily. Free.

Virginia Lodging Places

	Dates open	Rooms	Cabins	Private bath	Breakfast offered	*Included in room charge	Lunch offered	Dinner offered	Pool	Tennis court	Children welcome	Pets welcome	Rates: L - Low, less than $30; M - Moderate, $31-$60; H - High, $61 and up
Martha Washington Inn Abingdon, Va. 24210 703-628-3161	Year round	√		√	√	√	√				√		H
Trail Motel Big Stone Gap, Va. 24219 703-523-1171	Year round	√		√							√		M
Breaks Motor Lodge Breaks, Va. 24607 703-865-4414	April - October	√	√	√	√	√	√	√			√		M

Virginia Parks

	Lodge	Campsites	Dumping station	Hook-ups	Cabins	Pool	Picnicking	Boating: R-Public ramp M-Marina L-Horsepower limits	Boats to rent: C-canoe P-paddleboat F-fishing boat	Hiking trails	Fishing	Water skiing	Primitive camping	Supply store	Museum	Leashed pets welcome
Breaks Interstate Park Breaks, Va. 24607 703-865-4413	√	122	√	√	4	√	√	R L	P	√	√		√		√	√
Natural Tunnel State Park Duffield, Va. 24244 703-940-2674		25	√			√	√			√	√					√
Shenandoah National Park Luray, Va. 22835 703-999-2243	√	625	√		10		√			√	√		√	√	√	√
Hungry Mother State Park Marion, Va. 24354 703-783-9234		70	√	√	20		√	R L	PF	√	√		√		√	√
Mount Rogers National Recreation Area Marion, Va. 24354 703-783-5196		400	√	√			√			√	√		√		√	√

	Lodge	Campsites	Dumping station	Hook-ups	Cabins	Pool	Picnicking	Boating: R-Public ramp	M-Marina	L-Horsepower limits	Boats to rent: C-canoe	P-paddleboat	F-fishing boat	Hiking trails	Fishing	Water skiing	Primitive camping	Supply store	Museum	Leashed pets welcome
Grayson Highlands State Park Mouth of Wilson, Va. 24363 703-579-7092		73	✓				✓							✓	✓		✓		✓	✓
Jefferson National Forest Roanoke, Va. 24001 703-982-6370		400	✓	✓			✓	R		L				✓	✓		✓		✓	✓
Cumberland Gap National Historical Park Middlesboro, Ky. 40965 606-248-2817		160	✓		1		✓							✓			✓		✓	✓

Virginia
Chambers of Commerce

Abingdon
304 Depot Square
Abingdon, Va. 24210
703-628-8141

Big Stone Gap
765 Park Ave.
P.O. Box 226
Norton, Va. 24273
703-679-0961

Bristol
20 Volunteer Pkwy.
P.O. Box 519
Bristol, Va. 37620
615-968-4399

Grundy
West End of Grundy Rt 460
P.O. Box 672
Grundy, Va. 24631
703-935-4147

Marion
200 E. Main St.
P.O. Box 924
Marion, Va. 24354
703-783-3161

Pulaski
42 First St. N.W.
P.O. Box 168
Pulaski, Va. 24301
703-980-1991

Roanoke
14 W. Kirk Ave.
Roanoke, Va. 24011
703-344-5188

Wytheville
First & Main St.
P.O. Box 563
Wytheville, Va. 24382
703-228-3211

North Carolina

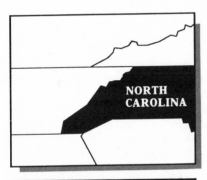

NORTH CAROLINA

Chapter Four

Western North Carolina is mountain country. When you top the Great Smokies at Newfound Gap and look south, all you see is mountains. If your length of vision were doubled, still all you'd see would be mountains. They stretch south all the way to Georgia and South Carolina, west beyond the Tennessee border and east to the Piedmont.

Western Carolina has about 6000 square miles of mountains. It has 43 peaks higher than 6000 feet, more than any other state in Eastern America. It has 6684-foot Mt. Mitchell, highest peak east of the Mississippi, and it shares with Tennessee the second and third highest, Clingmans Dome and Mt. Guyot. Forest covers most of these steep mountains. Many of them lie within the Great Smoky Mountains National Park and Pisgah and Nantahala National Forests. Nestled, like jewels in wrinkled green velvet, among these steep valleys and lofty highlands are small towns with populations ranging from 200 to more than 10,000. The biggest western North Carolina city is Asheville, with a population of more than 53,000. Although it has numerous charms, we'll stay out of it.

Swift, brawling creeks and rivers drain these highlands. They plunge white-foamed and furious over waterfalls and down rapids and linger briefly in dark pools. Thrill-seekers in canoes, rafts and kayaks float them. Thrill-seekers of another type carefully work their waters for rainbow, brook and brown trout.

One of the loveliest of the rivers is the Oconaluftee. It drains a wide swath of the south side of the Great Smokies, stretching from west of Newfound Gap eastward almost to Mt. Guyot. The Oconaluftee and its tributaries race recklessly down steep slopes until the main stream reaches land with gentler pitch a few miles north of where it joins the Tuckasegee River.

On this gentle land along the Oconaluftee live many of the Eastern Band of the Cherokee. Few people in North America have dwelt so long beside the same rivers as the Cherokees have lived near the Oconaluftee and the Tuckasegee. They claim they have lived there more than 10,000 years. Though they may not be able to prove this to everyone's satisfaction, there's no question that they have lived there a very long time, far longer than white people have lived anywhere in North America. They were there when the first white explorers arrived, and they obviously had been there a long time before that.

On a wide, flat bottom near the confluence of the Oconaluftee and the Tuckasegee stood ancient Kituwah, one of the seven "Mother Towns" of the Cherokee.

The Cherokees once claimed dominion over a large area lying in what now are parts of Tennessee, Kentucky, Virginia, West Virginia, North Carolina, South Carolina, Georgia and Alabama. They used most of this land for hunting. They actually lived on the rich bottomlands of the Little Tennessee and Hiwassee Rivers and their tributaries in Tennessee and North Carolina and on the headwaters of the Savannah River. Most of them lived within the Little Tennessee watershed.

Many still do, for the Tuckasegee is a Little Tennessee tributary. The Eastern Band of the Cherokees had an enrollment of 8822 members in 1982, and nearly 6000 of them lived on the 56,573 acres of land in 52 tracts in five western North Carolina counties. Most of this group lived in six communities: Cherokee, Birdtown, Painttown, Soco, Big Y and Big Cove. All these are clustered close together. A few hundred others lived several miles away in the Snowbird Mountains of Graham County. Still others live on Cherokee lands north of Hiwassee Lake, in Cherokee County.

Nearly 3000 members of the Eastern Band lived elsewhere, off reservation land. This is the largest Indian reservation east of the Mississippi.

Most Indians in Eastern America moved — or were driven — west of the Mississippi River before 1838. And most of those remaining went that year, on the infamous Trail of Tears. But by hiding, negotiating and sacrificing, about 1200 Cherokees managed to remain near the Oconaluftee and the Tuckasegee. Most of those there now are descendants of the 1200.

An account of how they managed to remain and survive is told in the outdoor drama, "Unto These Hills," presented each year by the Cherokee Historical Association. Performances are held every night except Sunday from near the middle of June through late August. More than 4 million visitors have seen the drama since it was first presented in 1950. Phone 704-497-2111 for reservations.

"Unto These Hills" isn't all that's outstanding in Cherokee. Oconaluftee Indian Village is another attraction. It's a living replica of a Cherokee town of the middle 1700s. Visitors can see the kind of houses Cherokees lived in, how they made clothing, pottery and baskets and grew herbs. They can watch men fashion blowguns, darts, arrows and dugout canoes. They can see inside a seven-sided council house like those in which Cherokees long ago held religious and secular meetings. The village opens about the middle of May and closes in late October.

Some of the best examples of Indian arts and craft work in America are in the attractive building that houses the Qualla

Canoe making at Oconaluftee Indian Village, Cherokee

Arts and Crafts Mutual. About 300 Cherokee craftspeople and artists sell baskets, beadwork, pottery, wood carvings, handwoven rugs, finger weavings and other craft products through the mutual. Carol Welch fashions white oak baskets that sell for as much as $500. Eva Wolf makes beautiful double-weave rivercane baskets, some of which have found homes in the Smithsonian. They sell for up to $1000 and become household treasures. They are long-lasting. A woman in Robbinsville has several double-woven rivercane baskets Cherokee friends gave her great-grandmother nearly 150 years ago. When I visited the mutual outlet recently, the most expensive item in it was priced at $10,000. This was a walnut sculpture of an Indian clutching an eagle. The artist, Virgil Ledford, spent 100 hours just on the eagle and the hand that holds it. Richard and Berdina Crowe make exquisite dolls. He carves them of wood. She dresses them in Cherokee clothing of the 1800s.

To learn the history and myths of the Cherokees, visit the Museum of the Cherokee Indian, a few yards from the Qualla Arts and Crafts Mutual building. With the help of more than 20 video presentations, visitors learn about past and present life of the Cherokees. They listen to the musical Cherokee language on special "hearphones."

For a small fee, visitors can fish for trout in the Oconaluftee and some of its tributaries on the reservation. The tribe operates the fishing program and stocks good-sized fish.

An early autumn attraction is the annual Indian fair at Cherokee. It lasts a week, usually the last part of September or the first part of October. It features native Cherokee foods, stickball games and blowgun contests.

Cherokee has several motels. But if you want to stay in one owned by the tribe and eat in an Indian-owned restaurant, try the Boundary Tree Motor Lodge, the Boundary Tree Dining Room or the Boundary Tree Restaurant. You also can buy gasoline at the Boundary Tree Service Station. The Cherokees also operate Mingo Falls

Campground.

Of course, you don't have to stay in Cherokee. If you plan to stay several days in the area, you may want to consider two excellent inns. One is Hemlock Inn, snug against the Great Smokies, near Bryson City. The other is Snowbird Mountain Lodge, near Robbinsville and within a 10-minute drive of the Joyce Kilmer-Slickrock Wilderness. (I should mention a third inn, the Swag, near Waynesville and the Great Smokies. I haven't stayed there, but many people have told me it's good.) From these inns, you can make one-day trips to such places as Cherokee, Bryson City, Fontana Village, Dillsboro, Sylva and Franklin.

But you probably won't want to take long drives *every* day from either Hemlock or Snowbird. For there are many things to do near them. From Snowbird, you can be on Joyce Kilmer-Slickrock hiking trails within minutes. One of the best, especially when wildflowers are blooming in the second half of May, is the Haoe Lead Trail. Two others are the Stratton Bald and Naked Ground trails.

Why's it "Naked Ground"? It's on the divide separating the headwaters of Slick Rock and Santeetlah creeks. A long time ago, well before the region became an official wilderness area and probably before it became part of Nantahala National Forest, cattle grazed and browsed in the mountains. The Naked Ground was one of the spots where herders placed salt for the cattle.

One day, two big bulls got mad at each other. They fought for hours, pushing, butting, shoving, sweating. By the time they grew too tired to continue, their hooves had cut up the ground and killed all vegetation. So, Naked Ground. That's one story.

The bulls probably fought there, all right. But a more likely reason the ground was naked is that the salt killed the vegetation. Or maybe it was a combination of the fight and the salt. Now, years later, the area doesn't look particularly naked.

A good all-day hike, only for those with considerable stamina, is to start up the Haoe Lead Trail, follow it to the Jenkins Meadow Trail and continue on that one to

Haoe. A short side trip to the right will take you to Hangover, a peak that offers a fine view on a clear day. Retrace your steps to Haoe and continue on the mountain crest to Naked Ground. Turn left down the Naked Ground Trail. It follows the valley of Little Santeetlah Creek to a parking area. That's a walk of 11 or 12 miles. (Remember to arrange transportation to get back to your car at the Haoe Lead trailhead. Also, remember to buy a Joyce Kilmer-Slickrock map.)

You don't want to miss the short Joyce Kilmer Memorial Trail winding among the giant tulip poplars and hemlocks. It starts and ends near the Joyce Kilmer parking area.

When you're at the parking area, you may see a tall mountain woman named Oleta Nelms. She works parttime for the U. S. Forest Service. Her main duty is to answer questions.

I asked her one day about John Denton. I knew this legendary mountain man had lived nearby, and I wanted to know where. She put me on an old trail that leads to the homesite. But before doing this, she told me more about Denton.

I already knew that he was tall and tough and that he had moved his family over the mountain from Polk County, Tenn., in the late 1870s. I knew that Robbinsville bullies had picked a fight with him and that he had whipped five of them, all in the same encounter.

But Oleta Nelms told me more. She said John Denton first built a small log house, about as little as the family could live in, when he arrived. Then he started clearing land for corn and a garden. He built his small house close against a huge fallen chestnut tree. When winter came and John was no longer working with his crops, he expanded his house. With axe and other tools, he expanded it right into that chestnut log. He hollowed out a room tall enough for him to stand erect without bumping his head. He was 6-feet-3.

When Oleta Nelms finished her story, I said, "You know a lot about John Denton."

She smiled proudly and said, "I'm his granddaughter."

If it's fishing you want, you can try for

trout in nearby Santeetlah and Little Santeetlah creeks. Only a little farther from Snowbird Lodge is Snowbird Creek, also good for trout. For lake fishing, try nearby Santeetlah and Cheoah lakes.

Snowbird Lodge, operated by Bob and Connie Rhudy, provides three meals a day for its guests. If you plan to be gone at lunchtime, they'll pack a picnic lunch you can take on the trail or in the car. If you're in a party of four or more, your group will be seated together at a table. If you're one or two, chances are you'll be seated with others who are one or two. The food is good and plentiful.

While driving near the lodge, you may see Cherokee Indians. And you may see mailboxes bearing Cherokee names. Look at the Robbinsville and Santeetlah quadrangle maps and you will notice small geometric areas marked with such words as "Upper Cornsilk," "Teeoatlah," and "John Teeseteska." These are Cherokee tribal lands, and the names indicate which individuals owned possessory rights to them.

These are called the Snowbird Cherokees. One of them is Maggie Wachacha, a wrinkled brown little woman who has been one of the clerks of the tribal council for about 45 years. Every time the council meets in Cherokee, Maggie Wachacha attends. She records the minutes in the Cherokee language, using the syllabary devised by Sequoyah. Another clerk writes the minutes in English. In earlier years, before the present system of highways was built, Maggie Wachacha sometimes had to walk much of the considerable distance from Robbinsville to Cherokee. The Cherokee Tribe a few years ago bestowed upon her the title of Beloved Woman. She's believed to be the first Eastern Cherokee to bear that title since the famed Nancy Ward, a Cherokee leader at the time of the American Revolution.

In the town of Robbinsville, only a few miles from Snowbird Lodge, is the grave of Junaluska, a Cherokee chief during and before the presidency of Andrew Jackson. In fact, Junaluska is said to have saved Jackson's life at the Battle of Horseshoe Bend, in Alabama in 1812. Junaluska and his men were fighting with Jackson's troops against the Creek Indians. Junaluska later said he was sorry he saved Jackson's life, for it was President Jackson who set in motion the series of events that led to the Trail of Tears. Junaluska walked the Trail of Tears to Oklahoma. He lost his wife and children on it. And a few years later, he walked all the way back from Oklahoma and squatted on a piece of land in Robbinsville. He got along well with the white people and the other Indians in this Snowbird country. The State of North Carolina later felt so well disposed toward him that it made him a citizen and gave him 337 acres of land and $100. When Junaluska died, his red and white friends buried him on a hill near an old Cherokee dance ground. Later, in 1910, the Daughters of the American Revolution provided an appropriate and lasting monument at the old chief's grave.

Hemlock Inn, operated by John and Ella Jo Shell, offers good breakfasts and dinners, but guests are on their own for lunch. Everybody is expected to arrive at about the same time for meals, because John always says a blessing. Guests are seated at large round tables. You serve yourself from serving plates on lazy susans in the center of the tables.

The inn is near the Deep Creek section of the Great Smokies. Tubing is a popular sport on the creek. Farther up the creek, and on Indian Creek, a Deep Creek tributary, there's trout fishing. Not far to the west is another Great Smokies trout stream, Noland Creek.

If you want a good downhill hike, get someone to drive you from Hemlock Inn to the top of the mountain, on the Clingmans Dome Road, and then to the Noland Divide Trailhead. From there, it's about 11½ miles down to Deep Creek Campground. You're likely to see few other hikers. Last time I did it, I didn't meet another person. In the high country, lots of winter wrens sang to me. Saw many wildflowers. Alberta met me at the campground and took me back to the inn, where the Shells laid out enough food for somebody who'd hiked twice as far.

Rates at Snowbird and Hemlock are moderate, considering the meals you eat and the recreation available.

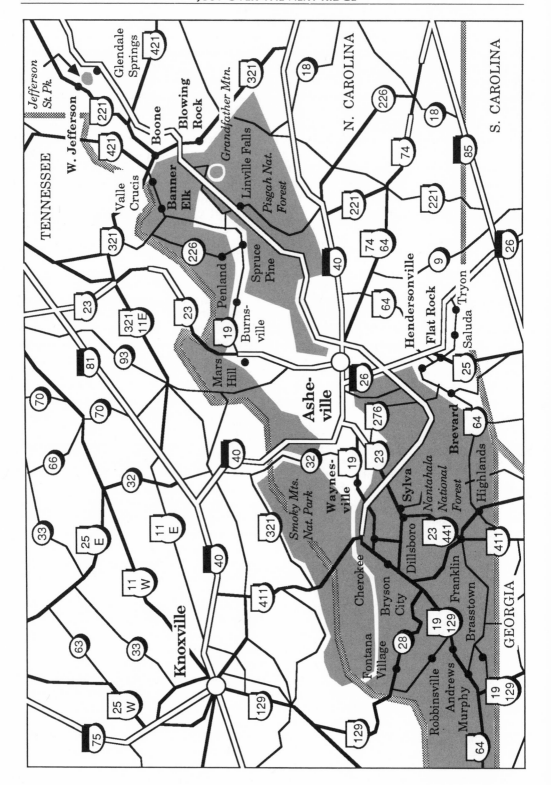

Dillsboro, a distinctive little town (population fewer than 300) on the Tuckasegee River, is within an easy roundtrip drive of either Snowbird Lodge or Hemlock Inn. But if you're not lingering long in the area, you might rather spend a night at the Squire Watkins Inn or the Jarrett House, both in Dillsboro.

Squire Watkins Inn, operated by Tom and Emma Wertenberger, is a bed-and-breakfast place. Western North Carolina has lots of bed-and-breakfast places. Tom at this writing was president-elect of the North Carolina Bed and Breakfast Association. He'll probably be president by the time you read this.

Bed-and-breakfast establishments are for those of adventurous spirit. If you want to be sure of a TV set and phone in the room, reading lamp at just the right angle over the bed and the ice bucket right were you expect to find it, you'd better stick with the Holiday Inn people. Also, if you like a real breakfast, you'd better find out ahead of time just what is breakfast at your prospective bed-and-breakfast place.

Tom and Emma serve a real breakfast. And Emma's "herbed" eggs are about as good as any eggs I ever ate.

Some — but not all — bed-and-breakfast places are in old homes. The Wertenbergers' place was built as a residence about 100 years ago. The owner was J. C. Watkins, and he really was a squire, or magistrate. It has five guest rooms. On the grounds are "efficiency cottages" and a "family cottage" which are rented at weekly rates.

Bed-and-breakfast rates usually compare well with motel rates, and breakfast is a dividend.

I have not stayed or eaten recently at the Jarrett House, that big three-story framed building whose owners have fed and housed Dillsboro visitors for more than 100 years. Because of the building's age, its floors are not precisely level. I recall that when Alberta and I stayed there a dozen years ago, our portable typewriters kept trying to slide off their tables because of the slant of the floor.

Food at the Jarrett House was good the last time I ate there, and a News-Sentinel colleague who ate there more recently says it's still delicious. Room rates and meal prices are reasonable. Jarrett House opens near the middle of April and stays open through October. The dining room is open four to six weeks longer.

When Alberta and I stayed at Squire Watkins Inn, we ate dinner at the Well House. The name comes from the fact that in one corner of the dining room there is an old well. I ate barbecue chicken. It was delightful. A specialty of the house is smoked salmon, but it was not available that night. Bob Leveille, the chef-operator, makes his own barbecue sauce and smokes the salmon, we were told. Prices are low to moderate.

The Well House is the restaurant part of a large rambling complex called Riverwood Shops, situated on a hilltop above the Tuckasegee. The owners of the buildings in which the shops are housed are Dr. Ralph Siler Morgan Jr. and his wife, Ruth. A physician, Dr. Morgan has done much to bring the benefits of modern medicine to this rural area.

The Morgans established Riverwood Shops — or what became Riverwood Shops — in 1959. Dr. Morgan's father had started producing hand-hammered pewter in nearby Sylva in 1930. Dr. Morgan and his wife brought the pewter operation to Riverwood. She still manages the pewter shop, where visitors can see workers hammer and polish pewter. A Morgan daughter, Susan Leveille (wife of the restaurant operator), runs a weaving shop in the complex. There also are pottery, leather and glass shops, as well as a large gift shop which specializes in crafts produced over a wide area of the Southern Highlands.

The main building of Riverwood Shops was the home of C. J. Harris, an early Jackson County developer.

Down off the Riverwood hill is the main portion of Dillsboro, stretched three blocks along Front and Haywood Streets. Nearly all the buildings house businesses catering to visitors. It's attractive any time, and it's particularly bright and cheerful when the whole town decorates for Christmas. One weekend, usually the first one in December, the area is outlined with luminarias (lighted candles in weighted paper bags).

Next stop is Franklin. If you're already in Dillsboro, the shortest route to Franklin is by way of US 441. But I'd rather make that trip southward from near Bryson City, on State Highway 28. That route takes you up the valley of the Little Tennessee. Lovely river, lovely country.

The Little Tennessee probably is the most dammed river of its size in America. The Aluminum Company of America built Cheoah, the first Little T dam, before 1920. Then it built Calderwood, and then TVA built Fontana, and then ALCOA built Chilhowee, after which TVA built Tellico. ALCOA also built 12 other dams on Little Tennessee tributaries and on their tributaries. Probably no other U.S. river of comparable size is such an electricity factory.

So the Little T now provides two kinds of recreation water. Those who like to swim and fish and boat and ski on flat water have all those lakes. And those who want to fish or float in hurrying water can use the Upper Little T, above Fontana Lake.

Fontana is an outstanding fishing lake. Calderwood, narrow, deep and cold, grudgingly gives up big trout to those who know how to fish for them. The place to put a boat in Calderwood is just downstream from the bridge immediately below Cheoah Dam on US 129.

If you want to fish Fontana Lake (or square dance or hike) spend a few days at Fontana Village near Fontana Dam. A family can stay in one of the many cabins built by TVA to house workers' families during construction of the dam. These housekeeping cabins rent at low to moderate rates. You can buy groceries at the village store. If nobody wants to cook, you can eat at the cafeteria. Or if you want to spend more and have a touch of luxury, stay and eat at Fontana Inn. The village is a leading square dance center of Southern Appalachia.

We have strayed from Franklin, county seat of Macon County, a town of fewer than 3000 persons, sitting there on both sides of the Little Tennessee. The same site has been a town far back in time. Before Franklin, this was the Cherokee's Nikwasi.

Nikwasi Mound still stands a few yards from the river.

Besides being one of the few — maybe the only — Indian mounds in the middle of a modern city, Nikwasi is known for at least two other reasons. It was to this very spot that Scotsman Sir Alexander Cumming came in 1730 to meet and negotiate with the Cherokees. Chiefs from towns all over the Cherokee nation attended.

In myth, the Cherokees remember Nikwasi for another reason. A formidable enemy tribe of long ago attacked them here along the Little T. The battle was going badly for the Cherokees until the Nunnehis, or the Immortals, raced out of Nikwasi Mound and joined the Cherokees in crushing the attackers. The enemies could not see the Nunnehis; they could see only their spears and arrows. Much later, in 1760, the Nunnehis were credited with helping the Cherokees defeat a British army in a battle near the Little Tennessee.

If you arrive in Franklin at the right time in spring, you may find a wild strawberry ripening on Nikwasi Mound.

This has been great wild strawberry country for centuries. Quaker botanist William Bartram followed the Little Tennessee Valley down out of North Georgia before the American Revolution. His horses trampled so many strawberries that strawberry juice dyed "my horse's feet and ancles (sic)." Bartram also wrote a flowery account of watching "companies of young, innocent Cherokee virgins, some busy gathering the rich fragrant fruit."

Instead of picking red strawberries now, lots of visitors search for red rubies and garnets near Franklin. Alberta and I have a tiny bag of those stones we dug years ago. I also still have memories of a sore back. Some also find sapphires; we didn't.

You can stop at at least 12 ruby mines within a 10-mile radius of Franklin, pay a fee and go out and search for a big ruby that will make you rich. You won't find it. At least, the odds are a few million to one that you won't. A very few have found stones that some claimed to be worth about $10,000. You have some chance — I won't guess how good — of finding a stone worth using in a ring or pendant. You'll find

Water recreation at Fontana Village Resort, Fontana Dam

Franklin shops where experts will appraise it and mount it for you. The Franklin Gem and Mineral Museum is in an old jail, built in the 1850s and used as a jail until 1972. Members of the Gem and Mineral Society of Franklin renovated it and established the museum.

A few mines operate throughout the year. Others open in April and May and close before cold weather. Before selecting a mine, you may want to find out whether it's been "enriched" or has only native gems. The tourist ruby mining business is so good that some operators buy rubies elsewhere and hide them in their own soil and gravel. A brochure distributed by the Franklin Area Chamber of Commerce identifies mines which have "native stones only" and those which are "enriched." Some mines have both.

Some visitors to Franklin — mostly hikers and Episcopalians — may want to make a side trip, a pilgrimage to a tiny Episcopal Church, Saint John's, Cartoogechaye, near Cartoogechaye Creek, a sparkling tributary of the Little T.

To reach it, turn west off US 441 onto US 64. After driving about five miles, look for Carl Slagle Road. Continue on 64 to the next road beyond Carl Slagle Road. Turn right on this road, which bore no name

marker when we were there. Go a half-mile and turn right again. By then, you will see markers leading you to the church.

Look around the little cemetery beside the church. You will find a rough stone on which is lettered: "Albert Rufus Morgan, 1885-1983. Thanks be to God who Gives the Victory."

Rufus Morgan was — and remains — a legend, from a legendary family. His maternal ancestors, the Silers, were first settlers in this region. Their name is on Silers Bald in the Nantahalas and on the other Silers Bald, in the Great Smokies.

On the western side of the Nantahalas lived the Cherokees when the Silers came. They got along well, the Silers and the Indians. The Indians helped William Siler build his house. But these friendly neighbors had to leave the Nantahalas in 1838, to go into stockades before moving west on the Trail of Tears. Two of them, Chief Chuttahsotee and his wife, Cunstagih, escaped from their stockade and went into Tennessee. Then, in roundabout ways, they made their way back into North Carolina and to the Siler home. William Siler, Rufus Morgan's great-grandfather, gave them land to live on and made them a deed to it.

And they lived on it until they died in 1879. According to one account, after

Chuttahsotee died, Cunstagih called a son and told him, "I am going with your father when the sun goes down." And she did.

Their tombstone stands in the little cemetery, not so far from Rufus Morgan's. "Chief Chuttahsotee Wife Cunstagih 1879."

Rufus Morgan's grandparents had donated land for a church in this spot in 1879. Chuttahsotee and Cunstagih were the first members buried there. Episcopal officials had the church torn down in 1925 and were preparing to sell the land. This church and other small ones were consolidated into one church in Franklin.

By then, Rufus, a graduate of the University of North Carolina and of the General Theological Seminary in New York City, was the rector at a church in South Carolina. He heard what was happening and persuaded church officials not to sell the land his grandparents had given.

Later, he moved back to western North Carolina, where he served 11 small Episcopal churches. At the same time, he hiked. He also single-handedly maintained the entire 55-mile section of the Appalachian Trail along the Nantahala crest. (When he grew too old to do the job alone, he formed a hiking club which took on the maintenance job.)

He longed to rebuild the Cartoogechaye church. And he finally did, without telling his bishop, without borrowing a cent of money. Most of the remains of those buried in the old cemetery had been taken to the cemetery at the church in Franklin. The old tombstones were left. Rufus used some of them in the foundation of the new church. The church exterior is of wormy chestnut, given to Rufus from long-dead trees in Nantahala National Forest. The interior is of white pine cut in the churchyard. Friends helped Rufus build the church.

It's so small that if 40 worshipers crowded into it, some probably would have to stand. But it's lovely, all in good taste. Rufus served without salary as its minister for many years. When his health became such that he could not continue, another minister followed him on the same no-salary basis, and now a third is doing the same.

One of Rufus' favorite hiking destinations was Mt. Le Conte in the Great Smokies. He hiked there more than 170 times. He liked to go there on his birthday, Oct. 15. A crowd of friends always went with him. There was the birthday cake at supper at Le Conte Lodge. Then a group walk to Cliff Top to await the sunset. Rufus said a prayer and led hymn-singing as the sun sank and the red sky dimmed. His last Le Conte hike was on his 92nd birthday. He died at 97, and the bell at Saint John's was tolled 97 times.

At Franklin, you decide whether you want to go east or west. On this particular trip, we went east. But on earlier trips we've gone west, and we'll discuss that territory first.

Going west on 64 will take you across Nantahala Mountain and the Appalachian Trail and to another church that is part of the legacy of Rufus Morgan. This is Chapel of the Ascension, a roof, open sides, a rustic low wall of fieldstone. It stands near the Rainbow Springs community, and it replaced a church that was torn down in 1917. Rufus conducted services there on a when-needed basis, mostly for summer visitors.

Going on west on 64 will take you to the vicinity of Brasstown and the John C. Campbell Folk School. Actually, Brasstown and the school are two miles south of 64.

John C. Campbell died before this school was founded in 1925. He had wanted to help people of the Southern Appalachians preserve their mountain ways and still make a decent living. He founded the Conference of Southern Mountain Workers, which continues today as the Council of the Southern Mountains, at Berea, Ky. His widow, Olive Dame Campbell, and others founded the school at Brasstown and gave it Campbell's name. School officials call it America's first folk school.

The school offers courses in woodcarving, woodworking, basketry, blacksmithing, casting, enameling, knife making, lap quilting, pottery, spinning, music and dance. Though some courses last 12 weeks, others are aimed at people who can spare only a weekend or a week or two of vacation time.

Special events, such as the annual Fall Festival the first weekend of October, draw thousands of visitors to this remote rural setting near Carolina's western tip. For about $240, a person can take a one-week course. The price includes meals. The school can accommodate 90 students and 12 instructors. You can folk dance every Saturday night.

Resuming your westward way on 64, you soon find yourself driving beside a pretty river. It's the Hiwassee. Then comes Murphy, county seat of Cherokee County, Carolina's westernmost county.

This route into Murphy is all right. But there's a prettier one. If you should find yourself at either Snowbird Lodge or Hemlock Inn and wanting to take a pleasant drive to Murphy, follow US 129 from Robbinsville, or US 19 from Bryson City until it joins 129. You soon reach Andrews, and the drive from Andrews most of the way to Murphy is through as lovely a mountain valley as you're likely to find. This is Valley River Valley, bounded on the north by the Snowbird Mountains and on the south by Valley River Mountains.

We've discussed places of interest to Episcopalians. The next stop is at a place with meaning to members of another church, the Church of God of Prophecy, which has its world headquaters at Cleveland, Tenn. In Cherokee County, it has Fields of the Wood, which the church calls a Biblical theme park. It is situated on more than 200 acres of landscaped mountain land. To reach it, continue west from Murphy on US 64. Go to State Highway 294 and turn right on it. Follow it several miles to Fields of the Wood.

There, you'll find the Ten Commandment Mountain, the Place of Prayer, the Honor Roll (of churches which have "met certain spiritual qualifications"), the All Nations Cross, a stairway ascending Prayer Mountain, and what's said to be the "world's largest Testament."

Ten Commandment Mountain probably is the most striking. The commandments are written in white letters, each five feet high and four feet wide. They cover an entire mountainside. It's claimed they can be read from a plane 5000 feet above the mountain. Somebody with good eyes might do better than that.

Maybe you don't want to go to Brasstown, Murphy and Fields of the Woods. Alberta and I didn't, either, on this particular trip. So instead of turning west on 64 in Franklin, we turned southeast on it and followed it up the Cullasaja River. The Cullasaja is one of the prettiest, wildest rivers I know. You're usually only a few yards from it as you drive up 64.

Cullasaja Falls is the first waterfall you see. There's no good parking space to pull off and have a look. Wait until you get to Dry Falls. It's "dry" because the water pitches off an overhung cliff. You can walk under the overhang and stay dry as you watch the curtain of water falling in front of you. The next is Bridal Veil Falls. It's on the left side of the highway, on a small tributary to the Cullasaja.

At Bridal Veil, I looked for jewels. Someone in Franklin had told me that the easiest place to find gems in Macon County is among the sand and pebbles beside the highway at this waterfall. Within five minutes, I found a few garnets. They were so tiny I needed my glasses to see them. But that's all right; I wasn't expecting riches.

As you drive up 64 and the Cullasaja, you may see a marker pointing to a community called Gold Mine somewhere across the Cullasaja. Don't resist the temptation to cross the bridge and have a look. It's not quite the postage-stamp paradise it was when Alberta and I explored it more than 15 years ago. The real estate developers have found it but they haven't ruined it. Not yet. We stopped at the home of Nettie McClure, 90 years old. She remembers that her father, Uncle Billy McCoy, who lived to be nearly 104, searched for gold in Gold Mine Branch off and on most of his life. On his best day, he found 30 particles. Nobody ever got rich on gold from Gold Mine Branch. But Gold Mine Valley has been a golden place to live. Most of the hidden little valley is more than 3000 feet in altitude; so it's comfortable on all but the hottest days. The soil is rich and the land slopes gently. Dwellers in the valley can look up at protective mountains called Fishhawk, Little Fishhawk, Buckhorn and Whiterock. But too many dwellers can ruin it, and that may be about to happen.

Next stop, Highlands. Highlands had no humble beginning with scruffy log cabins. More than 100 years ago, town builders Samuel Truman Kelsey and Charles C. Hutchinson drew a line from New York to New Orleans and another from Chicago to Charleston. The lines intersected in North Carolina, atop the Blue Ridge Mountains. There, Kelsey and Hutchinson built Highlands. They built it for rich people. The rich spend only the summers there, when the population is estimated to be between 12,000 and 20,000. The winter population is only 971. An estimated one-half the summer families have assets of $1 million or more. The other half isn't far behind.

A Highlands real estate agent told me a three-bedroom home had just sold for $525,000. Another, "just a shack," he said, went for $60,000. He had a four-bedroom, three-bath home on a "good lot" listed for $935,000. The owners live in these only six months of the year.

For their amusement (and yours, if you stay a few days in Highlands), there is the Highlands Playhouse, featuring actors from New York and Atlanta. It's open from the second week in June to the second week in August. The Highlands Chamber Music Festival has performances each Sunday and Tuesday of July. There's much more to whet your cultural appetite. And if culture is not what you're hungry for, you can go to afternoon auctions. Auctions are big in Highlands. If that doesn't tempt you, you can always get a map from the U. S. Forest Service office in Highlands and go for a hike in nearby Nantahala National Forest. Or you can play golf, tennis or ride a horse.

Highlands has a fine small library, in which you can find the poetry of the Benet brothers, William Rose and Stephen Vincent. They spent summers in Highlands when they were growing up. So did their sister Laura, whose poetry is not so well known. Laura helped raise funds to build the library.

The oldest place of lodging in Highlands is the Highlands Inn, more than 100 years old, and it has just been refurbished. Two other recommended inns are the Old Edwards Inn and King's Inn. Rates are moderate to high. I have not stayed at any of these. (The one we stayed in and liked was Lee's Inn, but it burned.)

The average altitude of Highlands is 4118 feet. Its people used to boast that it was the highest incorporated city in Eastern America. But that was before the ski community of Beech Mountain, five or six counties northeast of Highlands, got itself incorporated. Its altitude is 5506 feet and its people now boast that it is the highest city in Eastern America.

Even though it's now only the second-highest city east of the Mississippi, Highlands is still high enough to stay naturally cool through the worst summers. It's in a region of very high rainfall. So it stays green, beautiful and comfortable.

And rich.

Back to 64. This time we follow it northeast through mountain country that makes you want to stop and look: Great rolled-edge cliffs, bare of vegetation. For miles along 64, you're near the divide separating the Tennessee River drainage from land whose water flows to the Atlantic Ocean by way of the Savannah River. Most of Highlands drains to the Tennessee, but water that falls on a few acres of it goes to the Atlantic.

Down we go past Fairfield-Sapphire Valley, 5800 acres of landscaped resort — golf, fishing, riding, snow skiing. It has its own gem mine.

We cross Toxaway River just above where it glides down the glistening brown stone face of Toxaway Falls.

Brevard. If you're a music lover, you probably know Brevard. The Brevard Music Center presents more than 50 concert events from late June through early August. These range from symphony and chamber music to opera and Broadway musicals. Internationally known guest artists perform on weekends. Talented amateurs work the weekdays. Admission to some events is free; others cost $3.50 to $10.

Alberta and I hurried through Hendersonville on 64, got on I-26 and headed south to Tryon, last populated place before the South Carolina line. Mill Farm Inn, a bed-and-breakfast place in a large old stone house, was our immediate destination.

Mill Farm Inn, Tryon

It was deep dusk by the time we got there, and innkeepers Chip and Penny Kessler had left, leaving in charge some guests who had been there many times before. These were friends and relatives following their long-established custom of having an annual reunion there. They were using seven of the inn's eight bedrooms, and they showed us to the eighth. They also recommended that we go to George's for dinner and marked a map to guide us there. George's serves dinner seven days a week. Good food. Moderate prices. Alcoholic beverages. You get the impression that George's has been in Tryon a long time and is comfortable there.

Tryon is more relaxed than Highlands. While Highlands is for summer-home people, Tryon is mostly for retired people, fairly well-heeled retired people. Besides being an innkeeper, Penny Kessler is in real estate. She says home prices there range from $35,000-$40,000 up to $1.5 million. The latter price is for a plantation-type layout, with main house, guest house, barn, caretaker's cottage and about 100 acres.

Tryon became a resort community in the late 1800s. Rich South Carolinians and some people from other areas came to en-joy the coolness. Some built homes and spent much of their time there. It was a genteel place with much socializing. One custom was the "party call." After a party, each woman guest was supposed to thank the hostess by paying her a visit. This has been replaced by a hand-written note or a chat on the phone.

Though Tryon has a population of fewer than 2000, it supports a Fine Arts Center and at least 17 eating places. It also has the Tryon Riding and Hunt Club, whose fox-hunting members ride to the hounds.

One reason for Tryon's special ambiance seems to be that it is in what Carolinians call a "thermal belt." They tell you it's on the "south slope of the Blue Ridge Thermal Belt." They say this takes the extreme edges off both winter and summer, and "makes autumn and spring very long." Fruit grows well there. Tryon grapes are regionally renowned.

Writers seem to like Tryon. F. Scott Fitzgerald and John Burroughs put in time relaxing and writing there. Poet Sidney Lanier came to nearby Lynn to die.

I learned the next morning that eggs and bacon are not part of the breakfast provided by Mill Farm Inn. But I loaded up on my favorite healthful dry cereal, a banana, toast, jelly and coffee.

Then we headed up the road to Saluda, where we stopped at the M. A. Pace Co. I went in to look for a newspaper. I bought a paper, and the woman who sold it to me asked whether I also wanted tomorrow's paper. I thought she was joking. No, she meant did I want her to put me on her list for the Sunday paper. Good business woman.

I looked around the store. Toys, denim overalls, duct tape, nails, fertilizer, yard goods, candles, washtubs, seed, mattocks, shovels, over-the-counter drugs, magazines, newspapers, gas pumps out front. The list could go on and on. It's one of the best old-fashioned general stores I've seen in years.

We weren't expecting to stay long in Saluda. So I didn't order the Sunday paper. But I'd like to stay there some time. So I asked what was a good place to spend the night. The old Saluda Inn, I was told.

We went to look at it. The outside of the place wasn't very inviting. I was tempted to leave without going inside. But I didn't, and the inside turned out to be clean, neat, attractive. Sandra Miser said she and her husband Jim run it. She showed me all nine rooms, and they all looked good enough to sleep in. It's a bed-and-breakfast place, and she said breakfast is a "complete meal." Prices are in the medium range.

Our next stop up the line was Flat Rock. Flat Rock isn't very large. Only about 1200 people. But it's famous for two things, and they're right across the road from each other: Connemara, the Carl Sandburg home; and the Flat Rock Playhouse. The playhouse is the State Theater of North Carolina and one of the top summer theaters in the country. The season runs from about the middle of June through August. Performances are at 8:30 p.m. Tuesday through Saturday and at 2:30 Wednesdays and Saturdays. The theater sits on part of Flat Rock's flat rock.

The Sandburgs came from Michigan to Flat Rock in 1945, not so much because it was a good place for him to write but because the 240 acres of Connemara were an excellent place for Paula Sandburg's prize-winning herd of milk goats. Some of those goats' descendants still nibble the fields of Connemara, now the Carl Sandburg National Historic Site.

In the 22 years they lived there before his death, he wrote his only novel, "Remembrance Rock;" his autobiography, "Always the Young Strangers;" several volumes of history and a volume of poetry, "Complete Poems," that won a Pulitzer Prize. His wife did pretty well, too. One of her goats produced nine quarts of milk per day, establishing a record that lasted until two or three years ago. She sold great amounts of goats' milk, and she sold goats for high prices.

A tour of the place takes about an hour. Hours are 9 to 5. It's closed on Thanksgiving, Christmas and New Year's Day. The big two-story white house, the rolling fields and the trees continue to make it a great place for goats, writers and visitors.

We went three miles on up the road to Hendersonville. Apples are big in Hendersonville and Henderson County. There is a 10-day Apple Festival that starts in late August and sometimes spills into September. It features such attractions as the Apple Jack Open golf tournament, an apple baking contest, a tour of an apple juice plant, a tour of apple orchards, an apple breakfast, road races, a folk dance jamboree and lots of other apple goodies.

Alberta and I went to Murphy's, on Fourth Avenue, for lunch. Ordered the house specialty, Dublin Grill, which turned out to be hot roast pork and Swiss cheese on French bread. Very good. Came with chicken-noodle soup.

I asked Red Murphy whether he serves alcohol. He said he did and told why. "I came downtown one day during the Apple Festival (two or three years earlier) and couldn't find a place to buy a beer. So I decided to start a little place." Earlier, he had come from Florida to Hendersonville to retire.

Then we drove home and started planning the next North Carolina exploration.

Dean and Susan Peake at Grassy Ridge, Peake land for five generations

The treasures of the North Carolina high country are many, and it isn't surprising that fights flare over a few of them, for they're worth fighting for.

When Alberta and I next went into Carolina, we drove through East Tennessee, to Elizabethton, then up the mountain to Carvers Gap, the Carolina line and the Highlands of Roan. I wanted to walk northeast on the Appalachian Trail to a treasure in dispute.

This is a piece of property on Grassy Ridge owned by heirs of a North Carolina mountain farmer named C. Rex Peake. But Peake ownership of the land goes back much farther — five generations from the present owners. The U. S. Forest Service was trying to buy some of the ridge to add to the Apppalachian Trail corridor.

It's precious land, part of the grassy highlands along the Tennessee-Carolina border that some think is among the most beautiful parts of the earth's surface. Grassy balds — similar to but much larger than Spence Field and Gregory Bald in the Great Smokies — stretch for miles. They rise and fall from ridge to gap and back to ridge like towering ocean waves. They are dotted and fringed with Catawba rhododendron, lovely in June bloom.

Animosity has risen between the Peakes, who say they don't want to sell their land at any price, and the Forest Service, hikers and others who want this beauty preserved as part of the AT corridor.

The two sides have had at least two confrontations. Susan Peake threw rocks at one man she said identified himself as a member of a conservation organization supporting the Forest Service effort to buy the land. She told News-Sentinel outdoors writer Lowell Branham she was glad she did. She said one of her rocks hit the man, whom she accused of using bad language and making an obscene gesture. The other angry meeting occurred when supporters of efforts to buy the land were met at the property line by Peakes and their friends. No rocks were thrown, no blows struck. But a shotgun lay on a rock nearby during the whole angry conversation. The supporters of adding the land to the AT did not cross the property line.

The 54 acres of Peake land the Forest Service wants has been appraised at $119,500, more than $2200 an acre. The Peakes say it's worth far more. They say less desirable land nearby has sold for $7000 an acre.

On this day that Alberta and I stopped at Carvers Gap, some would say the land wasn't worth a nickel an acre. It was a wintry day. Alberta, nursing a sprained ankle, didn't walk with me. Fog choked visibility in the gap, and Alberta said the wind was so fierce it rocked the car while I was gone.

I headed up over Round Bald, the first climb northeast of the gap. On top, the wind staggered me a step or two off trail. Wind-lashed rain sometimes mixed with the fog. Visibility was never more than a few yards. There are no trees up here to bear the white AT markers. So they're painted on rocks every few yards. No danger of getting off trail — as long as snow doesn't cover the markers. I followed the trail from the top of Round Bald down to Engine Gap and then up Jane Bald and then down to the point where the AT swings north and a spur trail forks south down Grassy Ridge, the land in dispute.

There stood a Forest Service marker, warning hikers to stay off the spur trail because it was on private property whose owners do not want "people using their land."

Legally, this dispute probably will be settled soon, perhaps already is. But the anger it has caused will live for years. This is part of the price paid in disputes over precious treasures.

I walked the 1½ miles back to the car, and we headed for Boone, Banner Elk, Blowing Rock and the Blue Ridge Parkway.

We've been going infrequently to a mountain above Banner Elk ever since I bought a dulcimer for Alberta's Christmas present nearly 25 years ago. Ed Presnell, the mountain man who made the dulcimer, lives at the end of the road on that mountain. Back then, Ed was one of only three

or four dulcimer makers in the Southern mountains; there are dozens now. Ed's long beard was black then and the mountains around him were lonely. His beard now is salted with white and the mountains are not so lonely. Nor so beautiful. Rich outlanders have come and bought land and built outrageously large summer homes that break the symmetry of the mountain crests.

This is ski-resort country, Christmas-tree country, land of swift rivers and cool summer winds. Some of its people are getting rich catering to the wishes of visitors who come to partake of its pleasures. Adjoining Avery and Watauga Counties have six of the top ski slopes in the southern mountains.

Boone, with more than 10,000 population, is the biggest city in the area. It has an average elevation of 3333 feet. Blowing Rock is even higher at 4000 feet. And Beech Mountain, with a population of fewer than 300, is the highest city in Eastern America, 5506 feet above sea level.

The high-country counties have dozens of resorts, restaurants, motels and bed-and-breakfast places. On an autumn run on the Blue Ridge Parkway, Alberta and I stayed a night at the Azalea Garden Motel in Blowing Rock. Inside, it's OK, about the same as other motels that charge reasonable prices. But it's outstanding outside. Good landscaping. Flowers everywhere.

On somebody's recommendation, we ate dinner that evening at the New River Inn. To get to it from the highway, you cross a small stream, one of the tributary forks of New River. New River, you may remember, is the second oldest river in the world, second only to the Nile. So that may be one reason I thought the food was good. The chef does great things with herbs. I may never forget a big mushroom stuffed with herbs. Salubrious! New River Inn is on the northern fringe of Blowing Rock, on US 321, just south of the Blue Ridge Parkway.

On our more recent trip to the area, we stayed in Boone, at the High Country Inn. Since we were late arriving, we'd hoped to eat at the inn's Water Wheel Restaurant, which is supposed to be pretty good. For some reason, it was closed that evening. Go to Mike's Inland Seafood, somebody at the inn suggested. I thought it was OK, but not outstanding. Alberta said her fish was dry. She pledged not to eat again at a seafood restaurant with "inland" in its name. We ate breakfast at the Water Wheel. Good.

Christmas trees grow by the millions in the Carolina high country. Avery County alone grows 10 percent of the nation's Christmas trees, a Chamber of Commerce executive said. Ashe, Watauga and Jackson counties also produce lots of Christmas trees. They are mostly Fraser firs. Yes, the tree that balsam woolly aphids have just about killed out of the Great Smokies. Christmas tree growers kill aphids and other pests with heavy chemical spraying.

Boone, of course, is named for Daniel. Daniel never stayed long any place. But he lived in the general area of Boone from 1760 to '69, part of that time in a cabin where Appalachian State University now sits.

Daniel lives again in "Horn in the West," Kermit Hunter's outdoor drama that in 1987 is playing its 36th season in Boone. It deals with events leading to the Battle of Kings Mountain. It opens in late June and continues through the middle of August. Show time is 8:30 nightly, except Mondays. Daniel Boone Native Gardens, featuring hundreds of mountain plants, is on the theater grounds.

West of Boone, nestled beside the Watauga River, is the village of Valle Crucis (means Valley of the Cross, because the route of two streams flowing toward each other form a St. Andrews Cross as they empty into Dutch Creek). A family named Mast apparently has lived there for generations. The Mast General Store is more than 100 years old and is the only general store I know of that's a National Historic Landmark. The Valle Crucis post office is in the store, and there's not a very substantial partition between. There also is a Mast Farm Inn in Valle Crucis, and you may drive on Mast Gap Road. The village also is the home of an Episcopal mission founded in 1842.

The Blue Ridge Parkway runs through this high country. You can get on it from US 321 at Blowing Rock and from US 221 near Linville. Of course, you also can get on it at many other places, including its southwestern starting place, just north of Cherokee, where it intersects US 441. From there, it twists and curves and climbs and dips 470 miles through some of the loveliest country in Eastern America, to Shenandoah National Park at Rockfish Gap, Va. Alberta and I made that run in early fall 1986 and then continued on the Skyline Drive through the national park to Front Royal, Va. Fall, with its splendor of colors, and spring, with its wildflowers, are the best times to do the parkway.

The parkway construction is taking a long time to finish. Crews started working in 1935. They are scheduled to finish this fall (1987). But there have been long lapses between jobs. The unfinished part, a 7½-mile stretch around Grandfather Mountain, is in extremely rugged and fragile terrain. To protect this land, the road builders are putting much of the road above ground on 12 bridges. The most spectacular of these is the 1243-foot Linn Cove Viaduct. Work started on it in 1979 and ended in 1983. Cost was nearly $10 million.

Parkway officials say the viaduct is "the most complicated segmental concrete bridge ever built." It sweeps around boulder-strewn Linn Cove in a graceful S-curve. The structure consists of 153 segments that weigh 50 tons each. Only one of the 153 is straight. Each new segment was cast against the segment preceding it. Computers kept measurements accurate to 0.0001 foot. Each batch of concrete was tinted to match colors of the granite boulders and outcrops nearest it. The viaduct itself was the only route to the construction site. So construction moved from the top down. Crews lowered each pre-cast segment into place against the preceding segment and stuck them together with epoxy glue. This bridge itself is so unusual and graceful that it's expected to rival the parkway's natural attractions.

Among those natural attractions are Linville Falls of the Linville River and Linville Gorge downstream from the falls. It's a National Wilderness Area. But we run

Linn Cove Viaduct, Blue Ridge Parkway

into conflict here. Boastful North Carolinians say Linville Gorge is "the deepest cut in the earth east of the Grand Canyon." But equally boastful Virginians say the gorge cut by Russell Fork through Pine Mountain in Breaks Interstate Park is "the deepest gorge east of the Mississippi." (We will touch on this matter again when we discuss a Georgia gorge.)

Grandfather Mountain is another natural attraction on the Parkway. But this mountain and the nearby Blowing Rock are unlike most natural attractions Tennesseans are accustomed to visiting: These are privately owned; you pay to visit them.

But the last time Alberta and I were on the parkway, we didn't pay to see Grandfather. Officials there may have been surprised that we wanted to see it at all. An ice storm had devastated the area a few days earlier. Portions of the parkway were closed. Pieces of broken trees still littered even the parts of parkway that had been opened. The road up Grandfather was closed. But I persuaded somebody to permit me to drive to the top. After all, the broken power lines had been collected. A few phone cables were still on the road, along with an occasional boulder and tree branch. Grandfather wore fog for whiskers and raging winds combed them.

When we reached the top, an attendant alone there looked at us in astonishment and asked: "Did somebody sell you a ticket to drive up here?"

The view that is great in clear weather was nothing but fog. Still, it was an interesting experience, a little scary. Walking a wind-shook swinging bridge from one crag to another, with fog so thick you can't see either end of the bridge, is a tad different from taking the same walk on a clear, calm day.

Lots of activities go on at Grandfather. One of the biggest is the Highland Games and the Gathering of the Scottish Clans the second weekend of every July. Scots arrive from all over this country and from Scotland. Governors proclaim, senators speak, thousands of knobby knees are exposed under tartan kilts, pipers pipe and athletes compete. They toss the caber, throw the hammer, race and wrestle.

Another annual event is Singing on the Mountain, a gospel sing the fourth Sunday in June. The Masters of Hang Gliding Championship is the third weekend of August. But hang gliders take off from Grandfather on exhibition flights four times daily, weather permitting, May through October.

One of the earlier visitors to reach the summit of Grandfather was French botanist Andre Michaux. It was on Aug. 30, 1794. He wrote in his journal that he had "reached the summit of the highest mountain in North America." He and his companions sang "La Marseillaise" and shouted, "Long live America and the Republic of France, long live liberty."

Of course, he was wrong about Grandfather being the highest mountain in North America. At 5964 feet above sea level, it's a pretty good mountain, but Western North Carolina alone has nearly 50 higher peaks.

The Blowing Rock, naturally, is at Blowing Rock. Its name comes from the fact that northwest winds hitting the gorge below the rock funnel upward. They lift light objects, such as a piece of paper or handkerchief. Sometimes it snows upside down.

There are at least three good reasons for going to Ashe County. Both the north and south forks of New River flow through it and join just before the river flows out of Carolina into Virginia. Beautiful river. For the most part, gentle, good for canoe floats, good for fishing. The second reason is the Ashe County Cheese Co., in West Jefferson. The third is what most people call simply "the frescoes."

Like Grassy Ridge, the frescoes are treasures in dispute.

What's a fresco? It's a piece of art, a painting on a wall. Sand, lime and water are mixed to make plaster which is applied to the wall. Colors — made by grinding dry powder pigments in pure water — are applied to the wet plaster. The colors dry with the plaster, becoming a permanent part of the wall. Michelangelo's paintings on the ceiling of the Sistine Chapel are frescoes. But that method of painting has suffered a long, steady decline since Michelangelo.

However, Ben Long, a North Carolinian, studied fresco painting in Italy and came back to Carolina in the early 1970s. He was determined to paint a fresco, or maybe several frescoes. He offered his free services to one church after another. No takers.

But he finally met Faulton Hodge, an Episcopal priest for three small churches of the Parish of the Holy Communion. The churches are St. Mary's at Beaver Creek, just outside West Jefferson; Holy Trinity at unincorporated Glendale Springs; and St. Matthew, just across the county line in Watauga County. Hodge had not been there long. The churches were in poor condition. Membership and attendance were low. It would have been hard for Ben Long to do anything to make matters worse. Hodge accepted the offer.

Long first painted a very pregnant Mary at St. Mary's. According to one account — which I could not confirm because Long was in Europe and Hodge was never available for an interview — Long said, "I feel great expectations about this place."

And Hodge said, "This church is called St. Mary's. Why don't you paint Mary expecting?"

The result is called "Mary Great with Child."

Long also did a fresco of John the Baptist and then a Crucifixion scene in which a resurrected Christ towers above Jesus on the Cross. These also are at St. Mary's.

Then, at little Holy Trinity Long did what many think is his masterpiece, "The Last Supper." It covers the entire rear wall of the church. Long used local people for his models. A dog wandered in and Long painted it into the scene. So great was the undertaking that Long had to call in other artists to help.

You can walk into St. Mary's and Holy Trinity and see the frescoes, while listening to Hodge's taped account of their creation. There is no charge, but you may leave a contribution. About 250,000 persons a year visit. Many leave contributions that have helped the churches.

After Alberta and I admired the frescoes at both churches, I picked up the local West Jefferson paper, the Skyland Post, at our motel that evening. The top story on page one was under the headline, "Move of

Fresco Churches Put on Hold." On the back page was a full-page ad bought by "Friends to Preserve the Frescoes." It included statements from persons opposed to the move. Among those quoted were Ben Long, the artist; Pietro Annigoni, Florence, Italy, a man under whom Long studied; and three other art experts.

All opposed a proposal of the Episcopal Church to combine the three small churches into one new church at a new location. The proposal called for the frescoes to be moved to the new church.

Long and the art experts cited the risk of ruining the frescoes in such a move. Long wrote:

"It should be thought of as thin ice on still water — the churches where they are now are still water. To move them . . . would create waves in the still waters. Thin ice would shatter. The risk is immense. If destroyed, they are lost forever. If there was even only 1 percent chance of damage (I think it's more like 99 percent), isn't that too much?"

David Hoyle, a member of the church building and grounds committee, that night explained the reasons the church wants to move the three congregations and the frescoes to one new building. He said the great number of visitors to Holy Trinity had overtaxed the septic-tank sewage system at Glendale Springs. He said services are held only about twice a year at St. Matthew's and only spring to fall at Holy Trinity. Services could be held every Sunday at a new church at a central location, he said. He also said Hodge wants to retire in four or five years, and church officials fear it will be difficult to persuade another minister to come into the existing situation.

But he said the congregation is "split down the middle" over the proposal.

I wasn't able to talk with Hodge then. When I tried to phone him some months later, I was told he was on a year's medical leave. Another person was conducting services.

Ed Wheeler, general manager of the Skyland Post and a member of the parish, said that, "for the most part," Ashe Countians who are not members of the church have tried to stay out of the dispute. But he said there is concern in the community over any risk to the frescoes. He said Friends to Preserve the Frescoes quickly got 1500 signatures on a petition opposing the move. And he said the county commission adopted a resolution expressing hope that the church would reconsider the proposal.

That may be happening. The church backed off the proposal for a few months, pending further technical studies. Wheeler said, "There is hope for healing in the church."

There's no dispute over the Ashe County Cheese Co. It's a pleasant place and the only commercial cheese manfacturer in North Carolina. You can buy its products (Monterey jack, colby and sharp cheddar) on the spot. Among the cheeses Alberta and I bought was a bag of day-old cheese, a bit rubbery but good for nibbling. You can tour the plant with a guide and learn that it uses 300,000 gallons of milk per day and that the milk comes from North Carolina, South Carolina, Virginia and Tennessee. From that milk comes 20,000 pounds of cheese per day six days a week, plus lots of whey and butterfat. Farmers use the whey for feed and fertilizer. The butterfat is sent to another plant and made into butter.

From West Jefferson, we turned back in the general direction of home, but we had stops to make on the way. First stop is Penland. Take State 226 out of Spruce Pine and look for Penland signs. There are two Penlands. One is the little village beside the Toe River. The other Penland is Penland School, high on a ridge above the river.

Here, we cross Morgan tracks again. Remember Rufus Morgan, the Episcopal priest who built tiny St. John's, Cartoogechaye and who hiked to Mt. Le Conte on his 92nd birthday? Sometime before 1920, under auspices of the church, he started the Appalachian School on this ridge above Penland. It was for mountain youngsters who otherwise would have little chance of getting started on anything resembling a good education. But Rufus soon had to leave the school. His sister Lucy came to take his place in 1920.

He wrote to her about an old woman in the community who still did weaving, a dy-ing craft in the Carolina hills but one which both Morgans wanted to revive. Within a year or two, a girl graduate of the school received a scholarship to Berea College in Kentucky. Her parents wouldn't let her go, though, unless some adult would go with her and stay until she became settled.

Lucy went with her.

She had been wanting to go all along, for Berea was one place where she herself could learn hand-weaving. She learned and when she left Berea, she shipped three looms back to Penland. Then she started teaching adult women in the community to weave. One of her looms went into the home of a responsible mountain woman. She soon ordered more looms. Then husbands began making looms for their wives. Soon, Lucy arranged to sell the women's woven articles at resorts in the area. Then they sold at the North Carolina State Fair in Raleigh in 1924. They built a log Weaving Cabin at the school.

The Weaving Cabin is still there. And 44 other buildings have joined it on a campus of 400 acres. Penland people claim theirs is the largest craft school in the nation. As far as I know, nobody disputes them.

In her book, "Gift from the Hills," Lucy recalls a 1928 meeting in Knoxville, where Mrs. John C. Campbell of the John C. Campbell Folk School at Brasstown suggested scheduling a meeting to discuss forming a craft guild. Lucy invited those interested to meet at Penland. They accepted. They met. They established the Southern Highlands Handicraft Guild. No other organization has done so much to help crafts and craftspeople in the Southern mountains. Now, when potters, weavers, woodworkers, quilters, basket makers, blacksmiths and makers of musical instruments number in the thousands, it's hard to realize they had dwindled to a precious few in the 1930s.

Guild membership is difficult to attain. The standards committee sets high standards of design and craftsmanship. Only an estimated 15 to 20 percent of those who try at a given time make the grade. But many try repeatedly and finally make it. Blair White, now assistant director of the guild, said he tried four times before he gained membership as a jeweler. The guild now has an estimated 650 members. Most are from Western North Carolina and East Tennessee, but seven other Southern mountain states, from West Virginia to Alabama and Georgia, are represented.

Guild members have little worry about marketing their products. The guild has four marketing outlets of its own: Allanstand, on the Blue Ridge Parkway near Asheville; Parkway Craft Center, between Boone and Blowing Rock; Guild Crafts, in Asheville; and Guild Gallery, Bristol. Guild members are not required to sell through the guild and some don't. Being able to indicate guild membership on a label or letterhead is marketing aid enough.

Most of those who come to Penland don't expect to make a living in crafts. A physician friend of mine went there on vacation two or three years ago and studied sculpturing. He's proud of the likeness he did of himself. Many others take one-week or two-week courses.

Penland has drawn students from every state and from more than 50 foreign nations. Though it has never been able to afford high salaries for faculty, Penland has been able to get some of the world's best craft teachers because of the prestige and pleasure of working there.

Lucy retired as director of Penland when she was in her 70s. She moved to a home at Webster, near her nephew, Dr. Ralph S. Morgan (the physician associated with Riverwood Shops at Dillsboro). Like her brother Rufus, she lived a long time. She died in 1981 at the age of 92. The nephew is on the Penland Advisory Board.

From Penland, Alberta and I moved on to Yancey County. Yancey County has fish to catch in the North Toe and Cane rivers. It has Burnsville as its county seat, and Burnsville has the Nu-Wray Inn. In front of the inn is the town square, featuring the statue of Otway Burns, the man who introduced the legislation establishing the county.

And Burnsville has a story about the terrible fists of Jack Dempsey's grandfather. Not everyone can remember the grandfather's name. But one oldtimer is pretty sure he was Jack Johnson. He was Dempsey's maternal grandfather, and he was the town blacksmith. One day, he got mad at some people and gave such a terrible beating to six of them that the county was moved to declare his fists to be lethal weapons, illegal to use.

The Nu-Wray Inn has been providing food and lodging since 1833. It has been in the same family since 1867. The Wray family owns it now, and the manager is Betty Wray Souders, great-granddaughter of Garrett Ray, who bought it in 1867. One of Garrett Ray's daughters married a Wray. So the ownership bloodlines have been mingled Ray-Wray ever since and the pronunciation never changed.

Nu-Wray Inn is famous for the great platters of fried chicken and country ham on its long tables. Bowls filled with appropriate vegetables, plus desserts, are there, too.

But it also has 36 rooms. Among the people who have slept in them were writer Thomas Wolfe and entertainer Elvis Presley. Elvis may have played the 152-year-old piano on the second floor. But nobody plays it now; it won't hold tune. This year, for the first time, the inn is offering a bed-and-breakfast package. Rates are low to moderate. It's on the National Register of Historic Places.

One more stop, Mars Hill. I wanted to see the gift Pigeon Forge potter Doug Ferguson gave to his school, Mars Hill College. It's called the Douglas Ferguson Fountain. And it's beautiful. Doug designed it, sculpted it and presented it in 1982. It's 20 feet and 10 inches long, eight feet high and one foot thick. The north and south sides are made of 280 ceramic tiles, each bearing a design of an oldtime Southern Appalachian quilt. All told, Doug used 84 individual quilting designs in the tiles.

Very impressive.

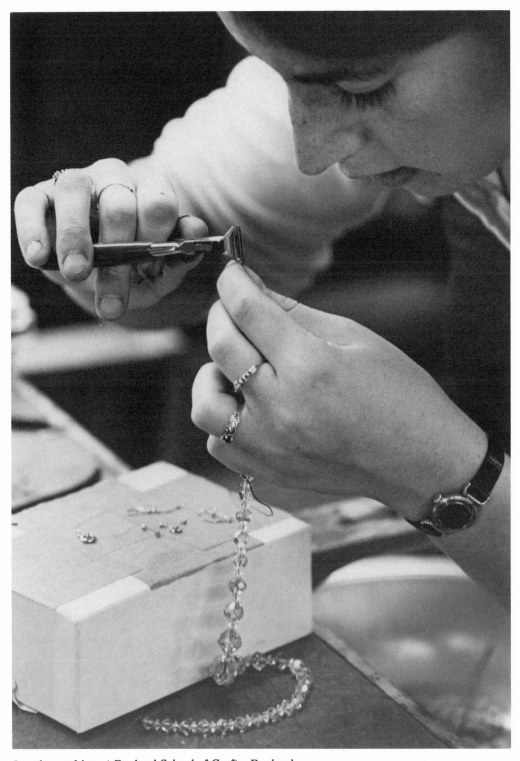

Jewelry making at Penland School of Crafts, Penland

North Carolina Attractions*

Blue Ridge Mountain Frescoes Ashe County, N.C. 28629 919-982-3076	For the present, Ben Long's beautiful frescoes decorate the walls of St. Mary's Church in West Jefferson and Holy Trinity in Glendale Springs. Open year round. No admission. For group information, please call office.
Southern Highlands Folk Art Ctr. Asheville, N.C. 28815 704-298-7928	Home of the Southern Highland Handicraft Guild. Sales, demonstrations, exhibits, conferences and library. Open year round. Admission.
Thomas Wolfe's Home Asheville, N.C. 28807 704-253-8304	The setting for Wolfe's novel, "Look Homeward, Angel," and a National Historic Landmark containing some of his furnishings and personal possessions. Open April-March. Admission.
Blue Ridge Hearthside Crafts Ctr. Banner Elk, N.C. 28604 704-963-7077	Folk and contemporary crafts from 400 members. Open year round, demonstrations on weekends. Admission charged for each of the three craft festivals during the year.
Ski Hawksnest Banner Elk, N.C. 28604 704-963-6563	Six slopes, two lifts open daily with night skiing. Ski rental.
Sugar Mountain Banner Elk, N.C. 28604 704-898-4521	Eighteen slopes, five lifts and three surface lifts, night skiing, nursery. Open Thanksgiving-February. Ski rental and lift tickets.
Ski Beech Beech Mountain, N.C. 28604 704-387-2011	Highest skiing east of the Rockies, 12 trails, eight lifts. Night skiing, ice rink, nursery for children. Open Thanksgiving-mid-March. Admission.
Biltmore Estate Biltmore, N.C. 28809 704-274-1776	This 255-room mansion was built by George Vanderilt in 1895 and contains art and antique furnishings from around the world. The estate also includes formal gardens, winery and restaurants. A National Historic Landmark. Open year round. Admission.
Appalachian Ski Mountain Blowing Rock, N.C. 28605 704-295-7828	Eight slopes, three lifts, including the state's first quad lift, which carries four skiers at a time. Open every day Thanksgiving-mid-March. Closed Dec. 24 and 25.
The Blowing Rock Blowing Rock, N.C. 28605 704-295-7111	Air flows upward from the Blowing Rock, making this a unique spot where "snow falls upside down." A snack bar, gift shop and observation tower also are at the site. Open April-October. Admission.
Blowing Rock Stables Blowing Rock, N.C. 28605 704-295-7847	Ride over 27 miles of trails on Cone Manor Estate. Rent by the hour. Barn open all year, horse rental April-November.
Cone Craft Center Blowing Rock, N.C. 28605 704-295-3782	High quality craft demonstrations and information center. Hiking and horse trails. Open May-October. Horse rental fee.

* We suggest you call and verify the information given in these listings when planning a trip or making reservations. See introduction to the tables on page 45 for further explanation.

Goodwin Guild Weavers
Blowing Rock, N.C. 28605
704-295-3577

Observe bedspreads and tablecloths being made on looms that have been in operation since before the Civil War. Slide show. Open year round. Free.

Mystery Hill
Blowing Rock, N.C. 28605
704-264-2792

Gravity is defied as water runs uphill and people walk on walls. Also browse the Lifestyles Museum, in which old customs and ways are preserved. Open year round. Admission.

Hound Ears Club
Blowing Rock, N.C. 28605
704-963-4321

Two slopes, two lifts. Open for skiing Thanksgiving-March 1. Lodge open all year. Tickets for lifts and ski rental.

Horn in the West
Boone, N.C. 28607
704-264-2120, 264-9089

Outdoor drama about the American Revolution in the Southern Appalachians. Late June-mid-August. Admission.

Ski French-Swiss
Boone, N.C. 28607
704-295-9311

Complete services for ski groups, including lodging and gear. Open Thanksgiving weekend-March 15. Fee.

Tweetsie Railroad
Boone, N.C. 28605
704-264-9061

This theme park features a train ride into American history, as well as rides, shops, a petting zoo, panning for gold and musical variety entertainment. Open May-October. Admission.

John C. Campbell Folk School
Brasstown, N.C. 28906
704-837-2775 or 837-7329

The school was founded in 1925 and offers weekend and week-long classes in a variety of crafts, music and dance. Open year round. Call for class schedule.

Kelischek Workshop for Historical Instruments
Brasstown, N.C. 28902
704-837-5833

Visit the showroom and see handmade dulcimers, lutes, psalteries, hurdy-gurdies and harps. Open year round.

Brevard Music Center
Brevard, N.C. 28712
704-884-2011

Sponsors more than 50 concerts late June-mid-August. Guest artists perform during weekend festivals. Admission. Call for schedule, ticket information.

Museum of the Cherokee Indian
Cherokee, N.C. 28719
704-497-3481

Prehistoric artifacts on display and multimedia exhibits tell the history of the Cherokee. Open year round. Admission.

Oconaluftee Indian Village
Cherokee, N.C.28719
704-497-9195

A re-created Indian village of the 1750s. Live demonstrations and guided tours of Cherokee crafts and skills. Open May 15-end of October. Admission.

Qualla Arts & Crafts Mutual Inc.
Cherokee, N.C. 28719
704-497-3103

Indian-owned and operated arts and crafts cooperative. Open year round. Free.

Unto These Hills
Cherokee, N.C. 28719
704-497-2111

An outdoor drama portraying the history of the Eastern Band of Cherokee Indians, including the infamous "Trail of Tears." Open mid-June-late-August. Admission.

Chimney Rock
Chimney Rock, N.C. 28720
704-625-9611

See 75 miles away from the chimney-shaped outcropping of rock. A 26-story elevator takes visitors to the top of the rock, gift and snack shops. Also features Hickory Nut Falls, one of the highest falls in eastern America. Open mid March-October. Admission.

Connemara Flat Rock, N.C. 28731 704-693-4178	Carl Sandburg's farm and a National Historical Site. Tours of the home available, as well as picnic grounds, hiking trails and lake. Open year round. Home tour costs $1 for those between the ages of 13 and 62 and is free for others.
Flat Rock Playhouse Flat Rock, N.C. 28731 704-693-0731	The State Theater of North Carolina and one of the top 10 summer theaters in the U.S. Call for schedules.
Franklin Gem and Mineral Society Franklin, N.C. 28734 704-369-7831	Housed in the 150-year-old county jail, the society offers exhibits of gems and minerals from North Carolina and around the world, as well as fossils and Indian artifacts. Open May-October. Free.
Grandfather Mountain Linville, N.C. 28646 704-733-4337	Spectacular views of the Blue Ridge Mountains, natural habitats for native bears, cougars, eagles and deer, hang gliding exhibitions, hiking, picnicking, museum and gift shop. Open April-November, plus some winter weekends. Admission.
Old Hampton Store Linville, N.C. 28646 704-733-5213	Historic country store circa 1921 includes working grist mill. Open year round. Free.
Linville Caverns Marion, N.C. 28752 704-765-4171	Guides escort visitors along lighted paths to the innermost caverns. Year round. Admission.
Penland School Penland, N.C. 28765 704-765-2359	The nation's largest crafts school offers instruction on crafts ranging from weaving to metal work, pottery and sculpture. Open March to December. Tuition and room-and-board.
North Carolina Mineral Museum Spruce Pine, N.C. 28777 704-765-2761	Exhibits show the history of mining of minerals and gems. Demonstrations. Open year round. Free.
Mast General Store Valle Crucis, N.C. 28691 704-963-6511	Established 1883 and listed in the National Register of Historic Places. Authentic and nostalgic emporium. Open year round. Free.
Vance Birthplace Weaversville, N.C. 28787 704-645-6706	Reconstruction of the 1795 log house in which Civil War Governor Zebulon Baird Vance was born. Pioneer exhibits. Open year round. Free.
Ashe County Cheese Co. West Jefferson, N.C. 28694 919-246-2501	See how cheese is made at this 57-year-old plant, and sample their products in the cheese shop. Open year round. No admission.

North Carolina Lodging Places

	Dates open	Rooms	Cabins	Private bath	Breakfast offered (* Included in room charge)	Lunch offered	Dinner offered	Pool	Tennis court	Children welcome	Pets welcome	Rates: L - Low, less than $30 / M - Moderate, $31-$60 / H - High, $61 and up
Albemarle Inn Asheville, N.C. 28802 704-255-0027	Year round	✓		✓	✓*	✓	✓	✓		✓		M-H
Cedar Crest Victorian Inn Asheville, N.C. 28802 704-252-1389	Year round	✓		✓	✓*							M-H
Flint Street Inns Asheville, N.C. 28801 704-253-6723	Year round	✓		✓	✓*							M
Grove Park Inn & Country Club Asheville, N.C. 28802 704-252-2711	Year round	✓		✓	✓	✓	✓	✓	✓	✓		H
Pine Cottages Asheville, N.C. 28802 704-645-9661	Year round	✓	✓	✓						✓		M
Ray House B&B Asheville, N.C. 28801 704-252-0106	Year round	✓			✓*					✓		L-M
Reed House B&B Asheville, N.C. 28803 704-274-1604	May - October	✓			✓*					✓		M
Old Reynolds Mansion Asheville, N.C. 28804 704-254-0496	April - November	✓		✓	✓*							M
Smoky Mtns. Inn on the Plaza Asheville, N.C. 28801 704-252-8211	Year round	✓		✓	✓	✓	✓	✓		✓		M
Beech Mountain Chalet Rentals Beech Mountain, N.C. 28604 704-387-4231	Year round		✓	✓						✓		H
Azalea Garden Motel Blowing Rock, N.C. 60473 704-295-3272	Year round	✓	✓	✓						✓		M
Blowing Rock Inn Blowing Rock, N.C. 28605 704-295-7921	April - October	✓	✓	✓				✓				M
Gideon Ridge Inn Blowing Rock, N.C. 28605 704-295-3644	Year round	✓		✓	✓*							H
Green Park Inn Blowing Rock, N.C. 28605 704-295-3141	May - October	✓		✓	✓	✓	✓	✓		✓		H

	Dates open	Rooms	Cabins	Private bath	Breakfast offered	*Included in room charge	Lunch offered	Dinner offered	Pool	Tennis court	Children welcome	Pets welcome	Rates
Hillwinds Inn Blowing Rock, N.C. 28605 704-295-7660	April - Nov. 15	√	√	√							√		M
Maple Lodge Blowing Rock, N.C. 28605 704-295-3331	April - October		√	√							√		M
New River Inn Motel & Rest. Blowing Rock, N.C. 28605 704-295-3056	April - October	√		√	√	√	√				√		M
Ragged Garden **Inn & Restaurant** Blowing Rock, N.C. 28605 704-295-9703	May - October	√		√	√*	√	√						M-H
Sunshine Inn Blowing Rock, N.C. 28605 704-295-3487	Mid-May - October	√	√	√	√*		√				√		M-H
High Country Inn Boone, N.C. 28607 704-264-1000	Year round	√		√	√		√	√			√		M
The Inn at Brevard Brevard, N.C. 28712 704-884-2105	March - December	√		√	√*	√	√				√		M
The Pines Country Inn Brevard, N.C. 28768 704-877-3131	May - October	√	√	√	√*		√				√		H
Fryemont Inn Bryson City, N.C. 28713 704-488-2159	Mid-April - October	√		√	√*		√	√	√	√			H
Hemlock Inn Bryson City, N.C. 28713 704-488-2885	April 29 - October	√	√	√	√*		√				√		H
Nantahala Village Bryson City, N.C. 28713 704-488-2826	April - December	√	√	√	√	√	√	√	√	√			M-H
Randolph House Bryson City, N.C. 28713 704-488-3472	April - November	√			√*		√				√		M-H
Nu-Wray Inn Burnsville, N.C. 28714 704-682-2329	Year round	√		√	√*		√				√		M
High Hampton Inn Cashiers, N.C. 28717 704-743-2411	April - October	√	√	√	√*	√	√				√		M

Rates: L - Low, less than $30   M - Moderate, $31-$60   H - High, $61 and up

	Dates open	Rooms	Cabins	Private bath	Breakfast offered * Included in room charge	Lunch offered	Dinner offered	Pool	Tennis court	Children welcome	Pets welcome	Rates: L - Low, less than $30 M - Moderate, $31-$60 H - High, $61 and up
Boundary Tree Motor Lodge Cherokee, N.C. 28719 704-497-2165	Year round	√	√	√				√	√	√		M
Jarrett House Dillsboro, N.C. 28725 704-586-9964	April - October	√		√	√	√	√					M
Squire Watkins Inn Dillsboro, N.C. 28725 704-586-5244	Year round	√	√	√	√*							M-H
Fontana Village Resort Fontana Dam, N.C. 28733 704-498-2211	Late March - Oct.	√	√	√	√	√	√	√	√	√		M
Buttonwood Inn Franklin, N.C. 28734 704-369-8985	April - October	√		√	√*							M
The Franklin Terrace Franklin, N.C. 28734 704-524-7907	May - October	√	√	√	√*							M
Glendale Springs Inn Glendale Springs, N.C. 28629 919-982-2102 or 982-2103	May - October	√			√*	√	√				√	H
Lee's Lodge & Mtn. House Rest. Glendale Springs, N.C. 28629 919-982-3286	April - October	√		√	√	√	√				√	M
Mountain View Lodge & Cabins Glendale Springs, N.C. 28629 919-982-2233	Year round	√	√	√	√*	√	√				√	M
Cabin Fever Hendersonville, N.C. 28739 704-692-9500, 749-9652	May - October		√	√								M
Claddagh Inn & Guest House Hendersonville, N.C. 28732 704-693-9368	Year round	√		√	√*			√			√	M
Echo Mountain Inn Hendersonville, N.C. 28739 704-369-8985	April - December	√	√	√	√	√	√	√			√	M
Cricket's Corner Highlands, N.C. 28741 704-526-4733	Year round	√	√	√	√*						√	M
Colonial Pines Inn Highlands, N.C. 28741 704-526-2060	April - December	√	√	√	√*						√	M

	Dates open	Rooms	Cabins	Private bath	Breakfast offered	* Included in room charge	Lunch offered	Dinner offered	Pool	Tennis court	Children welcome	Pets welcome	Rates: L - Low, less than $30 M - Moderate, $31-$60 H - High, $61 and up
Highlands Inn Highlands, N.C. 28741 704-526-9380	April-December	√		√	√*		√	√			√		H
King's Inn Highlands, N.C.28741 704-526-2161	April 15 - October	√	√	√	√		√	√			√		M
Old Edwards Inn Highlands, N.C. 28741 704-526-5036	April - November	√		√	√*		√	√					M-H
Phelps House B&B Highlands, N.C. 28741 704-526-2590	Year round	√			√*			√			√		M
Skyline Lodge Highlands, N.C. 28741 704-526-2121	May - October	√		√					√		√		M-H
Lake Lure Inn Lake Lure, N.C. 28746 704-625-2525	Year round	√		√	√			√	√		√		M-H
Greystone Inn Lake Toxaway, N.C. 28747 704-966-4700	May - October	√	√	√	√*			√	√		√		H
Eseeola Lodge Linville, N.C. 704-733-4311	Mid-May-Mid-Sept	√		√	√*			√	√	√	√		H
Twinbrook Resort Maggie Valley, N.C. 28751 704-926-1388	Year round		√	√					√		√		H
Baird House B&B Inn Mars Hill, N.C. 28754 704-689-5722	January - Nov.	√			√*						√		M
Blue Boar Lodge Robbinsville, N.C. 28771 704-479-8126	April - January	√		√	√*			√			√		H
Snowbird Mountain Lodge Robbinsville, N.C. 28771 704-479-3433	May - October	√		√	√*		√	√					H
The Orchard Inn Saluda, N.C. 28773 704-749-5471	Year round	√		√	√*			√					H
L'Auberge of Tryon Tryon, N.C. 28782 704-859-6992	March - December	√		√	√*						√		M

	Dates open	Rooms	Cabins	Private bath	Breakfast offered *Included in room charge	Lunch offered	Dinner offered	Pool	Tennis court	Children welcome	Pets welcome	Rates: L – Low, less than $30 / M – Moderate, $31-$60 / H – High, $61 and up
Melrose Inn Tryon, N.C. 28782 704-859-9419	Year round	√		√	√*	√	√			√		M
Mill Farm Inn Tryon, N.C. 28782 704-859-6992 or 859-6242	March - December	√		√	√*					√		M
Pine Crest Inn Tryon, N.C. 28782 704-859-9135	Year round	√	√	√	√	√	√			√		M
Mast Farm Inn Valle Crucis, N.C. 28691 704-963-5857	Jan.-Mar., May-Oct.	√		√	√*		√			√		H
The Taylor House B&B Valle Crucis, N.C. 28691 704-963-4271	Mid-April - Nov.	√		√	√*							H
Pisgah Inn Waynesville, N.C. 28786 704-235-8228	April-October	√		√	√	√	√			√		M
The Swag Waynesville, N.C. 28786 704-926-0430, 926-9978	May-October	√		√	√*	√	√			√		M-H

North Carolina Parks

	Lodge	Campsites	Dumping station	Hook-ups	Cabins	Pool	Picnicking	Boating: R-Public ramp, M-Marina, L-Horsepower limits	Boats to rent: P-paddleboat, C-canoe, F-fishing boat	Hiking trails	Fishing	Water skiing	Primitive camping	Supply store	Museum	Leashed pets welcome
Nantahala National Forest Asheville, N.C. 28802 704-257-4200		365	√				√	R		√	√	√	√			√
Mount Mitchell State Park Burnsville, N.C. 28714 704-675-4611		9					√				√				√	√
Chimney Rock Park Chimney Rock, N.C. 28720 704-625-9611							√				√					√
Pisgah National Forest Pisgah Forest, N.C. 28768 704-877-3265		301	√				√			√	√		√		√	√

North Carolina
Chambers of Commerce

Asheville
151 Haywood St.
P.O. Box 1011
Asheville, N.C. 28802
704-258-3858

Blowing Rock
Main St.
P.O. Box 406
Blowing Rock, N.C. 28605
704-295-7851

Boone
701 Blowing Rock Road
Boone, N.C. 28607
704-264-2225

Brevard
35 W. Main St.
P.O. Box 589
Brevard, N.C. 28712
704-883-3700

Bryson City
Everett St.
P.O. Box 509
Bryson City, N.C. 28713
704-488-6381

Burnsville
2 Town Square Rm. 3
Burnsville, N.C. 28714
704-682-7413

Cherokee
P.O. Box 465
Cherokee, N.C. 28719
704-497-9195

Franklin
180 Porter St.
Franklin, N.C. 28734
704-524-3161

Hickory
470 Hwy. 64-70 S.W.
P.O. Box 1828
Hickory, N.C. 28603
704-328-6111

Maggie Valley
Stallard Mall
P.O. Box 87
Maggie Valley, N.C. 28751
704-926-1686

Robbinsville
129 By-Pass
P.O. Box 1206
Robbinsville, N.C. 28771
704-479-3790

Spruce Pine
Rt. 1
P.O. Box 796
Spruce Pine, N.C. 2877
704-765-9483

Sylva
18 N. Central St.
Sylva, N.C. 28779
704-586-2155

Tryon
401 N. Trade St.
Tryon, N.C. 28782
704-859-6236

Georgia

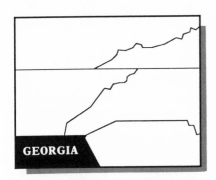

GEORGIA

Several routes lead from East Tennessee into the North Georgia mountains. I like to go the Little Tennessee River route: US 129 from Knoxville, past Maryville, along Tellico, Chilhowee and Calderwood Lakes, then North Carolina 28 along Cheoah and Fontana Lakes and then up the lovely river to Franklin, then US 441 along the river into North Georgia at Dillard.

If you want to follow the river to its beginning, you can continue south on 441 to a right turn onto Wolf Fork Road. Follow that road into Wolf Fork Valley and you may be able to see the point where Billy's Creek and Keener Creek join to form the Little T — a very little Little T at that point.

Adam Keener, who owned a dairy farm in Wolf Fork Valley, one morning a long time ago told Alberta and me how the valley got its name: Wolves killed lots of livestock in the valley during pioneer days. Some smart farmer found a leaning forked tree. He figured out how to position a bait just high enough above the fork. A wolf would jump high for the bait, and when he came down, his head would catch in the fork of the tree.

When Adam told us that story in 1969 or '70, Wolf Fork Valley was his Eden. Or so it seemed to us. It was an idyllic place, a Cades Cove with people. But not many people. The bloom is off it now; too many people, too many homes.

We've never stayed a night in Dillard that we didn't stay at the Dillard House. Dillards own large chunks of Rabun County. They tell the story that, more than 200 years ago, brothers John and James Dillard bought from the Indians all the land between the two mountain crests that flank this wide valley. They paid the Indians $3, a jug of apple brandy and a muzzle-loading rifle.

After the family had been there about 100 years, one of the Dillards decided to provide food and lodging for travelers: Dillard House. Jim Dillard, one of the third generation of Dillard innkeepers, does the job now. Members of the fourth generation are helping. Jim is a large genial man, obviously one of his own best customers.

Most of the food served in the dining room is grown on Dillard land. At an adjoining gift shop, you can buy Dillard apple butter, various jellies and other good things, including country hams, grown on Dillard land. One of the things that first impressed us years ago was that the corn-on-the-cob we ate for dinner was only about 15 minutes off the stalk. Little of its sweetness had fled.

You eat family style at Dillard House. To me, this means you're seated at a table with only those who are members of your family or party. You serve yourself from bowls and platters of food the waitress places on the table. Some places do it a little differently and call it family style, but I call it boarding house style: Sometimes, especially if the dining room is crowded, you may be seated at a table with people you never saw before.

Among the foods on our table during our most recent stop were country steak, fried chicken breast, country ham, marinated raw vegetables, green beans, creamed corn, yams, rice (with gravy optional), apple butter, honey and cherry cobbler. For breakfast: apple juice, coffee, bacon, sausage, country ham, redeye gravy, cream gravy, scrambled eggs and cooked apples.

Dining room prices and room rates are moderate. Rooms these days are in motel-like buildings only one story high. You look out at horses grazing on wide fields that blend into the mountains. You can rent one of the horses. Or you can play for free on the tennis courts and swim in the pool. Or you can go into nearby lands of Chattahoochee National Forest and hike and fish. War Woman and Coleman River wildlife management areas are nearby.

It was here in Rabun County, in 1966, that English teacher Eliot Wigginton decided to try a different approach to teaching. He put his ninth- and tenth-grade students into the writing and publishing business with a magazine called Foxfire. They interviewed their grandparents and other elderly persons in the community to learn how they long ago made apple butter and soap, how they built sleds and log houses and rail fences and lots of other things. Foxfire magazine evolved into Foxfire books. More than 7 million have been sold in one of the most successful publishing ventures of this century.

While some rain that falls on Rabun County drains down the Little T and eventually reaches the Gulf of Mexico, other Rabun rain flows the other direction by way of the Chattooga and Tallulah rivers, which are parts of the Savannah River system that flows into the Atlantic. At Rabun Gap, the divide between these drainages is so gentle that you are unaware you are crossing it. US 441 crosses the gap on what seems to be level ground. It was on the Chattooga that the movie "Deliverance" was filmed. The stream has been designated a Wild and Scenic River.

But on this trip, I was more interested in the Tallulah. US 441 crosses it in the town of Tallulah Falls. The bridge is just below where Tallulah Falls used to be and at the point where Tallulah Gorge begins. You can't see the waterfall any more because it's covered by a lake impounded by the Georgia Power Co.

If you've read the Virginia section of

this book, you know that Virginians and Kentuckians claim the gorge of the Russell Fork River in their Breaks Interstate Park is "the deepest gorge east of the Mississippi." And if you've read the North Carolina sections, you know that the Tar Heels boast that Linville Gorge is "the deepest cut in the earth east of the Grand Canyon." So I wanted to learn what Georgians say about their Tallulah Gorge.

You're right. They claim it is "spectacular and is the deepest east of the Mississippi River."

The quotes above are from literature about the three gorges. I don't know why this matter hasn't been settled years ago. For about 10 minutes, I had aspirations of taking on the job myself. Then I decided there are more ways to lose than win in this kind of thing.

In their literature, the Breaks people say the Russell Fork "has carved the largest canyon east of the Mississippi. Its craggy, untouched beauty reaches more than five miles long and 1600 feet deep."

I don't think the 1600 feet is right; I think that's the altitude above sea level for the top of the gorge at one particular point. Park Supt. James L. Childress said the gorge is about 1000 feet deep. In a small book, "Scenic Geology of Pine Mountain in Kentucky," published by the University of Kentucky, author Preston McGrain says, "Breaks Interstate Park . . . is situated on top of Pine Mountain, 1000 feet above Russell Fork."

I don't know for sure how deep the Russell Fork has cut that gorge. But I do know the horseshoe bend of the gorge is one of the most awesome and beautiful sights of the Southern Appalachians. The river itself is fearsome inside the gorge. Only expert canoeists attempt to run it, and they use decked boats, according to the canoeists' book, "Appalachian Whitewater." At a place called El Horrendo there are drops of 10 and 15 feet only a few feet apart. In difficulty for boaters, the river through the gorge is rated Class IV through Class VI. Class VI is the highest on the scale.

Nowhere did I find North Carolinians saying exactly how deep Linville Gorge is. So I asked officials of Blue Ridge Parkway for figures. Jim Ryan, Parkway management assistant, answered in part:

"The U. S. Forest Service, which manages the area, tells me the highest point on the rim is approximately 3400 feet above sea level and that the lowest point on the Linville River in the gorge is some 1400 feet. However, the gorge is 12 miles in length, and everyone agrees that the highest point is not directly above the lowest point. But no one seems to know precisely what the depth is on any single vertical line.

"The USFS does say the river falls about 2000 feet in those 12 miles," Jim continued. "I pointed out to them that if the lowest point on the river within the gorge is 2000 feet, and if the river falls 2000 feet within the gorge, that means it enters the gorge at an altitude of 4000 feet, which is 600 feet above the highest point of the rim. Since no flooding has been reported in that area, this bit of mathematics caused some consternation, but produced no additional information . . ."

Georgia people will tell you right quickly how deep is their Tallulah Gorge, but they don't all use the same figures. First, though, you need to know where to look. As you go south, the first place you can look is at Tallulah Gorge Park, a small commercial park just south of the bridge. It wasn't open when we stopped. But someone told me not to fret, that a better look, without cost, was only a mile down the road.

People there love the gorge. One man, Terry Green, said he had strewn the ashes of his father in the gorge only a few weeks earlier.

One person told me the gorge is 1125 feet deep. But at Tallulah Point, the place where you look for free, a sign says it's 1200 feet deep. Another marker says Karl Wallenda walked a high wire across the gorge at the point.

However, a piece of promotional literature from the Rabun County Chamber of Commerce carries a different figure. It says the chief attraction of the town of Tallulah Falls "is still its scenery, in particular the two-mile Tallulah Gorge which reaches depths of just under 1000 feet in places."

Maybe all these gorge boosters in Georgia, Carolina, Virginia and Kentucky ought to persuade a Wallenda to walk a wire above the deepest points of all three gorges. From there, he could drop a weighted tape measure until it hits rock. On the other hand, maybe the situation is more interesting unsettled.

On south we go, to Clarksville. Then northwest a short distance on State 17. We're looking for Beaver Dam Road and one of the main outlet stores of the Habersham Plantation Co. Here is the scene of one of those storybook business successes that pop up infrequently. It has East Tennessee connections.

Less than 20 years ago, Joyce Eddy was at a low point in her life. She was just divorced. Her uninsured home had burned. She had one son in service and another in school. She and a brother were trying to make a living selling craft items.

She heard that a nearby textile company wanted to sell thousands of wooden spools. She bought 20,000 of them for two cents each and turned them into chandeliers, towel bars, bookends, candlesticks and other useful items. They sold well. She bought more spools. Then she and the brother and a retired minister began making small pieces of furniture. She decorated them in the primitive style early American settlers used.

About that time, Gatlinburg business partners Lloyd Blaker and Mack Bryant chanced to stop at the little shop in Clarksville. The furniture impressed them. They offered to sell it in Gatlinburg. They gave her an advance on the first order, and that's when the Habersham Plantation Co. went into business. She credits Blaker and Byrant with giving her the boost that led to big success.

At the Dogwood Arts Festival House and Garden Fair in Knoxville in 1983, Habersham Plantation replica 17th- and 18th-century furniture was used in a log cabin.

Habersham Plantation business is running about $7 million a year now. The company ships to 400 outlets over the country. The building on Beaver Dam Road once housed the factory. Now, Joyce's son Craig uses it as a retail outlet, mostly for his mother's products. The main factory now is in nearby Toccoa.

Ironically, a hitch developed in the relationship between Joyce Eddy's company and the Gatlinburg firm owned by Blaker and Bryant. She said they wanted their Lloyd's of Gatlinburg label on the furniture, and she wanted her Habersham Plantation label on it. They couldn't resolve their difference. So she no longer sells to them.

This North Georgia region is chicken country. You pass farm after farm dotted with long commercial chicken houses. It's also peanut country. Signs in nearly every town advertise boiled peanuts.

Our next stop was the old gold-mining town of Dahlonega. We didn't mine any gold that day, but we arrived in time for lunch at Smith House. This was our first stop at Smith House, though we had heard about it for years. Alberta and I had a table to ourselves, but if the place had been crowded we would have been seated with others. The waitress loaded our table with enough food for a half-dozen: blackeyed peas, turnip greens (with pepper sauce if you like it with your greens), fried okra, yams, excellent squash relish, creamed corn, green beans, coleslaw, mashed potatoes, fried chicken, cured ham, cream gravy, strawberry shortcake. For dinner, there is a third meat, usually roast beaf. Friday and Saturday night dinners feature fried shrimp, catfish, fried chicken, rainbow trout and barbecued beef ribs. Prices are reasonable.

Some Sundays, Smith House feeds as many as 2500 hungry people, says Fred Welch Jr., who, with his wife Shirley, owns the inn. Probably not that many people sleep at the inn in six months. It has only 19 rooms, and they're not always filled. However, Alberta and I stayed a night there. It was OK. Rates are low to moderate. There are several other lodging places in Dahlonega, including inns, resorts and bed-and-breakfast places. A colleague at The News-Sentinel stayed at Worley Homestead, a bed-and-breakfast place, and found it very pleasant.

In 1884, a man named Hall bought an acre of land one block east of Dahlonega's town square. According to the story hand-

Hot air balloons over Helen

ed down from that day, Hall began exca-
vating a home site. But he struck a rich
vein of gold and decided to mine instead of
build. But the Dahlonega city government
wouldn't permit a gold mine just one block
from the town square. Hall sued the city
and lost. So he built his house over the gold
vein.

Henry and Bessie Smith bought the
house in 1922, after Hall's death. They
turned it into an eating and lodging place.
The Welch family began operating the dining room in 1946. Fred Welch was a young-
ster then. He and Shirley became part of
the business in 1966, and they've owned it
since 1970. They have enlarged the building
considerably.

Smith House is busiest when the town is
filled with visitors to Gold Rush Days the
third weekend of October.

After lunch, Alberta and I drove to Amicalola Falls State Park, in Chattahoochee
National Forest. The waterfall is pretty.
Park officials say it's 729 feet high. If you
consider it to be a true waterfall, it's much
higher than Tennessee's 256-foot Fall

Creek Falls, which Tennesseans claim is
the highest waterfall in the East. "The
World Almanac" lists Fall Creek Falls as
the highest in Tennessee, and it lists no
higher falls east of the Rockies. It doesn't
mention Amicalola. This probably is because Amicalola really is a steep cascade,
rather than a straight-drop fall.

This park is where most people leave
their cars when they start hiking the Appalachian Trail at its southern end, Springer
Mountain. The walk from the park to
Springer is 8½ miles. You can park at a
place closer to Springer but it's unprotect-
ed, and several hikers have come back to
find their cars looted. Amicalola is safer.
The AT runs 79 miles through Georgia,
from Springer to the North Carolina line.

The state park contains more than 700
acres, has 15 rental cabins and 17 campsites. Rates are reasonable.

On to Helen. You've probably heard of
Helen, perhaps visited there. It's the little
North Georgia lumber mill town trans-
formed into an Alpine village. An Alpine
village in North Georgia doesn't appeal to

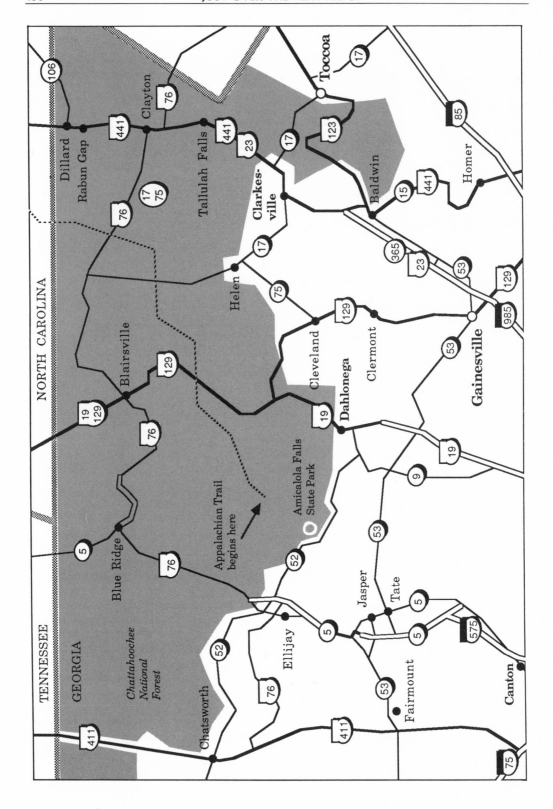

me. It doesn't fit. I feel about it the same way I felt about those porpoises that used to live far from the ocean in Pigeon Forge.

I suppose this just shows what I feel doesn't matter. For Helen has been successful. And even I have to admire the people of Helen for the way they did it. They asked for no help from government at any level. They didn't even go out of North Georgia to hire a planning expert. They knew of John Kollock, an artist over in Clarksville. They invited him to come to Helen and see if he could come up with ideas for painting or decorating the buildings that might help. He did. He'd had an idea for 18 years, ever since he was a U.S. soldier stationed in Bavaria. He fell in love with Alpine villages. And he thought Helen, sitting there astride the lovely Chattahoochee River, would make a fine Alpine village.

He presented his idea to the businesspeople of Helen, and they bought it. They redid their buildings to look like shops and hotels and restaurants in villages in the middle of Bavaria. Tourists seem to like the result. The place is full of restaurants and hotels with names like Gesellschaft Haus, Hofbrauhaus Inn, Helendorf Inn. How about Motel Heidi?

Motels and hotels in and near Helen can accommodate more than 300 visitors. One of the claims of Helen is that women can spend a day in their shops while their husbands catch trout in the Chattahoochee. Most rate sheets and menus I checked had prices on the high side of moderate. You can buy German food, beer and wine.

Helen has Oktoberfest on September weekends and then nightly except Sundays until the middle of October. German bands, polka and alpine dancers and Georgia cloggers are all helped by the flow of German beer.

Just outside of Helen, something else jarred my feeling of what is appropriate. It's an Indian mound, in a field at the junction of Georgia Highways 17 and 75. Excavators in 1915 found that it was a burial mound with about 75 burials. In more recent years, somebody has put a white gazebo on top of the mound.

Next morning in Dahlonega, I had a brief look at Georgia gold connections, past and present. The most obvious thing in town is the gold-leaf spire atop Price Memorial Building, which is the administrative building of North Georgia College. The gold is from local mines, of course. (The dome of the Georgia state capitol in Atlanta is covered with the same thin gold plate.)

Price Memorial Building stands on the foundation of the old U.S. Mint in Dahlonega. The government operated the mint from 1838 until the Civil War, and it burned in 1878.

Though Hall never was able to work his gold vein a block from the town square, you can pan for gold on the lawn of Smith House. Lots of dirt supposedly containing gold particles is in barrels on the lawn. But we passed up that opportunity in favor of a visit to the Gold Museum in the old Lumpkin County Courthouse. The museum is operated as a Georgia historic site.

You learn there that gold was discovered in what's now Lumpkin County in 1828. The region then was the Cherokee Nation. The Indians had moved there from Tennessee. You learn little about this in the museum, but the fact is that the discovery of gold there brought great trials to the Cherokees. Greedy white people poured into the region in this country's first major gold rush. They ignored Cherokee rights and took Cherokee property. The eagerness of the miners to chase out the Cherokees was a major factor in the chain of events that put the Cherokees on the Trail of Tears in 1838, 10 years after the gold discovery. Just 11 years later, many of the same miners left to become forty-niners in the new gold rush in California.

From 1828 through 1933, 858,000 ounces of gold were mined in North Georgia. At modern gold prices (about $400 an ounce at this writing), that much gold would be worth $343.2 million. But it was worth less than $8 million when mined because gold prices were much lower.

Most commercial gold mining in North Georgia stopped about the time of World War II. But several places cater to recreational miners.

As we left town, we stopped at the Crisson Mine, operated both as a commerical mine and tourist mine. When I saw owner John Crisson, I recognized him as one of the persons shown in a film at the Gold Museum. A pan of gold-bearing dirt costs a visitor $1.50. I found a few flecks of gold and a tiny nugget. Naturally, I had to buy small pendants to contain these little goodies. So I spent about $15. I suspected the Crissons take more from the tourists than they do from their honest-to-goodness commercial mining, but Mrs. Crisson said the reverse is true.

Incidentally, an assayer of the Dahlonega mint tried to persuade the Dahlonega miners not to go to California. He pointed to a ridge called Findley and said, "There's millions in it." Mark Twain heard of the remark, so the story goes, and in his "Gilded Age," it became, "There's gold in them thar hills."

So there is.

Georgia Attractions*

Brasstown Bald Blairsville, Ga. 30512 404-896-2556	The highest mountain in Georgia, offering a view of the Chattahoochee National Forest. Ride the mini-bus or walk 930 yards to visitors center/museum on top. Open daily May-October, weekends March 15-April 30 and Nov. 1-Dec. 15. Free except for mini-bus.
Lake Lanier Islands Buford, Ga. 30518 404-945-6701	Outdoor recreational resort has one of the largest boat rental fleets in the Southeast, a 3/4-mile wide beach, water slide, golf course, hotel and cottages, campgrounds, picnic areas, fishing. Special spring and summer events.
Vann House Chatsworth, Ga. 30705 404-695-2598	James Vann, son of a white trader and a chief of the Cherokee nation, built this mansion in 1804. It was abandoned in 1834 and restored in 1950s. Admission. Open all year except Mondays.
Grace Episcopal Church Clarkesville, Ga. 30523 404-754-2451	Built in 1838 and restored in 1975, the building is listed in the National Register of Historic Places and houses its original 1849 organ. Only one other like it still exists in the U.S. Open daily.
Habersham Plantation Marketplace Clarkesville, Ga. 30523 1-800-221-3483	A showplace of handcrafted Colonial furniture. Open year round. Free.
Habersham Vineyards and Winery Clarkesville, Ga. 30523 1-800-221-3483	Winery open to public year round. Reservations recommended. Free.
Mark of the Potter Clarkesville, Ga. 30523 404-947-3440	See pottery made on a kick wheel at this 51-year-old water mill. Other local Georgia handicrafts on display. Located on the Soque River. Open year round. Free.
Rabun Gap Crafts Clayton, Ga. 30568 404-746-5736	An outlet for local crafts. Specialties include weaving, pottery, and woodcarving. Open year round. Demonstrations free.

* We suggest you call and verify the information given in these listings when planning a trip or making reservations. See introduction to the tables on page 45 for further explanation.

Babyland General Hospital Cleveland, Ga. 30528 404-865-5505	Formerly a doctor's clinic, this is the home of the original Cabbage Patch Kids. Open year round. Free.
Gourdcraft Originals Cleveland, Ga. 30528 404-865-4048	Museum of gourds. Open weekends year round. Free.
The Gold Museum Dahlonega, Ga. 30533 404-864-2257	This refurbished county courthouse tells the story of the nation's first major Gold Rush city. Some say the museum, located on the town square, sits atop the city's major gold vein. Open year round. Admission.
Gold Panning at Crisson Mines Dahlonega, Ga. 30533 404-864-6363	An opportunity for would-be prospectors to pan for gold throughout the year. Admission.
Hot-Air Balloon Rides Helen, Ga. 30545 404-878-3526	Tethered ride, night rides and champagne flights available. Fee.
Museum of the Hills Helen, Ga. 30545 404-878-3140	Depicts the lifestyles of the area at the turn of the century. Includes Fantasy Kingdom. Open year round. Admission.
Nacoochee Indian Mound Helen, Ga. 30545 404-878-2181	Romantic tales surround this ancient Indian burial site, which was later used by the Cherokee tribe for ceremonies and tribe meetings. Free.
Sunburst Stables Helen, Ga. 30571 404-878-2095	Overnight and weekend trips into the national forest. Open year round. Rental charge.
Up-River Tube Rentals Helen, Ga. 30545 404-878-3526	Float two miles downriver through Helen. Rental fee.
Tekawitha Helen, Ga. 30545 404-878-2938	This shop features the work of more than 50 Indian tribes. A member of the Indian Arts and Crafts Association.
Andy's Trout Farm and Square Dance Resort Rabun County, Ga. 30537 404-746-2134	Rent cottage or camping facilities and fish March 15 - Nov. 15. Square dance April-October. Reservations required for dance program.
Sky Valley Ski Area Rabun County, Ga. 30537 404-746-5301	Southernmost ski resort in the nation includes a 2200 ft. slope, rope tow, double chair lift, ski school, ski shop and rental equipment. Open year round, ski when weather permits.
The Old Sautee Store Sautee, Ga. 30571 404-878-2281	A 115-year-old store/museum. One of the largest collections of general store memorabilia in Georgia. Open year round. Free.
Stovall Mill Bridge Sautee, Ga. 30571 No Phone	One of the few covered bridges still standing in Georgia. Free.
Traveler's Rest Toccoa, Ga. 30577 404-886-2256	The stagecoach inn and plantation house of a Georgia planter and businessman. Built early 1800s. Now a National Historic Landmark. Admission. Closed on Mondays.

Georgia
Lodging Places

	Dates open	Rooms	Cabins	Private bath	Breakfast offered	*Included in room charge	Lunch offered	Dinner offered	Pool	Tennis court	Children welcome	Pets welcome	Rates: L - Low, less than $30 / M - Moderate, $31-$60 / H - High, $61 and up
Cohutta Lodge & Restaurant Chatsworth, Ga. 30705 404-695-9601	Year round	✓		✓	✓	✓	✓	✓	✓	✓			M
Blue Ridge Motel Clayton, Ga. 30525 404-782-3415	Year round	✓	✓	✓							✓	✓	L-M
Downtowner Motor Inn Clayton, Ga. 30525 404-782-4258	Year round	✓		✓	✓		✓	✓	✓		✓	✓	L-M
English Manor Clayton, Ga. 30525 404-782-5780	Year round	✓		✓									M
LaPrade's Cabins & Marina Clayton, Ga. 30525 404-947-3312	April - December		✓	✓							✓	✓	M-H
Mountain View Cottages Clayton, Ga. 30525 404-782-4582	Year round		✓	✓							✓	✓	L-M
Ole Clayton Inn Clayton, Ga. 30525 404-782-4207	Year round	✓		✓	✓	✓	✓	✓			✓		L-M
Small Hotel & Lodge Clayton, Ga. 30525 404-782-6488	Year round	✓	✓	✓								✓	L-H
Stonebrook Inn Clayton, Ga. 30525 404-782-2214	Year round	✓		✓	✓*				✓		✓		M
The York House Clayton, Ga. 30525 404-746-2068	Year round	✓		✓	✓*						✓		M
B&B at RuSharon Cleveland, Ga. 30528 404-865-5738	Year round	✓		✓	✓*						✓		M
Towering Oaks B&B Cleveland, Ga. 30528 404-865-6760	Year round	✓		✓	✓*								M
Mountain Top Lodge Dahlonega, Ga. 30533 404-864-5257	Year round	✓		✓	✓*								M-H
Smith House Dahlonega, Ga. 30533 404-864-3566	Year round	✓		✓	✓	✓	✓				✓		M-H

	Dates open	Rooms	Cabins	Private bath	Breakfast offered * Included in room charge	Lunch offered	Dinner offered	Pool	Tennis court	Children welcome	Pets welcome	Rates: L - Low, less than $30 M - Moderate, $31-$60 H - High, $61 and up
Worley Homestead B&B Dahlonega, Ga. 30533 404-864-7002	Year round	√	√	√	√*					√		M-H
Dillard House Inn Dillard, Ga. 30537 404-746-5348	Year round	√	√	√	√	√	√	√	√	√	√	L-M
Alpehnof Motel Helen, Ga. 30545 404-878-2268 or 2191	Year round	√		√				√		√		M
Derdenhof Inn Helen, Ga. 30545 404-878-2141	Year round	√		√				√		√		M
Helendorf Inn Helen, Ga. 30545 404-878-2271	Year round	√		√						√	√	M
Hilltop Haus B&B Helen,Ga. 30545 404-878-2519, 878-2388	Year round	√	√	√	√*					√		M-H
Hofbrauhaus Inn Helen, Ga. 30545 404-878-2248	Year round	√		√		√	√			√	√	L-H
Tanglewood Cabins & Inn Helen, Ga. 30545 404-878-3286	Year round	√	√	√						√		H
Anapauo Farm Lakemont, Ga. 30552 404-782-6442	Year round	√	√	√	√*					√		M
Moon Valley Cabins Rabun Gap, Ga. 30568 404-746-2466	Year round	√	√	√	√	√	√	√		√		H
Stovall House Inn & Restaurant Sautee, Ga. 30571 404-878-3355	Year round	√		√	√*	√	√			√	√	H
White Pines Mtn. Cabins Sautee,Ga. 30571 404-865-5204	Year round		√	√								H
Forest Lodges Tallulah Falls, Ga. 30573 404-782-6250	Year round		√	√						√	√	M-H

Georgia Parks

	Lodge	Campsites	Dumping station	Hook-ups	Cabins	Pool	Picnicking	Boating: R-Public ramp, M-Marina, L-Horsepower limits	Boats to rent: C-canoe, P-paddleboat, F-fishing boat	Hiking trails	Fishing	Water skiing	Primitive camping	Supply store	Museum	Leashed pets welcome
Vogel State Park Blairsville, Ga. 30512 404-745-2628		76	√	√	36	√			P	√	√		√	√		√
Fort Mountain State Park Chatsworth, Ga. 30705 404-695-2621		75	√	√	15	√			P	√	√		√			√
Moccasin Creek State Park Clarkesville, Ga. 30523 404-947-3194		53	√				√			√	√					
Amicalola Falls State Park Dawsonville, Ga. 30534 404-265-2885		17	√		15	√				√	√				√	√
Chattahoochee National Forest Gainesville, Ga. 30501 404-536-0541		507	√				√	R		√	√	√	√		√	√
Unicoi State Park Helen, Ga. 30545 404-878-2201	√	96	√	√	29	√		L	CP	√	√		√	√	√	√
Black Rock Mountain State Park Mountain City, Ga. 30562 404-746-2141		64	√	√	10	√				√	√		√	√		√
Cloudland Canyon State Park Rising Fawn, Ga. 30738 404-657-4050		75	√	√	15	√	√			√			√			√
James H. Floyd State Park Summerville, Ga. 30747 404-857-5211		25	√	√			√	R L	PF	√	√		√			√

Georgia Chambers of Commerce

Index of Places

Abingdon, 85, 86, 88
Abraham Lincoln Museum, 48
Abrams Creek, 39, 40
Audubon Acres, 45
Alamo, 23
Albemarle Inn, 123
Allanstand, 118
Allardt, 5
Allegheny, 63, 65
Alley Ford, 3
Alpenhof Motel, 141
Alpine Slide, The, 45
Alvin C. York Agricultural Institute, 9
Alvin C. York Highway, 31
Alvin C. York Memorial Park, 9, 48
American Museum of Science and
    Energy, 51
Amicalola, 135
Amicalola Creek, 3
Amicalola Falls State Park, 135, 142
Amis House, The, 14, 52
Anapauo Farm, 141
Anderson Branch Coal Mine, 11
Anderson County Courthouse, 42
Andrew Johnson National Historic Site,
    24, 48
Andrew Johnson's tailor shop, 12, 23
Andrews, 107
Andy's Trout Farm and Square Dance
    Resort, 139
Angel Falls, 11
Angel Falls Overlook, 11
Appalachia, 91
Appalachian Museum at Berea College,
    70, 78
Appalachian School, 117
Appalachian Ski Mountain, 120
Appalachian State University, 113
Appalachian Trail (AT), 20, 23, 37, 39,
    86, 106, 111, 112, 135
Apple Festival, 110
Apple Jack Open golf tournament, 110
Armstrong-Lockett House, 49
Arrowmont School of Arts & Crafts,
    36, 48
Ashe County, 113, 115
Ashe County Cheese Co., 115, 117, 122
Asheville, 98, 118
Ashland Henry Clay Estate, 79
Asylum House, 5
Atlantic Ocean, 108,132
Austin Nichols Distillery, 79
Avery County, 112, 113
Azalea Garden Motel, 112, 123

B&B at RuSharon, 140
Babyland General Hospital, 139
Baird House B&B Inn, 126
Bald River, 29
Bald River Falls, 27
Bald River Gorge, 29
Bald River Road, 27
Banner Elk, 112
Barter Theater, 88, 92
Baxter, 77
Bays Mountain Park, 15, 16, 57
Beal Farm, 14
Bean Station, 13
Bean Station Inn, 13

Beaumont Inn, 65, 80
Beauty Spot, 22, 23
Beaver Creek, 116
Beaver Dam Road, 134
Beck Cultural Exchange Center, 49
Beech Mountain, 108, 112
Beech Mountain Chalet Rentals, 123
Beersheba Springs, 33
Beggar's Castle, 8
Bell County, 74, 77
Bent Creek Mountain Inn, 54
Berea, 69, 106
Berea College, 69, 117
Big Branch, 5
Big Cove, 98
Big Creek, 14, 33
Big Ridge State Park, 44, 58
Big Sandy River, 91
Big South Fork, 3, 9, 11
Big South Fork National River and
    Recreation Area (BSFNRRA), vii, 9,
    11, 58
Big South Fork Scenic Railway, 80
Big Spring, 31
Big Spring Inn, 55
Big Stone Gap, 91, 92
Big Valley of Union County, 41
Big Y, 98
Bijou Theater, 49
Billy's Creek, 131
Biltmore Estate, 120
Bird's Creek Road, 35
Birdtown, 98
Black Mountain, 74
Black Rock Mountain State Park, 142
Black's Fort, 88
Blakely House, The, 55
Bledsoe County, 30
Blount Mansion, vii, 27, 49
Blowing Rock, 112, 113, 115, 118, 120
Blowing Rock Inn, 123
Blowing Rock Stables, 120
Blue Hole, 3
Blue Ridge, 89
Blue Ridge Hearthside Crafts
    Center, 120
Blue Ridge Motel, 140
Blue Ridge Mountain Frescoes, 120
Blue Ridge Mountains, 108
Blue Ridge Parkway, 112, 113, 118, 133
Booker T. Washington State
    Recreational Park, 57
Boone, 112, 113, 118
Boone Tavern, 69, 80
Boones Creek, 16
Boundary Tree Dining Room, 99
Boundary Tree Motor Lodge, 99, 125
Boundary Tree Restaurant, 99
Bourbon County, 91
Brady Mountain, 31
Brasstown, 106, 117
Brasstown Bald, 138
Breaks Interstate Park, 88, 89, 93,
    115, 133
Breaks Motor Lodge, 93
Breaks of the Sandy, 76
Brevard Music Center, 108, 121
Bridal Veil Falls, 107
Bristol, 70, 118

Bristol Caverns, 45
Bristol International Raceway, 45
Brookside Resort, 54
Brushy Mountain State Prison, 1
Bryan Station Inn, 80
Bryson City, 35, 100, 104, 107
Buckhorn Inn, 35, 54
Buckhorn Lake State Resort Park, 81
Buckhorn Mountain, 107
Buckhorn Road, 35, 36
Buckley Wildlife Sanctuary, 80
Buffalo Cove, 8
Buladean, 20
Buladeen, 20
Bullhead Trail, 38
Bulls Gap, 43
Burem Road, 14
Burgess Falls State Natural Area, 58
Burning Bush Restaurant, 36
Buttonwood Inn, 125
Bybee, 70
Bybee Pottery, 70, 78

Cabin Fever, 125
Cable Mill, 40
Cades Cove, 39, 71, 132
Cades Cove Loop Road, 40
Cades Cove Riding Stables, 53
Calderwood, 24
Calderwood Dam, 104
Calderwood Lake, 40, 131
California, 9, 20
Campbell Folk School, 106, 117
Campbell House Inn, 80
Cane Creek Falls, 32
Cane Creek Gorge, 32
Cane River, 118
Carl Sandburg National Historic
    Site, 110
Carl Slagle Road, 105
Carr's Northside Cottages/Motel, 54
Carriage House Motor Hotel, 81
Carriage House Restaurant, 39
Carter, 20
Carter-Johnson County Line, 20
Cartoogechaye Creek, 105
Carvers Gap, 19, 111, 112
Caryville, 70
Catoosa Wildlife Management Area, 3
Cave House, 88
Caylor, 72
Cedar Bluff, 89
Cedar Crest Victorian Inn, 123
Chained Rock, 74, 75
Chanticleer Lodge, 54
Chapel of the Ascension, 106
Charleston, 25
Chattahoochee National Forest, 132,
    135, 142
Chattahoochee River, 3, 137
Chattanooga, 8, 44
Chattanooga Choo-Choo Hilton, 54
Chattanooga Choo-Choo, 46
Chattooga River, 3, 132
Cheoah, 131
Cheoah Dam, 104
Cheoah Lake, 101
Cherokee, 98, 100, 101, 113
Cherokee County, 98, 107

Cherokee Dam, 12
Cherokee Historical Association, 98
Cherokee Lake, 12, 13
Cherokee National Forest, 3, 20, 22, 27, 29, 57
Cherokee Orchard, 38
Cherokee towns, 26
Chester Inn, 22
Chestnut Top Trail, 39
Chickamauga-Chattanooga National Military Park, 46
Children's Museum of Oak Ridge, 51
Chilhowee Dam, 104
Chilhowee Lake, 27, 40, 131
Chimney Rock, 2, 121
Chimney Rock Park, 127
Chimney Top Trail, 2
Chimneys Trail, 37
Chota, 24, 25, 26, 27
Christ Church, Episcopal, 4
Christmas at Rugby, 5
Churchill Weavers, 78
Citico Creek, 27, 29
Citico Road, 27
Civilian Conservation Corps (CCC), 74, 75, 76
Claddagh Inn & Guest House, 125
Clarksville, 134, 137
Clear Creek, 2, 3, 43
Clear Fork, 3, 9, 76
Clear Fork River, 4
Cleveland, 107
Cliff Top, 38, 106
Clinch Mountain, 13
Clinch River, 3, 43, 44
Clingmans Dome, 86, 97
Clingmans Dome Road, 36, 37, 101
Clinton, 42
Cloudland Canyon State Park, 142
Cohutta Lodge & Restaurant, 140
Col. Sanders Original Restaurant, 78
Colditz Cove, 5
Coleman River Wildlife Management Area, 132
Collins River, 33
Colonial Pines Inn, 125
Cone Craft Center, 120
Confederate Memorial Hall, 49
Connemara, 110, 122
Constitution Square State Shrine, 78
Copper Basin, 24, 29, 30
Copperhill, 29
Corbin, 70
Cordell Hull Birthplace, 45
Cosby, 35, 38
Cosby Campground, 38, 39
Cosby Ramp Festival, 39
Council of the Southern Mountains, 106
Courthouse Square, 75
Cove Lake State Recreational Park, 44, 56
Covered Bridge, 18
Creech Overlook, 76, 77
Cricket's Corner, 125
Crisson Mine, 137, 138
Cristopher Taylor House, 49
Crockett Tavern, 24
Cross Mountain, 20
Cross-country ski center, Roan Mountain State Park, 19
Crossville, 30
Cub Motel, 39
Cudjo Caverns, 47
Cullasaja Falls, 107
Cullasaja River, 107
Cumberland, 1, 31, 33, 76
Cumberland Caverns Park, 51
Cumberland County Playhouse, 30, 47
Cumberland Falls State Resort Park, 70, 81
Cumberland Ford, 74

Cumberland Gap, 13, 72, 74
Cumberland Gap National Historic Park, vii, 58, 70, 82, 93
Cumberland General Store, 31, 48
Cumberland Homesteads, 30
Cumberland Mountain, 71, 72, 74
Cumberland Mountain State Rustic Park, 31, 57
Cumberland Mountains, vii, 3, 9, 11, 41, 89
Cumberland Plateau, 4, 31, 33
Cumberland River, 18, 70, 74, 76, 77

Daddys Creek, 2, 3
Dahlonega, 134, 135, 138
Damascus, 20, 85, 86
Damascus Road, 39
Dandridge, 24
Daniel Boone National Forest, 82
Daniel Boone Native Gardens, 113
Davenport, 39
Davenport Gap, 39
Davy Crockett Birthplace State Historical Area, 23
Davy Crockett Birthplace State Park, 57
Davy Crockett Stables, 53
Davy Crockett Tavern & Museum, 51
DeBord Falls, 2
Deel, 89
Deep Creek, 101
Deep Creek Campground, 101
Denmark, 20
Derdenhof Inn, 141
Devil's Jump, 11
Devil's Race Track, 70
Devils Breakfast Table, 3
Dillard House, 132
Dillard House Inn, 141
Dillsboro, 100, 103, 118
Dismal Creek, 89
Dixie Belle Riverboat, 79
Doe River, 18, 19
Doe River Covered Bridge, 18, 47
Dogwood Arts Festival House and Garden Fair, 134
Dogwood Arts Festival, vii
Dollywood, 35, 39, 51
Douglas Ferguson Fountain, 118
Douglas Lake, 24
Downtowner Motor Inn, 140
Dr. Thomas Walker State Shrine, 78
Dry Falls, 107
Ducktown, 29
Ducktown Basin Museum, 30
Dulin Gallery of Art, 50
Dupont Lodge, 70
Dutch Creek, 113

East Tennessee Historical Society, 50
Ebbing and Flowing Spring, 14
Echo Mountain Inn, 125
Edgar Evins State Rustic Park, 58
Edgewater Hotel, The, 54
El Horrendo, 133
Elizabethton, 18, 20, 21, 111
Elk Garden, 86
Elkhorn City, 76
Engine Gap, 112
English Manor, 140
Episcopal Church, St. John's, Cartoogechaye, 105
Erwin, 22
Eseeola Lodge, 126
Ewing, 70, 71, 72
Ewing Trail, 71
Exchange Place, The, 49

Fairfield Glade, 3
Fairfield Glade Resort, 54
Fairfield-Sapphire Valley, 108
Fall Branch, 11

Fall Creek Falls, 135
Fall Creek Falls State Resort Park, 30, 31, 33, 58
Fentress County, 1, 5, 8, 9, 31
Fields of the Wood, 107
Fighting Creek Gap, 37
Fine Arts Center, 109
Finland, 20
First Lady's Table, 87
Fishhawk Mountain, 107
Fittified Spring, 14
Flat Rock, 110
Flat Rock Playhouse, 110, 122
Flint Street Inn, 123
Flyaway, 51
Folklife Center of the Smokies, 47
Fontana Dam, 104
Fontana Inn, 104
Fontana Lake, 104
Fontana Village, 100, 104
Fontana Village Resort, 125
Foothills Parkway, 38, 40
Forbidden Caverns, 52
Forest Lodges, 141
Forge Creek Road, 40
Forge Creek Valley, 40
Fork Ridge Trail, 37
Fort Boonesborough State Park, 81
Fort Loudoun, 25, 26, 27, 41
Fort Loudoun State Historic Area, 26, 53, 58
Fort Mountain State Park, 142
Fort Watauga, 18
Four Seasons Hotel, 77, 78
Foxfire, 132
France's Argonne Forest, 9
Frankland, 21
Franklin, 100, 104, 106
Franklin Gem and Mineral Museum, 105
Franklin Gem and Mineral Society, 122
Franklin Terrace, The, 125
French Broad River, 3
Front Royal, 113
Frozen Head State Natural Area, 2, 59
Frozen Head State Park, 1, 2, 59
Fruit Hill, 87
Fryemont Inn, 124

Gatlinburg, 35, 36, 38, 134
Gatlinburg Sky Lift, 48
Gatlinburg Space Needle, 48
General Burnside State Park, 81
General Store of J. A. Kemmer & Son, 31
Georgia Attractions Table, 138-139
Georgia Chambers of Commerce, 142
Georgia Lodging Places Table, 140-141
Georgia Parks Table, 142
Germany, 8
Gideon Ridge Inn, 123
Gift from the Hills, 117
Glade Spring, 88
Glades Road, 35, 36
Glen Oby Road, 8
Glendale Springs, 116
Glendale Springs Inn, 125
Glenmore Mansion, 49
Glenstone Lodge, 54
Gold Mine, 107
Gold Mine Branch, 107
Gold Mine Valley, 107
Gold Museum, 137, 138, 139
Gold Panning at Crisson Mines, 139
Gold Rush Days, 135
Goodwin Guild Weavers, 121
Gourdcraft Originals, 139
Grace Episcopal Church, 138
Graham County, 98
Grainger County, 12, 41
Grand Guitar Museum, 45
Grand Hotel, The, 55
Grandfather Mountain, 113, 115, 122

Grape Patch Winery, 53
Grassy Cove, 31
Grassy Cove Creek, 31
Grassy Ridge, 111, 112, 115
Graustein Inn, The, 55
Grave of the Unknown Girl, 65
Grayson Highlands State Park, 93
Great American Dulcimer Convention,
    The, 76
Great Smokies, vii, 11, 14, 37, 71, 86, 97,
    98, 100, 101, 106, 111, 113
Great Smoky Arts & Crafts Community,
    35, 48
Great Smoky Mountains National Park,
    3, 33, 35, 57, 97
Great Stage Road, 21
Green Park Inn, 123
Greenbo Lake State Resort Park, 81
Greenbrier, 14
Greene County, 23
Greeneville, 12, 23, 24
Gregory Bald, vii, 39, 40, 86, 111
Gregory Ridge, 40
Gregory Trailhead, 40
Grenelefe Inn, 80
Gresham-Keys House, 21
Greystone Inn, 126
Grist Mill York operated on the Wolf, 9
Grove Park Inn & Country Club, 123
Gruetli, 30, 32, 33
Grundy, 89
Grundy County, 30, 33
Grundy Forest State Natural Area, 58
Grundy Lakes State Park, 58
Gsellschaft Haus, 137
Guild Crafts, 118
Guild Gallery, 118

Habersham Plantation, 134, 138
Habersham Plantation Co., 134
Habersham Vineyards and Winery, 138
Hale Springs, 14
Hale Springs Inn, 13, 56
Halifac, 21
Hangover, 100
Hannah Mountain, 40
Haoe Lead Trail, 100
Hardware Company Restaurant, The,
    87, 88
Harlan, 77
Harlan County, 77
Harlan County Courthouse, 77
Harrison Bay State Park, 57
Harrodsburg, 63
Harrodsburg Springs, 65
Harrow Road Cafe, 5
Hawkeye Farm B&B, 81
Hawkins County, 13, 14, 15
Hawkins County Courthouse, 13, 52
Hawkins Cove, 33
Haywood Street, 103
Head of Sequatchie, 31
Headley-Whitney Museum, 79
Helen, 135, 137
Helendorf Inn, 137
Helicopter Rides, 51
Hemlock Garden, 76
Hemlock Inn, 100, 101, 103, 107, 124
Henderson County, 110
Hendersonville, 108, 110
Henley Bridge, 27
Hensley Settlement, 71, 72
Hensonville, 89
Henwallow Falls, 38
Hermitage, 13
Herndon Evans Lodge, 76
Hibbs Island, 43
Hidden Hollow Park, 47
High Adventure Sports, 46
High Country Inn, 112, 124
High Hampton Inn, 124

Highland Games, 115
Highland Inn, 126
Highland Manor, 8
Highland Manor Motel, 56
Highland Manor Winery, 5, 49
Highlands, 108, 109
Highlands Chamber Music Festival, 108
Highlands Inn, 108
Highlands of Roan, 18, 111
Highlands Playhouse, 108
Hilltop House B&B, 141
Hillwinds Inn, 124
Historic Rugby Inc., 4
Historic Rugby Visitors Center, 52
Hiwassee, 107
Hiwassee Lake, 98
Hiwassee Mine, 29
Hiwassee River, 3, 24, 25, 98
Hofbrauhaus Inn, 137, 141
Holly Flats, 27
Holston River, 14, 18, 85
Holston Valley, 13
Holy Trinity, 116
Homestead House, 54
Homesteads Tower Museum, 48
Horn in the West, 121
Hot-Air Balloon Rides, 139
Hound Ears Club, 121
Houston Antique Museum, 46
Hungry Mother State Park, 93
Hunt-Morgan House, 79
Hunter Museum of Art, 46
Huskey Gap, 37
Huskey Gap Trail, 37

Independence, 86
Indian Creek, 72, 101
Indian fair at Cherokee, 99
Indian Gap, 36, 37
Indian Grave Gap, 22, 23
Indian Mountain State Park, 57
Indian towns, 25
Indiana, 12
Inn at Brevard, The, 124
Iron Mountain, 20
Iron Mountain Stoneware, 50

"Jack" Jouett House, 80
Jackson County, 103, 113
James H. Floyd State Park, 142
James White Fort, 50
Jamestown, 8, 9
Jane Bald, 112
Jarrett House, 103, 125
Jefferson County Courthouse, 24
Jefferson County Museum, 47
Jefferson National Forest, 86, 93
Jellico, 76, 91
Jenkins Meadow Trail, 100
Jenny Wiley State Resort Park, 82
John C. Campbell Folk School, 106,
    117, 121
John Fox Jr. Museum, 92
John Muir Trail, 9, 11
John Sevier Historic Site, 50
John Teeseteska, 101
Johnson City, 16, 21, 26
Johnson County, 20
Johnson's Scenic Court, 54
Jonesborough, 21, 23
Jonesborough B&B, 55
Joyce Kilmer Memorial Trail, 100
Joyce Kilmer-Slickrock Wilderness Area,
    vii, 100
June Tolliver House & Craft Shop, 92
June Tolliver House, 92
June Tolliver Playhouse, 92

Keen Mountain, 89
Keeneland Race Course, 79
Kelischek Workshop for Historical

Instruments, 121
Kentucky Attractions Table, 78-80
Kentucky Bluegrass, 66
Kentucky Chambers of Commerce, 82
Kentucky Derby, 65
Kentucky Horse Park, 79
Kentucky Lodging Places Table, 80-81
Kentucky Parks Table, 81-82
Kentucky River, 18, 67
Kentucky State Park Commission, 74
Kentucky State Resort Parks,
    restaurants, 76
King's Inn, 108, 126
Kingdom Come State Park, 76, 81, 91
Kings Mountain, 18
Kingsport, 13, 15, 16, 25, 72
Kingsport's Boatyard Riverfront Park, 15
Kingstone Lisle, 4
Kissing Bridges, 18
Kituwah, 98
Knox County, 18, 43
Knoxville, 3, 8, 16, 22, 26, 27, 35, 43, 70,
    85, 117, 131, 134
Knoxville Zoological Park, 50
Kyle House, 13, 52

L'Auberge of Tryon, 126
Laager, 30, 32
Laager-Gruetli, 30
Lake Cumberland State Resort Park, 82
Lake Lanier Islands, 138
Lake Lure Inn, 126
Lake Winnepesaukah, 46
LaPrade's Cabins & Marina, 140
Laurel Bloomery, 20
Laurel Cove Amphitheatre, 76
Laurel Creek, 33
Laurel Creek Road, 39, 40
Laurel Fork, 9
Le Conte Lodge, 37, 106
Leatherwood Ford to Angel Falls, 11
LeConte Lodge, 55
Lee's Inn, 108
Lee's Lodge & Mountain House
    Restaurant, 125
Legend of Daniel Boone, The, 65
Lenoir Museum, 42, 43, 51
Levi Jackson Wilderness Road
    State Park, 82
Lexington, 8, 70
Lexington Cemetery, 79
Limestone, 23, 24
Lincoln, 65
Lincoln Memorial University, 78
Lincoln Museum, 78
Linn Cove, 113
Linn Cove Viaduct, 113
Linville, 113
Linville Caverns, 122
Linville Falls, 113
Linville Gorge, 113, 115, 133
Linville River, 113, 133
Little Bear Wallow Creek, 75
Little Fishhawk Mountain, 107
Little Pigeon River, 35, 37
Little River, 3, 37, 39
Little River Road, 39
Little Santeetlah Creek, 100, 101
Little Shepherd Trail, 76
Little Tennessee River (Little T), 3, 24,
    25, 26, 41, 98, 104, 105, 131, 132
Little Tennessee Valley, 24, 104
Lonesome Pine Arts and Crafts
    Association, 92
Long Island of the Holston, 13, 15, 25,
    26, 72
Lookout Mountain Caverns, 46
Lookout Mountain Incline Railway, 46
Lookout Mountain Museum, 46
Lost Sea, The, 53
Louisa Fork, 89

Low Gap, 39
Lumpkin County Courthouse, 137
Lynn, 109

Macon County, 104, 107
Mail Pouch, The, 49
Mansion House, 21
Maple Lodge, 124
Mark of the Potter, 138
Mark Twain Spring, 9
Mars Hill, 118
Martha Washington Inn, 85, 86, 87, 93
Mary Todd Lincoln House, 79
Maryville, 26, 39, 131
Massengill Museum of Overmountain
    History, 17
Mast Farm Inn, 113, 127
Mast Gap Road, 113
Mast General Store, 113, 122
Masters of Hang Gliding
    Championship, 115
Mauk's Jonesborough Pharmacy, 49
McCarter's Riding Stables, 48
McClung Museum, The, 50
McDowell House & Apothecary, 78
McKinney Tavern House, 13
McMinn County Living Heritage
    Museum, 45
McMinnville, 33
Melrose Inn, 127
Melton Hill Lake, 44
Mercer County, 66
Middle Fork of the Holston River, 85
Middlesboro, 77, 78
Middlesboro Basin, 74
Middlesboro Chamber of Commerce, 77
Middleton, The, 55
Mike's Inland Seafood, 113
Mill Cave, 31
Mill Creek Park, 52
Mill Farm Inn, 108, 109, 127
Mingo Falls Campground, 99, 100
Ministry's Workshop, 69
Mississippi River, 98
Missouri, 9
Moccasin Creek State Park, 142
Monteagle, 32
Moon Valley Cabins, 141
Moore Spring Shelter, 40
Morgan County, 1
Morristown, 13, 24
Motel Heidi, 137
Mount Mitchell State Park, 127
Mount Rogers National Recreation Area,
    85, 93
Mountain Breeze B&B, 55
Mountain City, 20
Mountain Home Inn, 56
Mountain Laurel Festival, 76
Mountain Top Lodge, 140
Mountain View Cottages, 140
Mountain View Lodge & Cabins, 125
Mountaineer Museum, 48
Mt. Cammerer, 39
Mt. Guyot, 37, 97, 98
Mt. Le Conte, 35, 37, 106, 117
Mt. Mitchell, 97
Mt. Rogers, 86
Mud Meeting House, 65
Murphy, 107
Murphy's, 110
Museum of Appalachia Tennessee Fall
    Homecoming, 42
Museum of Appalachia, The, vii, 41, 42,
    43, 51
Museum of Fine Arts, 51
Museum of the Cherokee Indian, 99, 121
Museum of the Hills, 139
Myrtle Point, 38
Mystery Hill, 121

Nacoochee Indian Mound, 139
Naked Ground Trail, 100
Nantahala Crest, 106
Nantahala Mountain, 106
Nantahala National Forest, 97, 100, 106,
    108, 127
Nantahala River, 3
Nantahala Village, 124
Nashville, 8
National Fish Hatchery, 47
National Knife Museum, 46
National Storytellers Festival, 22
Natural Bridge State Resort Park, 82
Natural Tunnel State Park, 93
Nature Center Building, 16
Nemo Bridge, 3
Netherland Inn Road, 15
Netherland Inn, The, 49
New Orleans, 13, 108
New River, 3, 9, 18, 115
New River Inn, 112
New River Inn Motel & Restaurant, 124
Newbury House, 56
Newbury House Inn, 5
Newfound Gap, 36, 37, 97, 98
Newport, 35, 38
Newport/Cocke County Museum, 51
Nikwasi Mound, 104
Noland Creek, 101
Noland Divide Trailhead, 101
Nolichucky River, 3, 23
Norfolk & Western Railroad, 89
Norris, 42, 43, 44
Norris Dam, 40, 43, 44
Norris Dam State Park, 42, 44, 57
Norris Freeway, 44
Norris Lake, 44
North Carolina Attractions Table,
    120-122
North Carolina Chambers of
    Commerce, 128
North Carolina Lodging Places Table,
    123-127
North Carolina Mineral Museum, 122
North Carolina Parks Table, 127
North Carolina State Fair, 117
North Fork of Citico Creek, 29
North Fork of the Catawba, 3, 4
North Fork of the New River, 3
North Georgia College, 137
North Old Mac Mountain Trail, 2
North Prong of Flat Fork Creek, 2
North River, 27, 29
North Toe River, 118
North White Oak Creek, 9
Northrup Falls, 5
Norton, 91
Nu-Wray Inn, 118, 124

Oak Ridge Energy Tour, 51
Oakwood, 89
Obed River, 2, 3
Obed Wild and Scenic River, vii, 2
Ober Gatlinburg Resort, 48
Observation Knob Park, 56
Ocoee River, 3, 29
Oconaluftee, 98, 99
Oconaluftee Indian Village, 98, 121
Oconaluftee River, 3
Oconaluftee Valley, 37
Ogle's Water Park, 52
Ohio River, 3
Old Edwards Inn, 108, 126
Old Fort Harrod Amphitheater, 65
Old Fort Harrod State Park, 63, 81
Old Hampton Store, 122
Old Harrodsburg Pottery, 79
Old Indian Road, 36
Old Jacobs House, 21
Old Mill, The, 43, 52
Old Mountain Village, 53

Old Reynolds Mansion, 123
Old Rutledge Pike, 18
Old Sautee Store, The, 139
Old Taylor Distillery, 80
Ole Brown Museum, The, 45
Ole Clayton Inn, 140
Oneida, 5, 11
Orchard Inn, The, 126

Painttown, 98
Pall Mall, 8
Panther Branch, 2
Panther Branch Trail, 2
Panther Creek State Recreational
    Park, 58
Parish of the Holy Communion, 116
Parksville Lake, 29
Parkway Craft Center, 118
Parson Branch Road, 39, 40
Parson's Table, 22
Peavine Railroad, 13
Penland, 117, 118
Penland School, 117, 118, 122
Perryville, 65
Petros, 1
Phelps House B&B, 126
Philadelphia, 13
Pickett State Rustic Park, 57
Pigeon Forge, 35, 118, 137
Pigeon Forge Pottery, 52
Pigeon River, 35
Pikeville, 31
Pine Cottages, 123
Pine Crest Inn, 127
Pine Mountain, 74, 75, 76, 115, 133
Pine Mountain State Resort Park, 74,
    75, 82
Pines Country Inn, The, 124
Pineville, 74, 75
Piney Creek Falls, 32
Pioneer Cottage, 5, 56
Pisgah, 97
Pisgah Inn, 127
Pisgah National Forest, 22, 23, 127
Pittman Center, 35
Pleasant Hill, 65, 66
Plum Alley Eatery, 88
Polk County, 100
Poor Fork of the Cumberland River, 77
Potter's Mark, 36
Pound, 91
Powell River, 74
Powell Valley, 13, 72
Price Memorial Building, 137
Primitive Settlement, 47
Proffitt Road, 36

Qualla Arts and Crafts Mutual, 98,
    99, 121

Rabun County, 132
Rabun Gap, 132
Rabun Gap Crafts, 138
Raccoon Mountain Caverns, 46
Ragged Garden Inn & Restaurant, 124
Rainbow Falls, 38
Rainbow Falls Trail, 38
Rainbow Springs, 106
Raleigh, 117
Ramsey House, 50
Randolph House, 124
Rattlesnake Rock, 27
Raven Run Nature Sanctuary, 79
Ray House B&B, 123
Read House, 54
Red Ash, 89
Red Clay State Historic Area, 47
Red Clay State Historic Park, 57
Red Mile Harness Track, 79
Reed House B&B, 123
Reflection Riding, 46

Renegade Mountain, 47
Renfro Valley Country Music Center, 80
Rhea County Courthouse, 47
Ridge Trail, 71, 72
River Terrace Motel, 55
Riverbluff Trail, 44
Riverchase, 56
Riverwood Shops, 103, 118
Roan Mountain State Resort Park, 19, 58
Roan Mountain, vii, 19, 20
Robbinsville, 27, 99, 100, 101, 107
Rock City Gardens, 46
Rock Creek Road, 22
Rock House, 52
Rock House Branch Falls, 32
Rock Island State Park, 58
Rockfish Gap, 113
Rocky Mount, vii, 16, 17, 21, 52
Rocky Mountains, 74, 135
Rocky Spur, 38
Rocky Waters Motor Inn, 55
Rogers Cemetery, 13
Rogersville, 13, 14
Rose Center, 51
Rough Creek, 37
Rough Creek Trail, 37
Round Bald, 112
Ruby Falls, 46
Rugby, 4, 5
Rugby Printing Works, 4
Russell Fork, 3, 91, 115, 133
Rutledge, 12, 23

Sadie, 20
Salt River, 65
Saluda Inn, 110
Sam Houston Schoolhouse, 50
Samuel W. Doak House, 48
Sand Cave, 70, 72
Sand Cave Branch, 72
Santeetlah, 101
Santeetlah Creek, 100, 101
Santeetlah Lake, 101
Sassafras Ridge, 27
Savage Creek, 33
Savage Falls, 33
Savage Gulf, 30, 33
Savage Gulf State Natural Area, 30,
  33, 58
Savannah River, 98, 108, 132
Schoolhouse Gap Trail, 40
Scott County, 1, 11, 12
Sequatchie County, 30
Sequatchie River, 3, 31
Sequatchie Valley, 31, 33
Sequoyah Birthplace Museum, 26, 53
Settlement School, 36
Sevier County, 35, 36
Sevierville, 35
Shady Valley, 20
Shaker Village at Pleasant Hill, 66, 79, 81
Shakertown, 66
Shenandoah National Park, 93, 113
Silers Bald in the Great Smokies, 105
Silers Bald in the Nantahalas, 105
Singing on the Mountain, 115
Sisters' Row, 21
Ski Beech, 120
Ski French-Swiss, 121
Ski Hawksnest, 120
Sky Valley Ski Area, 139
Skyline Drive, 113
Skyline Lodge, 126
Slickrock Creek, 100
Small Hotel & Lodge, 140
Smith House, 134, 135, 137, 140
Smoky Mountain Car Museum, 52
Smoky Mountain Passion Play, 53
Smoky Mountain Passion Play
  Association, 39
Smoky Mountain Winery, 48

Smoky Mountains Inn on the Plaza, 123
Snapp Inn B&B, 55
Snowbird Creek, 101
Snowbird Mountain Lodge, 100, 101,
  103, 107, 126
Snowbird Mountains, 98, 107
Soco, 98
Song Bird Trail, 44
South Cumberland State Recreation
  Area (SCSRA), 32, 33, 58
South Cumberlands, 30, 33
South Fork of Citico Creek, 29
South Fork of the Holston River, 85
South Fork of the New River, 3
Southern Appalachia, vii, 41, 69, 74, 86,
  104, 106
Southern Highlands Folk Art
  Center, 120
Southern Highlands Handicraft
  Guild, 117
Southern Inn, 54
Southern Railway, 13
Southwest Virginia Museum, 92
Speedwell Manor, 50
Spence Field, 86, 111
Spendthrift Farm, 80
Spring Creek, 24
Springer, 135
Springer Mountain, 135
Spruce Pine, 117
Squire Watkins Inn, 103, 125
St. Mary's at Beaver Creek, 116
St. Matthew, 116
Standing Stone State Rustic Park, 58
State of Franklin, 21, 23
State Theater of North Carolina, 110
Steiner Bell, 55
Stone Door, 33
Stone Door Connector Trail, 33
Stonebrook Inn, 140
Stonehedge Golf Course, 3
Stony Creek, 20
Stovall House Inn & Restaurant, 141
Stovall Mill Bridge, 139
Stratton Bald Trail, 100
Stratton Gap, 27
Stratton Meadow, 27
Students' Museum and Akima
  Planetarium, 50
Sugar Mountain, 120
Sugarland Mountain Trail, 37
Sullivan County, 15
Sunbright, 3
Sunburst Stables, 139
Sunshine Inn, 124
Swag, The, 100, 122
Swiss Memorial School, 30
Sycamore Shoals of the Watauga
  River, 18
Sycamore Shoals State Historic Area,
  18, 57
Sylva, 100, 103

Tales from here to Kingdom Come
  Story-telling Festival, 77
Talley-Ho Motel, 56
Tallulah Falls, 132, 133
Tallulah Gorge, 132, 133
Tallulah Gorge Park, 133
Tallulah Point, 133
Tallulah River, 132
Tanasi, 26
Tanglewood Cabins & Inn, 141
Tate Spring, 13
Tate Spring Hotel, 12, 13
Tavern, The, 88
Taylor House B&B, The, 127
Tazewell, 70
Teeoatlah, 101
Tekawitha, 139
Tellico, 27

Tellico Blockhouse, 25, 26
Tellico Dam, 26, 104
Tellico Lake, 26, 131
Tellico Plains, 24, 27, 29
Tellico River, 3, 24, 27, 29
Tellico River Road, 27
Tellico Wildlife Management Area, 27
Tennessee Attractions Tables, 45-53
Tennessee Chambers of Commerce,
  59-60
Tennessee Lodging Places Tables, 54-56
Tennessee Parks Tables, 56-59
Tennessee River, 44, 108
Tennessee Theatre, The, 50
Tennessee Valley Authority (TVA) Map
  Office, vii, 25
Tennessee Valley Railroad Museum, 47
Tennessee Wildlife Resources Agency, 44
Territory South of the Ohio River,
  16, 21
Thames River, 27
Thomas Hughes Library, 4
Thomas Wolfe's Home, 120
Thompson-Brown House, 50
Three Chimneys of Knoxville, 55
Timberfell Lodge, 54
Tipton-Haynes Farm, 49
Toccoa, 134
Toe River, 117
Tombstone Junction, 78
Toqua Mound, 25
Towering Oaks B&B, 140
Townsend, 39
Toxaway Falls, 108
Toxaway River, 108
Tracy City, 32
Trail Motel, 93
Trail of the Lonesome Pine, 91, 92
Trainstation Marketplace, 93
Traveler's Rest, 139
Tryon, 108, 109
Tryon Riding and Hunt Club, 109
Tuckaleechee Caverns, 53
Tuckasegee River, 98, 103
Tudor Mountain Road, 35
Turkey Pen Bluff, 27
Turkey Pen Gap, 27
Turkey Pen Hollow, 27
Turkey Pen Resort, 27, 56
Turtle Back Rock, 75
Tuskegee, 26
Tweetsie Railroad, 121
Twinbrook Resort, 126

Unakas, 22
Unicoi County Heritage Museum, 47
Unicoi State Park, 142
Union County, 41
University of Georgia, 29
University of Tennessee, 40
Unto These Hills, 98, 121
Up-River Tube Rentals, 139
Upper Cornsilk, 101

Valle Crucis, 113
Valley River Mountains, 107
Valley River Valley, 107
Van Buren County, 30
Vance Birthplace, 122
Vann House, 138
Vansant, 89
Virginia Attractions Table, 92-93
Virginia Chambers of Commerce, 94
Virginia Lodging Places Table, 93
Virginia Parks Table, 93-94
Virginia Tidewater, 88
Visitor's Center and Museum, 49
Vogel State Park, 142
Vonore, 27

Walden Ridge, 31
Ward Hall, 78
Warren County, 30
Warrior's Path State Park, 57
Wartburg, 2, 3
Washington, 13
Washington County, 22
Watauga County, 112, 113, 116
Watauga Lake, 21
Watauga River, 3, 18, 113
Water Wheel Restaurant, 112, 113
Wear's Motel & Cottages, 56
Weaving Cabin, 117
Webster, 118
Webster Angus Farm, 14, 15
Well House, 113
West Jefferson, 115, 116
West Prong of Little Pigeon River, 37, 39
Westmoreland Coal Museum, 92, 93
White Hall State Shrine, 80
White House, 13
White Pines Mountain Cabins, 141
White Rocks, 70, 71
White Rocks Trail, 71
White's Mill, 92
Whiterock Mountain, 107
Whitetop Mountain, 86
Wild Plum Tea Room, 35
Wilderness Road, 13
Windy Hill B&B, 55
Wise, 91
Wolf Fork Road, 131
Wolf Fork Valley, 131, 132
Wolf Hill, 88
Wolf River, 8, 9
Worley Homestead B&B, 134, 141

Yancey County, 118
Yellow Creek, 74
Yellow Creek Valley, 74
Yellow Door, 1, 8
York House, The, 140
Yosemite National Park, 32

Photo Acknowledgments

The News-Sentinel would like to thank the following contributors for the use of photographs in this book: *front cover,* Photographic Services, State of Tennessee; *back cover,* Shawn G. Henry, The Knoxville News-Sentinel; *pages 4, 10, 17 and 19,* Photographic Services, State of Tennessee; *page 23,* Tennessee Tourist Development; *pages 28, 35,* Photographic Services, State of Tennessee; *page 38,* The Knoxville News-Sentinel; *page 42,* Museum of Appalachia; *page 64,* Beaumont Inn; *page 67,* Shaker Village of Pleasant Hill; *page 73,* National Park Service; *page 87,* United Coal Company; *page 89,* Breaks Interstate Park; *page 99,* Cherokee Tribal Travel and Promotion; *page 105,* Fontana Village; *page 109,* Joy Kelly, Mill Farm Inn; *page 111,* Lowell Branham, The Knoxville News-Sentinel; *page 114,* Hugh Morton, Grandfather Mountain; *page 119,* Penland School of Crafts; *page 135,* Helen Chamber of Commerce. All maps were produced by Martin Gehring, The Knoxville News-Sentinel.